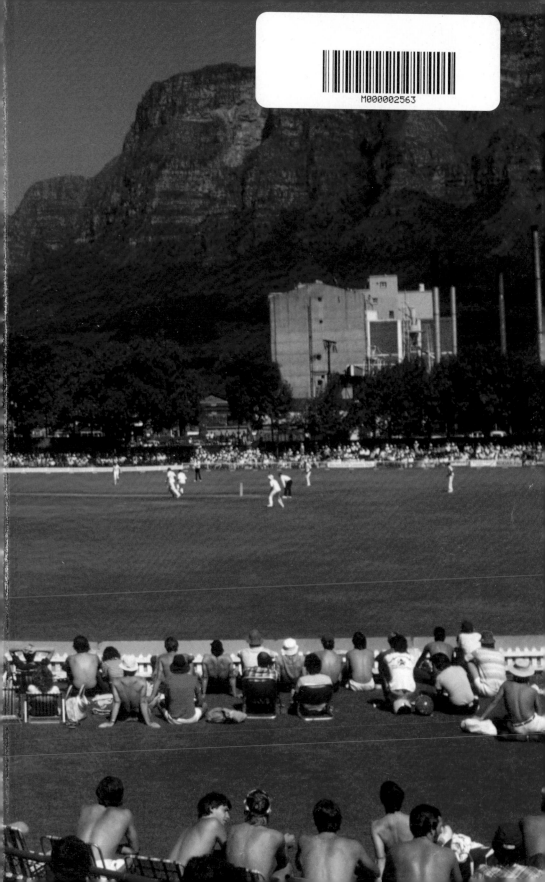

Also available at all good book stores

GUNNER
My Life in Cricket
IAN GOULD

9781785316302

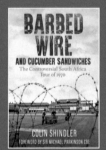

BARBED WIRE
AND CUCUMBER SANDWICHES
The Controversial South Africa Tour of 1970
COLIN SHINDLER
FOREWORD BY SIR MICHAEL PARKINSON CBE

9781785316340

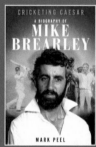

CRICKETING CAESAR
A BIOGRAPHY OF
MIKE BREARLEY
MARK PEEL

9781785316623

MARK PEEL
THE HOLLOW CROWN
ENGLAND CRICKET
CAPTAINS
FROM 1945 TO THE PRESENT

9781785316630

TIM BROOKS
A CORNER
OF EVERY
FOREIGN
FIELD
CRICKET'S JOURNEY

9781785316395

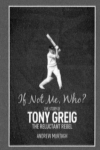

If Not Me, Who?
THE STORY OF
TONY GREIG
THE RELUCTANT REBEL
ANDREW MURTAGH

9781785316418

Tales from the Front Line
LUKE **FLETCHER**

9781785316876

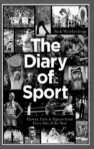

Nick Wotherhogg
The Diary of Sport
History, Facts & Figures from Every Day of the Year

9781785316289

GOOD OLD
Sussex by the Sea
A SIXTIES CHILDHOOD
SPENT WITH
HASTINGS UNITED,
THE ALBION AND
SUSSEX COUNTY CRICKET
TIM QUELCH

9781785316197

THE
UNFORGIVEN
Mercenaries or Missionaries?

T H E
UNFORGIVEN
Mercenaries or Missionaries?

The untold stories of the rebel West Indian
cricketers who toured apartheid South Africa

ASHLEY GRAY

First published by Pitch Publishing, 2020
Reprinted 2021

Pitch Publishing
A2 Yeoman Gate
Yeoman Way
Worthing
Sussex
BN13 3QZ
www.pitchpublishing.co.uk
info@pitchpublishing.co.uk

A CIP catalogue record is available for this book
from the British Library.

ISBN 978 1 78531 532 9

Typesetting and origination by Pitch Publishing

Printed and bound by TJ Books, Padstow, UK

Contents

Introduction. 9

Lawrence Rowe 26

Herbert Chang 56

Alvin Kallicharran 71

Faoud Bacchus 88

Richard Austin 102

Alvin Greenidge 125

Emmerson Trotman 132

David Murray 137

Collis King 157

Sylvester Clarke 172

Derick Parry 189

Hartley Alleyne 205

Bernard Julien 220

Albert Padmore 238

Monte Lynch 253

Ray Wynter 268

Everton Mattis 285

Colin Croft 301

Ezra Moseley 309

Franklyn Stephenson 318

Acknowledgements 336

Scorecards. 337

Map: Rebel Origins. 349

Selected Bibliography. 350

For Archie, Harriet and Simone

Introduction

IT WAS October 1982. Prisoner 220/82, Nelson Mandela, was settling into his new home – a cell in Pollsmoor Maximum Security Prison. He had just endured 18 years' imprisonment in the notorious Robben Island jail. Meanwhile, Hollywood superstar Liza Minelli was flying into Johannesburg for an 11-show engagement in Sun City.

On arrival at Jan Smuts Airport, she was mobbed by fans and journalists alike. The local newspaper couldn't contain its glee. 'Eat your heart out New York', it bragged, as Minelli 'swept into her hotel like a typhoon'. Unsurprisingly, the same reporter made no comparison between the room Ms Minelli occupied and the one Mandela was forced to endure, 870 miles away on the outskirts of Cape Town.

Minelli wasn't the first celebrity to find the lure of the krugerrand stronger than any ethical concerns about visiting the apartheid stronghold. British singers Shirley Bassey, Elton John and Rod Stewart were hot on her stiletto heels, while tennis champion Billie Jean King declared ahead of an international tournament in the Transvaal capital, 'I've been very keen to come to South Africa for a long time.'

For those big names, and the local white audiences who craved their visits, that spring must have seemed reassuringly normal – provided they turned a blind eye to the ugly reality within.

Furious white ratepayers in Durban, railing against black citizens having access to public toilets, alleging they would spread venereal disease. A gang of baton-wielding whites in Ermelo, attacking black guests at a Holiday Inn dinner-dance after learning of an interracial tryst. Frantic parliamentary debates over new influx controls, known as the Orderly Movement and Settlement of Black Persons Bill, which aimed to deny Africans the right to live in cities.

Racial discrimination buttressed by apartheid – the enforced separation of ethnic groups – was a feature of everyday life. It ensured the minority white population controlled the economic and social levers of the country.

But in a post-colonial world, South Africa's version of normal was becoming increasingly repugnant to the global community. Fierce condemnation gathered pace. Suspension from the United Nations (UN) and Olympic Games, sporting boycotts and trade and cultural sanctions isolated the republic, gnawing at the fragile self-esteem of its white citizens. By hosting a steady stream of international pop stars, entertainers and sportspeople at its gold-funded stages and fields, a people under siege could present a business-as-usual facade to the outside world.

But playing sport in the pariah republic was now a tug-of-war between money and conscience that fewer were willing to tolerate. In 1977, Commonwealth heads of government drafted the Gleneagles Agreement, which discouraged all sporting links with South Africa. Three years later, the UN drew up an ongoing blacklist of those who had played there.

The Springboks had been locked out of world competition since 1970 as cricket's controlling body, the International Cricket Council (ICC), demanded an end to segregated teams and integration on the pitch.

The likes of master batsman Graeme Pollock, dashing opener Barry Richards, and seasoned Test all-rounders Mike Procter and Eddie Barlow were confined to domestic or county competition in England.

The captain of that roll-call of Springboks legends was Ali Bacher. A doctor by profession, he became a successful administrator of Transvaal, transforming it into the feared 'mean machine' that dominated South African provincial cricket in the 1980s. In 1982, he sat on the board of the South African Cricket Union (SACU). The previous year he'd pulled off a major coup, luring West Indian left-hander Alvin Kallicharran – a man whose brown skin deemed him a second-class citizen in South Africa's racial hierarchy – as their overseas professional. For his enterprise, the 66-Test veteran earned a Test ban from the West Indies Cricket Board of Control (WICBC).

Throughout the 1970s, South African cricket had attempted to reinvent itself by embracing non-racial selection policies. However, most black, coloured and Indian players were aligned to the rival South African Cricket Board (SACB), which refused to cooperate with the dominant SACU while apartheid was still in place. Its leader Hassan Howa rightly pegged integration as a form of window dressing designed solely to appease white liberals and convince the ICC that the Springboks were worthy of readmittance to the Test arena. The ICC wasn't convinced either. Pressure from anti-apartheid campaigners was now so intense that resuming Test contact with South Africa would have brought world cricket to its knees and created a racial schism between white and non-white playing nations.

With the door shut firmly on a return and fears the game would wither without further international stimulus, the chequebook became the SACU's sole tool of survival. Bolstered by a generous tax break that allowed sponsors to claim back almost 90 per cent of their outlay for 'international events', it was near enough to a government-sanctioned blank cheque.

Early in 1982, a bunch of over-the-hill and fringe English Test players were paid close to £40,000 each to participate in an eight-match tour of the outlier republic. Despite a three-year Test ban and howls of protest from black-consciousness groups in South Africa and the left side of British politics – Shadow

Environment Secretary Gerald Kaufman said the players were 'selling themselves for blood-covered krugerrands' – the tour was a minor success. It set the template for a further half-dozen.

Ali Bacher had little to do with that spectacle. He had his eyes trained on a bigger prize: the all-conquering West Indies side. But Caribbean involvement – convincing black men to play in a country that systematically discriminated against people of their own colour – was no certainty, and fearing another summer without international competition, a Sri Lankan rebel side was quickly cobbled together for the pleasure of Pollock, Richards and Procter. That they were substandard surprised nobody; what was more significant was the warm reception they received. To interested watchers, it showed that 'non-white' sportsmen could tour the republic without incident.

Back on the subcontinent it was a different story. Slapped with a 25-year cricket ban by the Sri Lanka Board of Control, the 14 players now had more money than they could have expected to earn in a lifetime of cricket, but employers no longer wanted to be associated with men it was perceived had shamed a nation. The clubs where they had made their name gave them a wide berth. They were alienated from the sport they loved and the people who supported them. 'There's kind of an invisible difference between them and the others', a Colombo newspaper editor reported. It was a telling observation with haunting overtones for future rebel tourists.

While SACU president Joe Pamensky, an avuncular but hard-nosed Johannesburg businessman, took care of the Sri Lankan tour, Bacher pursued his Caribbean quarry. The West Indies were cricket titans. Reigning World Cup champions, they played with a swagger and charisma that thrilled spectators and critics alike. They were cricket's number one drawcard, but they were also vulnerable to opportunistic forces. Unlike first-world England or Australia, financial opportunities for West Indies cricketers in retirement were limited; there were few lucrative commentary positions and the economically challenged Caribbean was in no position to support them. It was a situation recognised by captain Clive Lloyd in a paper presented to West Indies' governments in 1982, warning of the spectre of South African raids:

'Several West Indies players ... many who do not have a secure playing future when their playing days are over ... may be tempted to respond favourably to these offers. If members of what might be considered the West Indies first and second elevens were to give in to the considerable temptations that could be offered, the implications for both West Indies and world cricket could be grave.'

At that point, West Indies players were paid less than a thousand dollars a Test match. Lloyd suggested a stipend of US$20,000 to US$30,000 a year to keep the sharks at bay.

While the authorities dithered, Bacher struck. It was on one of many fruitless trips to London to convince the ICC that South Africa should be welcomed back to Test cricket, that Bacher snuck away to meet Colin Croft in Manchester. The intimidating West Indian paceman was carrying a back injury that threatened his career, and Dr Bacher offered him treatment in South Africa and a cheque rumoured to be in excess of US$100,000. He also met with Malcolm Marshall and Sylvester Clarke, two Barbados fast bowlers on the fringes of West Indies selection; the very men Lloyd feared would be targets. They were interested.

When he returned to Barbados after the 1982 county season ended, it was Surrey-contracted Clarke who gave the business card of one of Bacher's associates to retired paceman Gregory Armstrong. Armstrong was a perfect choice for the conspirators. His career had petered out in the late 1970s but at his best he'd been good enough to open the bowling with Andy Roberts for the West Indies President's XI and hostile enough to break Bernard Julien's arm in a net session. He'd reinvented himself as a shrewd businessman, organising the first day-night cricket tournament on the island, sponsored by Cockspur Rum.

Armstrong immediately contacted Bacher with a plan to execute the doctor's vision. Bacher told Armstrong that without

Viv Richards or any of the 'big names', the tours would bomb. 'I'll have you know that any of these guys here could replace Richards or Holding or any of the others,' Armstrong shot back. But that didn't stop him contacting some of those big names.

Joel Garner, the giant Barbados quick, was one of them. A feared member of the West Indies Test team with 124 Test wickets, he would add instant cachet to any rebel side. 'It was about US$350,000 a year,' Garner says of the offer Armstrong made him. 'But at the end of the day I said, "Am I going to take their $350,000 to end my career?" I said, "You got to be joking. I can put away ten years of cricket. This is foolishness." But the money wasn't the catch. I said to them clearly, "I will not be an honorary white to go to South Africa to play cricket ... while the other blacks and coloureds were suffering."'

Even so, he made sure to check with the Barbados Prime Minister Tom Adams whether potential rebels would be banned from re-entering the island. 'He said, "You're a Barbadian. If you go to South Africa, no one can stop you coming and going to Barbados as you like." I said I wasn't going; I was just checking what the feeling of the people was.'

As a signatory to the Gleneagles Agreement, Adams's Barbados Labour Party government was strenuously opposed to sporting contact with South Africa, a position echoed across a British Caribbean built on the horrors of slavery. Opposition to apartheid was particularly trenchant in Jamaica, which, in 1957, was one of the first countries to enforce a trade embargo against South Africa. Former Prime Minister Michael Manley had built an international reputation as a warrior against racial segregation, going so far as to urge an air, sea and land boycott in the UN.

In Guyana, the government led by President Forbes Burnham had been prepared to sacrifice a Test match against England rather than allow English seamer Robin Jackman, an occasional coach in South Africa, into the country, such was the level of anti-apartheid sentiment. And Trinidad, scene of the Black Power uprising in 1970 that sought to alleviate Afro-Caribbean disadvantage, boasted a militant union movement that successfully orchestrated port boycotts of South African goods.

In this highly charged atmosphere, Bacher and Armstrong strove to keep negotiations under wraps. They devised a series of codes to keep telephone conversations secret as player recruitment continued at a frantic pace. Pre-internet, Bacher consulted *Wisden Cricketers' Almanack* to confirm the credentials of players he'd never seen in action. Little-known names such as Alvin Greenidge, Franklyn Stephenson, Albert Padmore, Ezra Moseley, Emmerson Trotman, Richard Austin and Everton Mattis, complemented fading Test men Lawrence Rowe, Bernard Julien, Derick Parry, Collis King and David Murray.

Croft was in, along with Johannesburg resident Kallicharran. So too was Clarke, every county batsman's worst nightmare, but forever destined to be a West Indies fill-in.

What united this disaffected mob of peripheral and slightly past-their-use-by-date cricketers was a belief that the West Indies side was a closed shop. Its successes meant that captain Clive Lloyd wielded unprecedented power. Individualists, eccentrics, rogues ... many of the rebel squad didn't fit the conservative Lloyd mould. Even some of Lloyd's own men were wavering. Desmond Haynes had only just established himself as Gordon Greenidge's opening partner, while fellow Bajan Malcolm Marshall was still banging at the door of the exclusive West Indies pace club. The SACU's generous lump sum, in the region of $US100,000 for two seasons, would set them both up for life.

They were so close to joining the tours that David Simmons, the chairman of Barbados National Sports Council, felt compelled to phone them in Melbourne, where they were playing grade cricket. 'I told them ultimately they would have to live with themselves,' he says. 'They'd be jeopardising their future.'

Sports minister Vic Johnson echoed his view. 'There is no price for which self-respect or human integrity can ever be bought,' he railed.

But it was Barbados, the home of the legendary 'three Ws' – Sir Frank Worrell, Sir Everton Weekes and Sir Clyde Walcott - and, one writer quipped, the 'three Cs' – conservatism, Christianity and cricket – that would supply nearly half the rebel contingent. There was even a report that its favourite son, Sir Garfield Sobers, was being lured to manage the rebels, though it was quickly rejected by his wife.

Up until the players boarded their flights, no one knew for sure whether the tours were going ahead. On the morning of Tuesday, 11 January 1983, cricket commentator Reds Perreira was driving to a practice session at Kensington Oval. A familiar presence on *Voice of Barbados*, he was reporting on the home side's preparation for its first Shell Shield match in ten days' time against the Leeward Islands. But as he stopped at a pedestrian crossing, he heard a tap on his car window and saw one of the most revered figures in West Indies cricket – a man whose name Perreira has sworn never to reveal. 'Rebel team going to South Africa,' the man whispered. 'Do your homework.'

It was potentially the biggest scoop of his career, so he called a friend at British West Indies Airways (BWIA) and asked her to check flights to Miami, one of the first stops for any international travel out of Barbados. He had to give her the name of someone he thought the rebel tour organisers would target; someone near enough to West Indies selection but far enough from ever making it. He suggested the hard-hitting Barbados batsman Emmerson Trotman. It worked; he was flying out the next day, along with seven other Bajan first-class cricketers.

'I went on air at about 1.05pm and broke the story,' Perreira says. 'I didn't want the BBC or Australia or anyone else to break it. This was a Caribbean story. But I didn't call out any names because I didn't want reporters and photographers at their house.'

The next day, Grantley Adams International Airport was packed with drama as Perreira sweated on the rebels' arrival, knowing he would be made to look a fool if they didn't show. When none of them boarded the proposed BWIA flight, he began to fret. A baggage handler he knew told him he'd seen Trotman's cousin, former Test opener Alvin Greenidge, rolling a suitcase to the American Airlines check-in. Perreira pounced on the American Airlines manager, who confirmed the rebels' booking.

The first plane had been a decoy. But the drama wasn't over. A van driven by 11-Test fast bowler Sylvester Clarke roared into the car park, tyres screeching. Six more international cricketers climbed out. The last to embark was two-Test off-spinner Albert Padmore. Perreira caught him on the tarmac. 'I knew him well,' he says. 'I said, "Paddy, are you going to South Africa?" His answer was, "No comment." Then I asked, "Why are you going to South Africa?" No comment again. Then the ramp came down and they let him on.'

A pattern of deception and denial characterised the lead-in to the rebel extravaganza as the SACU sought to confuse the world's press and take the pressure off their trailblazing recruits. In Kingston, Jamaica, batting great Lawrence Rowe and bowler Colin Croft seemingly gave assurances they had snubbed Bacher's pots of rand. WICBC president Allan Rae claimed that 'sportsmen have no respect for these cloak and dagger figures with their wallets full of money', and boasted that the much-loved Rowe 'was disgusted his name was being bandied around with the suggestion he would forfeit his pride for Krugerrands'. Within days Croft and Rowe, captain designate, would board a plane bound for Miami en route to Johannesburg.

Back in South Africa, SACU president Pamensky issued a statement abandoning the tour because press leaks were scaring off signings. It was hokum. He'd employed the same tactic before the Sri Lanka tour. But he wasn't done. As the rebels criss-crossed international airspace, the SACU leaked a story that nine of them were stranded in Madrid. But none had ever set foot in Spain.

The first to nudge South African terra firma were the Jamaicans Richard Austin, a two-Test all-rounder, and Everton Mattis, a four-Test batsman. They both hailed from Kingston's ghettos. En route, the string bean Mattis told a London reporter: 'Look, I am not supporting the apartheid regime, I don't agree with it. It's my living and I've got five children to support.'

White South Africa didn't care what his motivations were. The *Rand Daily Mail*, Johannesburg's liberal-leaning newspaper, splashed with '15 cricket rebels defy the world' and 'Cricket's impossible dream comes true'.

Ali Bacher and Joe Pamensky had pulled off the most daring cricket heist since World Series Cricket (WSC).

* * *

At Jan Smuts Airport, vice-captain Kallicharran, already into his second season with Transvaal, and according to Joe Pamensky a key figure in the tour's conception, greeted his jet-lagged teammates as three black protesters with anti-tour slogans pinned to their chests stood in silence in the concourse. News of the tour had barely registered in the townships.

The *Rand Daily Mail* editorialised: 'We are pleased to see the West Indians here and look forward to a stimulating sporting encounter ... it will we hope ... poke a few more holes in apartheid; help to demolish the ugly attitudes that bolster an ugly system.'

The reaction in the Caribbean was swift and merciless. The WICBC slapped each of the rebels with lifelong Test and first-class cricket bans. Jamaican Minister of Youth and Community Development Errol Anderson vowed never to let his country's rebels utilise their 'blood money', promising to purge Jamaica of their 'despicable qualities'. Trinidad Foreign Minister Basil Ince was more measured but equally as damning: 'They are mercenaries fighting for the cause of apartheid ... on the backs and blood of black people of South Africa.'

Perhaps the most surprising attack came from Roy Fredericks, a 59-Test veteran, and ex-team-mate of many of the rebels. He'd been a beneficiary of WSC and knew the hardships that several of his old friends faced. But in his role as Minister for Youth, Sport and Culture in the Guyanese government, he suggested they should 'not cause further discomfort to the West Indian population by attempting to live among us'. St Lucia and Grenada made sure they couldn't, barring them from ever entering their islands.

Fredericks wasn't the only former colleague to condemn the rebels. West Indies captain Clive Lloyd's worst fears had been realised. He called the tours 'an affront to the black man throughout the world'. Fast bowler Michael Holding and batting great Viv Richards had knocked back astronomical sums offered them to join the Bacher circus. Holding couldn't control his anger, 'If they were offered enough money, they would probably agree to wear chains.' Richards understood his friends' motives but insisted he would 'rather die than lay down my dignity' the way they had done. But some thought their criticism was over the top. It was easier, they said, for established stars Holding, Lloyd and Richards to take the moral high ground when their tenure in the West Indies set-up was much more secure.

Barbados-born Roland Butcher, the first black man to play for England, and himself a target of Mike Gatting's doomed 1989 rebel side, saw the problem of playing moral policeman. 'They were scathing but the question would be: had they been in a similar position to the others, would they be so scathing? They were coming from a privileged background. If they'd been in the same situation and taken the same stance that would have been fantastic, but you will never know.'

Black South Africa wasn't so equivocal. The Azanian People's Organisation claimed that the West Indians had 'soiled themselves by flirting with racism, white domination and black dispossession'. Gibson Thula, chief urban representative of the KwaZulu Homeland, invited the tourists to inspect the substandard facilities available to black cricketers in the Cape Town townships of Nyanga, Gugulethu and Langa. Hassan Howa of the SACB was unyielding in his belief that there could be 'no normal sport in an abnormal society'. All of them called for the rebels to return home while they still had some dignity intact.

Public condemnation from Mandela's African National Congress (ANC) was more muted – but with good reason: it had been banned since 1960 and reporting its leaders' opinions was a jailable offence.

What particularly irked Holding and Richards was the idea that the rebels would be accorded 'honorary white' status in order to travel to places and socialise in restaurants, hotels and bars that were normally off limits to black and coloured people. To a man, the rebels deny they ever signed documents that transformed them into honorary whites, but there's no question that they were afforded privileges the native population could only dream of. It lent the tour a bubble-like feel as they whizzed around the republic in five-star comfort and style.

Al Gilkes of Barbados's *The Nation* newspaper was the only Caribbean journalist to accompany the tourists. He saw through the deceit. 'I was very close to the guys,' he says. 'They had latitude to cross the colour bar. I don't think they knew they were in an unreal world. Every night in the hotels, white girls were in there partying and sleeping with them, in a country where cohabitation was banned. Jewellery stores would be opened on Sundays when they were normally closed, and the guys were able to shop at one-tenth of the price. On the planes everyone was sitting next to each other regardless of colour; there were black and white people in the international hotels they stayed at.'

It's little wonder it was reported post-tour that when one of them was asked what he knew of Nelson Mandela, he replied, 'I don't know him. He didn't play against us.'

At his first press conference, captain Lawrence Rowe was understandably nervous. 'Obviously we are feeling a bit jittery,' he said. 'I just hope the South African people will treat us and love us in the manner we would like to be treated.'

Away from the charged political debate, 'calypso fever' gripped white South Africa in a way even the tour's most strident opponents could never have foreseen. It prompted Graeme Pollock's brother, retired Test all-rounder Peter Pollock, to declare: 'This is the best thing to ever have happened to South African cricket.'

Spectators agreed. Grounds were packed as crowds flocked to witness history and the novelty of elite black sportsmen in action against their white counterparts. Pitch invasions were commonplace, and at stumps star-struck boys sporting tour-branded T-shirts begged the West Indies squad for autographs and mementoes. Collis King, the slashing Barbados all-rounder, was their number one target. 'They all wanted to have their picture taken with him,' Gilkes says. 'He was the superstar. The original Chris Gayle.

'They were worshipping him. You couldn't help but notice how they responded to these people they would normally see as inferior.'

Support for the tourists came from all corners of the republic – even rugby-loving Afrikaners. The Ficksburg Afrikaanse Sakekamer, a regional business association, sent 200 rand to the SACU to 'convey our heartfelt thanks and appreciation to your board and to the West Indies cricketers for what they have done for sport in South Africa'.

Brut 33 wasn't so impartial. Its ads featured blond fast bowler Garth Le Roux reclining in full-on hunk mode under the slogan 'Take on the world with the great smell of Brut', wishing the Springboks – it would be another decade before the apartheid-era nickname was replaced with the less controversial Proteas – every success in their encounter with Rowe's rebels.

Even record label EMI bought into the hype, releasing *The Cricket Song*, a steel band tune by novelty act Albie Dubbelyoo and the Fielders.

The *Rand Daily Mail* greeted the second 'Test' at the Wanderers in Johannesburg with a four-page colour wrap-around 'telling you all you need to know about the 'Bok and West Indies stars and their tactics' and set up a cricket score hotline for the match. It received more than 8,000 calls on the first day.

Supermarket chain Pick 'n Pay urged fans to 'stock up on the way to the Wanderers' with cheap cans of Coca-Cola and cheese wedges, while authorities warned those same fans not to bring cooler bags because there would be no room for them in the jam-packed grandstands.

They should have told them to cover their refreshments – medicos reported 15 spectators were stung by bees attracted by the sweet scent of soft drinks.

* * *

The rebels won the hearts and minds of a sizeable chunk of white South Africa, sometimes in spite of their own prejudices. When Port Elizabeth's Afrikaner mayor welcomed the West Indians to his city, the *Sunday Times* quoted a bemused white businessman at the city hall function: 'I never thought I'd see the day when we'd all be turning out at a civic reception in honour of 15 black sportsmen from overseas.'

A familiar argument put forward by the tour's supporters was that seeing a successful West Indian side would encourage greater black cricket participation at grass-roots level. But did black people see them? The rebels attended a few coaching clinics in townships, which Gilkes says were more about promotion and propaganda than genuine attempts to engage. Film footage and photographs show that crowds in the partially desegregated public stands were predominantly male, white and often shirtless, with a smattering of Indian and 'coloured' youths. But in the same *Sunday Times* story, correspondent Eric Marsden noted that the Border tour game in East London had 'more black spectators than had ever been seen there'.

The truth was that cricket was still the white man's domain and football the game of the townships. On the second day of the gripping Johannesburg 'Test', the front page of the township edition of the *Rand Daily Mail* ignored the action at Wanderers, and focused on the impending BP Cup semi-final between Iwisa Kaizer Chiefs and Orlando Pirates at Orlando Stadium in Soweto. Over 16,000 had savoured the rebels' play; more than 40,000 were expected for the soccer clash the following day.

Makhaya Ntini, the first black man to take 300 Test wickets for South Africa, is often cited as an example of the positive effect that the West Indies XI had in inspiring indigenous talent. But he was only five when the first tour kicked off. 'When we grew up there was no TV,' he says of his childhood in Mdingi, a small village in the Cape Province. 'There would have been nowhere to watch them.'

He's unsure whether the rebel tours spawned many black imitators but maintains the West Indies were admired as athletes by Africans, even if it wasn't their sport of choice. 'Our fathers were fans of the West Indies; black South Africans supported them anyway, because they were originally from Africa. We loved West Indian culture.'

* * *

If white South Africa enjoyed an orgy of self-congratulation over its unexpected love affair with the Caribbean tourists, the interim period leading up to the second tour was a reminder that race relations within the republic were still rotten to the core. In a move interpreted as progressive by most local commentators, white voters approved a change to the constitution which gave 'Indians' and 'Coloureds' their own parliamentary chambers and a direct voice in South African affairs. Unbelievably, the majority black population was left out.

In Jamaica, the rebels were heartened by a poll in the national *Gleaner* newspaper which indicated 68 per cent support for the South African tours, many of the respondents revealing they would have acted in the same way as their tainted countrymen. But the results were tempered somewhat by the knowledge only 34 per cent of those interviewed knew what apartheid was.

In South Africa, Bacher and the SACU weren't sitting on their hands. Aware the white sporting public would not tolerate a bland re-run of the first tour, they sought to strengthen the West Indies squad by raiding Lloyd's world-beaters. Except they were no longer that – at least not in the one-day format. In one of the great sporting upsets, they had gifted the 1983 World Cup Final to India. Bacher swooped on the disaffected losers. He snapped up classy Guyanese batsman Faoud Bacchus, but he craved a more recognisable name. In his autobiography, *Marshall Arts*, Malcolm Marshall, by now an indispensable cog in the West Indies pace machine, says Bacher met him at a Wimpy Bar in Southampton and tabled a US$1 million deal. When Marshall rebuffed him, a shocked Bacher spilt his cup of coffee down the front of his shirt. Instead, a clean-shirted Bacher would have to settle for Marshall's friend Hartley Alleyne, another product of the famed Barbados pace laboratory, and Monte Lynch, a promising, England-qualified Guyanese batter. The Jamaican trio of Richard Austin, Herbert Chang and Ray Wynter – the latter two were added to the first tour as injury cover – were axed.

The second campaign, a long, 10-week, 19-game affair, started in mid-November 1983. Wicketkeeper David Murray had endured a tough first campaign – Australian Prime Minister Malcolm Fraser had threatened to cancel his visa, stranding him from his wife and baby girl – but he was now relaxed and optimistic enough to declare his compatriots in the Caribbean were more interested in the rebels' fortunes than the progress of Clive Lloyd's official Test side in India. 'I think our people feel that our official Test team is now becoming a second-string side because some of our best players have been banned for coming to South Africa. I personally have no doubt that the West Indies' best fast bowlers are the ones in South Africa. At this moment, Colin Croft, Sylvester Clarke, Ezra Moseley and Franklyn Stephenson are the best we've got.'

Money and sponsorship tensions threatened to derail the summer. The tourists wanted a larger portion of the revenue they'd generated through record crowd receipts. With the tour in the balance, an improved deal was brokered but the goodwill between the SACU and its prized charges was permanently stained. Re-badged as the Yellow Pages One Day Series and the National Panasonic 'Tests', attendances remained high for the limited-over day-night games but dipped in the longer format because of over-exposure, and in the first Test at Durban, a featherbed pitch. However, the cricket was still top class. The West Indies' pace battery, led by Clarke, Moseley and new recruit Alleyne, a man Geoffrey Boycott maintained would command a spot in most Test teams, inspired a 2-1 'Test' and 4-2 one-day series victory.

The injured Croft's major contribution was getting himself thrown off a whites-only carriage in Cape Town. The incident provoked international outrage and anti-apartheid activists again ramped up their calls for a tour boycott.

But the rebels had an unlikely ally in world record-holding 1,500m runner Sydney Maree. He complained that an unfortunate side effect of the sporting boycott against South Africa was that it hurt black sportsmen like himself. He was already in the process of applying for US citizenship.

Meanwhile, European and American golfing greats Seve Ballesteros, Nick Faldo and Fuzzy Zoeller teed off in the Million Dollar Golf Challenge at Sun City, and Argentine Guillermo Vilas slugged it out with American Vitas Gerulaitis in the 1983 South African Open. It galled that these rich white sportsmen, unaffected by the Gleneagles Agreement, were able to flit in and out of South Africa with little condemnation, while the West Indians were universally slammed. It was hard enough being born with the wrong skin colour into virtual second-world poverty, let alone being forced to wear criticism for trying to escape it.

It was only when they returned to the Caribbean and the realisation that the life they had once cherished was gone forever, that the gravity of their transgressions kicked in. No one would escape the barbs, the cries of 'race traitor' and 'honorary white'. Cashed up, but ground down, some coped with ostracism by deserting their homelands, others sought refuge in drugs and religion. The tyranny of inter-island distance ensured that there would be no genuine rebel brotherhood. They were on their own.

Lawrence Rowe

'He was a hero here'

IT'S EASY to feel anonymous in the Fort Lauderdale sprawl. Shopping malls, car yards and hotels dominate the eyeline for miles. The vast concrete expanses have the effect of dissipating the city's intensity, of stripping out emotion. The Gallery One Hilton Fort Lauderdale is a four-star monolith minutes from the Atlantic Ocean. Lawrence Rowe, a five-star batsman in his prime, is seated in the hotel lounge area. He has been trading off the anonymity of southern Florida for the past 35 years, an exile from Kingston, Jamaica, the highly charged city that could no longer tolerate its stylish, contrary hero.

Florida is a haven for Jamaican expats; it's a short 105-minute flight across the Caribbean Sea. Some of them work at the hotel. Bartender Alyssa, a 20-something from downtown Kingston, is too young to know that the neatly groomed septuagenarian she's serving a glass of Coke was once her country's most storied sportsman. When it's pointed out to her, she giggles approvingly.

'Tell your father you met me,' Rowe jokes. He knows his demographic. There wouldn't be many men over 50 in his homeland who are unaware that he choreographed 214 and 100 not out against New Zealand at Sabina Park in 1972 – a Test record for most runs on debut that still stands – and followed it up two years later with 302 against Mike Denness's Englishmen in Barbados.

Choreographed is the word for it. Whereas Viv Richards blazed across the line, a boxer in creams, Rowe, compact and composed, caressed the ball in the classic batting arc. It wasn't the Bradmanesque weight of runs, but the way he scored them that so entranced. A young Richards hero-worshipped him, painting Rowe's nickname 'Yagga' on a fence post; Michael Holding rated him the most technically complete batsman he ever saw. Desmond Haynes and Malcolm Marshall idolised him. He was so cool that he had the temerity to whistle at the crease.

In Jamaica, he was the new George Headley, feted by prime ministers, adored by the public and media, who used the unique descriptor 'batting stylist' to encapsulate his artistry. It's said his beauty at the crease was such a distraction that fieldsmen, so transfixed by the quality of his stroke-play, sometimes forgot to chase the ball, which was always tantalisingly placed a yard to their right or left, or they found themselves applauding as they chased, like Geoffrey Boycott did from midwicket time and time again during Rowe's epic 1974 series.

'We look at Lawrence's batting with the same affection as when we see a pretty girl,' says Leonard Chambers, respected former national selector and mentor to Jamaica's batting elite.

The great Australia paceman Dennis Lillee, a formidable Rowe foe throughout the 1970s, brackets him among the very best. 'He was something to behold. He had so much time and such beautiful timing. He was in the top echelon; with Sobers, Richards, Lloyd, Haynes and Greenidge.'

Yet Rowe's demographic also knows that this son of a bus driver from Waltham Park Road in impoverished west Kingston captained the West Indies rebel side to South Africa in 1983. They know that he was forced to flee to Miami to rebuild his life when public reaction to the tours threatened to turn nasty. They know he's a fallen idol. It's why Rowe, seemingly so slick and carefree, is forever burdened with hauling a set of well-worn arguments and self-justifications that might one day, he hopes, restore his place in sporting history.

'I am one of the only sportsmen who reached the heights I did who hasn't been recognised by the Jamaica government,' he says. 'I've heard some radio programmes here in Miami where Jamaicans have called in saying, "Are they going to wait until this guy dies?"'

* * *

On the afternoon of 6 April 1981, during England's tour game against Jamaica, umpire Lindel Bell was temporarily the most hated man on the island. Officiating in his first major match, the police inspector, soon to become his country's assistant commissioner, raised his finger to a half-hearted lbw appeal from Ian Botham. The ball had struck crowd favourite Lawrence Rowe just below the hip as he pulled through midwicket. He was so disappointed with the decision that, despite making 116, he neglected to raise his bat or tip his cap to the Sabina Park faithful, whose boos turned to thunderous applause as he made his way to the pavilion.

Not that the crowd would ever hold it against him. This was the batting artist they had come to see, and he'd not disappointed. Describing one boundary, the *Jamaica Gleaner* reporter observed that Rowe had 'danced in Nijinsky style' to deliberately guide the ball past second slip. Yet for all the superlatives, it hadn't been a typical Rowe century, his 17th in first-class cricket. A risk-averse single-mindedness was evident as he 'abandoned some of his traditional gems of stroke play'. In truth, he'd been a man on a mission. The West Indies side for the fifth Test against England, controversially announced prior to the match, had once again found no room for the 32-year-old veteran of 30 Tests.

Mark Neita, just 20 at the time, was at the other end for the second half of his captain's century. He was witness to Rowe's fierce determination. 'Lawrence said to me, "I am going to embarrass the selectors." He said, "Churchill [Neita's nickname], stay down your end and watch this hundred. This is not going to be one hundred, this is going to be a big one." He wanted 200.'

How had the once-grand career of the mighty 'Lawrence of Jamaica' come to hinge on one dud decision from a greenhorn umpire in an inconsequential tour match? In some respects, Rowe was a victim of the impossibly high standards he'd set earlier. After a century in the first Test against Lillee and Thomson in Brisbane in 1975, his gargantuan run pile stood at 1,266 with a second-to-Bradman average of 70.33, including six centuries. Only Bradman himself could have maintained or improved on that kind of output. Rowe was 26 years old.

There was also the spate of injuries and ailments – an ongoing eye astigmatism diagnosed in 1974, which he says played havoc with his confidence, a grass allergy detected the following year, a broken hand that kept him out of action throughout 1977 and a dislocated shoulder suffered on the 1980 tour of England. It meant the second half of his career had a stuttering, staccato quality. There were occasional pearls such as the 175 against WSC Australia in Melbourne in 1979, an innings Richie Benaud described as one of the best he ever saw, but each time his once-glittering career threatened to reignite, misfortune seemed to strike.

It led to accusations that Rowe was soft, that his ailments were directly linked to a fragile state of mind. Former Jamaica Prime Minister Michael Manley, a one-time Rowe devotee, would ultimately conclude that he 'wasn't a man for the trenches of adversity'. Michael Holding wrote that his Jamaica and West Indies team-mate 'lacked self-confidence and determination'.

But where others saw fear and paranoia, Rowe saw perseverance and resilience, the capacity to forge a career in spite of the obstacles he faced. And in the late 1970s, he still had high-pedigree believers in his corner. His first Jamaica captain, former West Indies batsman Easton 'Bull' McMorris, remembers Clive Lloyd exhorting him to draw out more enthusiasm for the maroon cap from Rowe. 'He said to me: "Easton, try to see if you can get Lawrence to play cricket, please, because when I talk to him it's as if he does not want to play. But he is the best batsman we have." And this was with Viv, Lloydy and Greenidge on the team.'

It didn't help that Rowe was afflicted with the curse of the aesthetically pleasing batsman; that his effortless timing and elegance at the crease gave the impression he didn't care. It's a charge that still rankles. 'Right throughout my career, it got out there, it sounded like I was chicken,' Rowe says, 'that I didn't want to go out and play, heart not in it. Because of the way I played people said I was lackadaisical, but it was baloney. The injuries I had would have stopped other people, but I still managed to make a career out of cricket.'

He cites an incident during the Test match at Old Trafford on that injury-riddled 1980 tour of England as proof that his words were often manipulated to make him look weak. 'Clyde Walcott, the manager, never liked a bone in me from when my career started. We were sitting in the pavilion, when he said to me, "If you cannot play the next county game, we will have to replace you because the guys are tired."' Rowe told Walcott he might not be fit in time. 'I couldn't get my left elbow up if somebody bowled me a short-pitched ball. So, I said to him, "If I can't play the next game, then more than likely I will play the following one."'

Unpersuaded, Walcott informed Rowe he would be sent home immediately. 'But when they came off the field, Walcott met with them and told them I had requested to leave the team,' Rowe says. 'So, Viv [Richards] came up to me and said something like, "Yagga, why do you want to leave?" I said, "Nothing of the sort. Clyde Walcott came and told me I was going to be off the team," and Viv said, "That's not what he told us."'

It wouldn't be the first time a miscommunication tarnished Rowe's reputation, and nor was Rowe the first cricketer to fall out with the prickly Walcott, one of the famous 'Three Ws' and a certified member of West Indian cricket royalty.

By the beginning of that 1981 Caribbean series against England, Richards had long assumed from Rowe the mantle of the West Indies' premier batsman. Rowe's average had declined to a more terrestrial but highly respectable 43.55 and because of injuries he hadn't played Test cricket for over a year. Mere mortals Larry Gomes, Gus Logie and Jamaica team-mate Everton Mattis were now fighting over his vacant third drop spot. The perception was that Richards, unorthodox, aggressive and political, represented the zeitgeist. He was Bob Marley to Rowe's Barry White – smooth and immaculately turned out, but essentially a relic from another era.

Rowe's 116 at Sabina Park was a defiant middle finger to the establishment that had lost patience with him but also a reminder that he could cut it against international opposition. Yet earlier in the season, Clive Lloyd had approached Rowe with the offer of opening the West Indies batting in a one-day match as a replacement for the unwell Gordon Greenidge, whose star may have been momentarily on the wane because of negative comments he'd made about Lloyd's captaincy. The Guyanese had witnessed Rowe craft 51 and 58 not out in a Shell Shield match in Berbice; he could see that the Jamaican was back to his princely best. But in the second innings, Colin Croft had battered Rowe on the hip with a short ball, and the bruised Jamaica captain decided to turn down Lloyd's advances.

The incident again fed into perceptions that Rowe wasn't made of the right stuff; that he didn't want it enough, that when the going got tough he was nowhere to be found. Even his Jamaica team-mate, wicketkeeper Jeffrey Dujon, was mystified by Rowe's snub. 'From what I understand, Lawrence told Clive, "I'll get back to you." At this point in time, the West Indies is the top team. Clive Lloyd is the premier of WI cricket. You don't tell Clive Lloyd I'll get back to you. You're being offered a chance. You could be walking on one leg – yes, I'll play. You prove me unfit.'

Rowe, fated, in his own mind, to be eternally misunderstood, tells a different story. 'We were travelling across to Trinidad after the game. In the back of the plane, Lloydy came to see me. He said, "If you were selected to open in the next one-day game, would you be comfortable with it?" I said, "Sure." The problem was that I had been hit – I thought I'd broken something. I was going to get an X-ray and depending on what that was, I'd do it.' He says he was concerned that his injury would hamper the side's effectiveness. 'I said, "It would be a gamble if you pick me, my fielding would be a liability."'

What sticks in his craw is that when the story came out, he was portrayed as disrespecting the West Indies. 'I was told I'd turned him down; I didn't want to play. No heart. But I didn't tell him that. I had told him I would play but I would be restricted.'

Was he once again the victim of miscommunication or was there a susceptibility to injury that rendered him a now permanent selection risk? WICBC officials took the latter view. He was duly left out of the 1981/82 tour to Australia – although Lloyd publicly stated that he hoped Rowe would return to the Test side at some point – and there was even talk that he would be relieved of the Jamaican captaincy. Missing the campaign Down Under was a heavy psychological blow. The 116 against England counted for nothing. If a century against top-line international opposition wasn't good enough to turns selectors' heads, what was?

Uncertain about his future, and guiding a Jamaica side dogged by internal friction – the strong-willed Herbert Chang and Richard Austin attempted to engineer a coup to install Jeffrey Dujon as captain during the game in Barbados – the 1982 Shell Shield was poor by Rowe's standards.

Off the field, he was still the revered champion of old; a man whose commercial appeal as an ambassador was invaluable. His employer, Carrier Air Conditioning, where he worked in accounts, was so pleased to have him on the books that they built a concrete pitch at the office for him and the office team to practise on. They also boosted his bank account with a dollar for every run scored over 100. Property developer Matalon felt that the benefit of being associated with the 'batting specialist' was worth paying off the balance on his new home. He also owned a sports goods store with Jamaican team-mates Michael Holding and Basil Williams.

Always immaculately attired, Rowe, supported by his beautiful wife Violet, an air hostess with Air Jamaica, and their young daughter Stacey, projected an attractive package to the Jamaican people. But he was under no illusion as to where he stood. 'I thought without a doubt my career was over,' he says.

In the second half of 1982, rumblings across the Caribbean about a West Indies rebel tour to South Africa grew louder. Former Barbadian paceman Gregory Armstrong was the recruitment agent for Ali Bacher's dream of bringing a West Indies side to the republic. Fearsome fast bowlers Colin Croft and Sylvester Clarke had already shown interest, but the SACU needed to lock down a man whose stature and stainless reputation would add gravitas and star power to the concept. They needed the triple-century prestige of a Lawrence Rowe.

When Armstrong first approached Rowe, the Jamaica captain wasn't convinced, but he was interested enough in the idea to pass on the names of team-mates Everton Mattis and Richard Austin as potential recruits. It was Ali Bacher's call to Rowe at his home in the uptown Kingston suburb of Forest Hills that made him reassess his stance. He offered him the captaincy and a deal close to US$150,000. For Rowe, there were two main considerations. 'I asked myself: if we go there, could we make it any worse for the black people? And I thought: I can't see how we can make it worse. And could we inspire if we play well and win? The whites who could see us play and realise these are black people who can play – they are this good; then the blacks – it would be a victory for them if we win. I won't lie, of course, the money was important, too.'

Black-consciousness groups and the SACB had made it known that a tour would be seen as a validation of the whites-only government. They united around the slogan 'No normal sport in an abnormal society' and wondered aloud how black Caribbean cricketers could accept gargantuan sums of money to play sport in a country that discriminated against people of their own colour.

Rowe heard their pleas, but like African-American tennis star Arthur Ashe, who, defying public opinion, vowed to 'put a crack in the racist wall' by playing in the South African Open in 1973, he felt interaction, not isolation, was the best form of progress. 'Ashe said, "If you want black people to see you, you have to go through the white. They are using you, but you are using them." That's what we were doing.'

With the SACU circulating rumours that the tour had been cancelled to confuse the international media, at a Kingston press luncheon on 5 January, just seven days before the rebels would leave for South Africa, WICBC president Allan Rae expressed gratitude to Colin Croft and Rowe for apparently resisting Bacher's approaches. 'I believe the cricket fraternity of the West Indies ought to say a big thank you ... the gentlemen have put temptation behind them,' Rae beamed. Rowe and Croft said nothing.

What peeved many of Rowe's keenest supporters was that he'd seemingly deceived the public into thinking he was staying when it was his intention to go all along. Rowe's first Jamaica captain Easton McMorris says, 'I love Lawrence. I knew his situation – a poor fella growing up, and the opportunity to make some money. You can't give up that. I wasn't against him going to South Africa but denying it was childish, because you're a man, you've made a decision. My brother had a poster of Lawrence cover-driving and he turned it upside down when he found out he went to South Africa.'

Rowe maintains that he hadn't made up his mind at that point, and that it was in fact sports reporter and friend Tony Becca who told Rae that he wasn't going.

* * *

As Jamaica Prime Minister, Michael Manley had spoken out many times against apartheid in the UN. He was also a cricket tragic. In the early 1970s, when Rowe's star was in the ascendant, the People's National Party (PNP) leader took a personal interest in the development of the affable, well-mannered batting star. When Rowe twisted his ankle against the Australians in 1973, and his recovery dragged on, Manley intervened to have an orthopaedic specialist X-ray his foot. He invited Rowe ringside for the famous Frazier vs Foreman 'Sunshine Showdown' at the National Stadium and made a habit of congratulating Rowe publicly on his most recent century.

There's a 1974 photo of Rowe, gleaming belt buckle and sideburns, shaking hands with a safari-suited Manley at a government presentation. It was taken after Rowe's golden series against England when he made 616 runs at an average of 88, including three centuries. Manley was unable to attend the final Test in Port of Spain, but such was his devotion to Rowe, who scored 123, that he telephoned McMorris, a spectator at the ground, for a report on his innings.

'I told Manley you could not believe that he wasn't striking the ball through the off side like in Barbados when he scored 302. Because of the off cutters Greig was bowling – he got 13 wickets in the match – he was playing through midwicket and on the on side, a totally different innings. That was batsmanship of the highest class. Heady days – the prime minister calling me about cricket.'

When Manley received word the SACU was courting Rowe to captain the rebels, he attempted to broker a meeting to divert the classic batsman from what he saw as a 'course that could only bring disgrace and disaster'.

Rowe was having none of it. 'Manley was a giant of a man when it came to dealing with the sportsmen of this country,' he says. 'But I knew he only wanted to change my decision, and by then I had made it.' Stung by the snub and betrayal, Manley would later write that Rowe 'suffered from a flaw at the centre of his character'. Heavily weighing on Rowe's mind was the knowledge that if he pulled out, the whole tour would be in jeopardy, threatening the futures of players such as Everton Mattis, who had clambered out of the ghetto and was barely surviving as a professional cricketer.

Jeffrey Dujon, a product of Wolmer's School, which has nurtured six Test wicketkeepers, was Rowe's heir apparent as Jamaica captain. On the strength of his elegant batting, he'd edged out David Murray as West Indies gloveman on the 1981/82 tour of Australia. Rowe stood beside him at slip in the 1983 pre-season four-day match at Sabina Park against Bermuda. It was the last time they would play together. 'One day they, Rowe, Austin and Mattis, were there, the next day they were gone. Lawrence had come over and said, "What do you think about going to South Africa?" They really wanted the current team. It took me by surprise because I had only just made the West Indies team. I brushed it off and said, "I'll have to think about that," because I had no intention of going.'

The rebel tours permanently stained their friendship. Dujon had a lot to thank Rowe for; he'd helped to resurrect the young wicketkeeper's career when he was dropped after a run of low scores the previous season. 'It was the first time I'd been dropped from the Jamaica side since I was 18,' Dujon says. 'Lawrence put his hand up for me. I'd missed a few games and he said, "I need a wicketkeeper who can bat," and he got me into the next one-day game. I scored a half-century, kept wicket well and got my career going.'

But he felt let down by what he saw as Rowe's decision to sell out. 'Of all the Jamaicans who went, he was the one who needed the money least. It was quick money, but it came at a price. He was a hero here. He could have had a good life. I'm disappointed because he could have done a lot for our cricket. Viv Richards was a genius, but Lawrence knew the right way to play. He could teach kids the right way.'

As is often the case with perceptions of Rowe, the next generation, less encumbered by career tensions and dressing room politics, were more sympathetic. Jamaica team-mate Mark

Neita, 11 years Rowe's junior, gave him the benefit of the doubt. 'I did not support apartheid, I did not agree with the tours, but I understood the point where Lawrence Rowe reached. I don't think he would ever have played for West Indies again.'

Wayne Lewis, a former Kensington club team-mate whose rise through the ranks coincided with the tail end of Rowe's career, is the deputy president of the West Indies Players' Association. He's also a fan. 'A lot of the older guys were jealous of Lawrence. But we revered him. He was like the godfather. We could understand why he and the others went to South Africa for financial reasons.'

* * *

The rebels' flight from New York's Kennedy Airport to Johannesburg had started merrily. 'We sat drinking, having a gold old time,' Rowe says. 'Everybody was giving their experiences of leaving their respective countries and whether the press was there.'

Ten minutes before they landed, the atmosphere changed. 'The pilot announced we were about to arrive at the Jan Smuts International Airport, and everything went silent. You could hear a pin drop. It was like the reality is here; there is no turning back. As the plane started to get low, I looked through the window and saw some black guys working at the airport. I wondered what they were thinking about these black guys coming into South Africa.'

The truth is they probably weren't thinking much. Cricket barely registered on black South Africa's radar; football was their sport of choice. The *Rand Daily Mail* splashed their front page with 'Cricket rebels are on their way'; its township edition buried the same story underneath a political lead. It was the most prominent coverage the tour would get in black areas.

From the first, Rowe shouldered the dual burden of negotiating the daily grind of an international cricket tour and repeatedly justifying the rebels' presence to the world's media. 'It is no use trying to isolate people and keep them apart,' he told the press after the first match against Western Province. 'That is the very system we are trying to break down. The only way to persuade people to change things is to get together and exchange views – and this is exactly what we are doing on this tour. I'd be a fool if I didn't recognise there were problems in South Africa. But I'm from a Christian family and I pray we can do some good by giving the whites here a different perspective on black people.'

Being constantly under the spotlight took its toll. 'I've barely slept four hours. I've just been lying in my bed thinking about what we have done and the price we will pay.'

At the packed grounds, Rowe found solace. He was heartened to see white boys embracing their new black heroes. Television footage shows young fans in T-shirts and bucket hats streaming on to the field to snare West Indian autographs. 'They were holding on to our trousers and wanting to touch us. We were like gold. It was remarkable to see. You can't change that kid's mind now,' Rowe says proudly. 'Normally they were so distant from black people. A black man – I can't touch him or talk to him.'

There was also the matter of winning cricket matches. It was important to Rowe that his West Indies XI were competitive. 'We could have relaxed, got beat, gone sightseeing – we would have been paid just the same. But we wanted to show people back in the Caribbean. To this day we are still the only West Indian side to win in South Africa.'

* * *

The one word all his team-mates use to describe Rowe's captaincy is 'smooth'. Barbados all-rounder Franklyn Stephenson, just 23 at the time, says Rowe was the right leader for such a controversial tour. 'He'd look at the guys and say, "Okay, go ahead and do it." He's a cool kind of guy, not a dictating captain in a sense. I'm not sure that tour could have handled a dictating captain anyway. We were all in awe when he walked out to bat and how he moved on the field.'

The younger players soaked up the older man's wisdom. Surrey recruit Monte Lynch credits Rowe with improving his technique against quick bowlers by making him aware that he had much more time than he realised once the ball had been released. Off-spinner Derick Parry was just happy to get the chance to roll his arm over after feeling neglected under Clive Lloyd's pace-at-all-costs regime.

In 13 years of top-tier cricket, Lawrence Rowe had never bagged a pair until the second 'Test' in Johannesburg – castled twice, first by Vintcent van der Bijl and then by the inswing of Stephen Jefferies in the second innings. If Rowe was out of sorts, it was with good reason. In the back of his mind was his fracturing relationship with Michael Holding. 'Nothing shook me up so badly in South Africa as what he did to me,' Rowe says.

When it became clear that the injured Colin Croft wasn't going to play a role on tour, Rowe called his friend and business partner Holding, who was contracted to Tasmania in the Sheffield Shield, hoping he might secure his services as a bowling replacement for the remaining games. 'He told me he wouldn't come, but he also said, "Even if I could come, how could I get out of my contract with Tasmania?"' Rowe says.

When he read about their conversation in the newspaper a few days later, Rowe was furious. Holding had told Hobart's *Mercury* newspaper that Rowe had offered him US$250,000, and was quoted as saying, 'Principle is more important than the money.'

What particularly angered Rowe was that he felt that Holding was using their private conversation to 'make himself look virtuous' to the cricket world, demonising his former captain in the process. 'He never said anything about apartheid to me,' Rowe says. Holding refuses to be engaged on the subject, but in his book *Whispering Death* he wrote that he told Rowe during their telephone conversation that by being there, he was 'supporting apartheid'.

'What he writes in his book is not true. That is garbage,' Rowe says. 'Why mention me unless you want to destroy me as well? I also asked Patrick Patterson, but he didn't tell the whole world. And Larry Gomes. It hurt me so bad I made a pair in the next game.' And if there is no doubting, now, the strength of anti-apartheid conviction held by Holding and others like him, there is also no question of the passion animating Rowe. 'Everyone was trying to make themselves look good. They wanted to be able to say they turned it down because of their principles.'

* * *

Welkom is a mining city in the Free State. In 1983, its welcome didn't always include people of 'colour'. The final match of the first tour, a benefit for South African all-rounder Clive Rice and the retiring Barry Richards, was scheduled for the Rovers Club. What should have been a social, spectator-friendly finale to the tourists' campaign threatened to turn sour when Rowe found out the council had recently barred blacks from attending a concert given by a visiting Welsh choir. He wondered whether the colour bar would extend to the game, violating a non-negotiable standard he'd insisted on during contract talks: that people of all races be allowed into stadiums played at by the rebels.

He quickly informed Joe Pamensky, who reiterated the SACU's commitment to the non-racial treatment of spectators and threatened cancellation of the match. Chastened, the white-led council observed Pamensky's terms, but insisted the tourists would have to apply for permission to play squash or swim in municipal facilities.

It was a troubling reminder that the ugly manifestations of apartheid were never far from view, leavened, no doubt, by the presentation of krugerrand cufflinks to each of the tourists at a farewell banquet. It also demonstrated that Rowe, as a leader, was prepared to put principle before play.

* * *

Even before the second tour began ten months later, relations between the rebels and their South African paymasters began to fray. Rowe says he had to intervene to ensure countrymen Chang,

Austin and Wynter were paid in full when Bacher cut them from the squad in order to bring in new faces.

But sponsorship was at the crux of the fallout. As Rowe tells it, the SACU informed team manager Gregory Armstrong there was a lack of commercial support behind the tour. The West Indian brains trust of Padmore, Armstrong, Kallicharran and Rowe quickly enlisted an agent to find their own sponsors, and when they did, the SACU wasn't impressed, fearing a conflict with any sponsors they might secure.

At a hastily arranged meeting between the warring parties in the West Indies' Johannesburg hotel before the first one-day international (ODI), all hell broke loose. 'Pamensky got so mad he swore at us and walked away,' Rowe says. 'They didn't expect us to get any sponsors. Pamensky started going, "The tour is over, you breached the contract," so I told him to eff off out of here. You should have seen the look. He wasn't expecting that, especially from a black man.'

With their professional cricket careers within weeks of ending, the West Indians were anxious to eke as much money as they could from the remaining games. They also knew that gate receipts were at record levels and demanded a bigger slice of the pie. There was suspicion, too, that the SACU wasn't being entirely transparent about the level of their own sponsorship negotiations.

Rodney Hartman, in Bacher's biography, *Ali: The Life of Ali Bacher*, suggests that the West Indies wanted to boycott the game, throwing the future of the tour into chaos. When tempers cooled, the West Indies took to the field, but not in the maroon-coloured clothing they had been issued; instead they wore their whites as a protest at the way they had been treated. Eventually a deal with Yellow Pages worth 250,000 rand was struck guaranteeing 80,000 rand in bonuses, but the dynamic of the tour was irrevocably changed. Plans that Armstrong says were in train to make the West Indies tours an annual event for the next five years were binned for good.

A congested itinerary, dissatisfaction with the umpires' strict interpretation of the two bouncers per over rule, which Rowe saw as an attempt to rein in the effectiveness of the West Indies pace attack, and the grind of a ten-week campaign added to the lingering discontent.

The presence of Violet and daughter Stacey, four, who became something of a team mascot, precociously telling reporters when it was their turn to sit down to interview her father, went some way to alleviating the tour's stresses. Yet the batting stylist was still able to block out the off-field white noise and produce in the middle. Sporting a navy blue helmet, he claimed man of the one-day series honours. And there was room for one last 'Lawrence of Jamaica'-style innings, a typical widescreen effort of 157 in Durban.

At the end of the first tour, Rowe acknowledged that his side had offended some black South Africans who didn't want them there. At the second tour's conclusion he was convinced that at least some of those people appreciated his side's feats in conquering the all-white Springbok side, but his main concern now was where he and his family would live. The febrile, anti-rebel atmosphere in Jamaica, stoked by politicians and media upset at what they saw as a betrayal of the island's fundamental values, was, he and Violet concluded, an unsafe environment to bring Stacey up in. As the figurehead of the tours, his name was a lightning rod for vicious personal abuse and, Rowe says, threats of violence.

Violet had British citizenship, but Rowe wasn't confident of picking up a county contract, and he wanted to be close to his ageing parents, who still lived in Waltham Park Road. In a newspaper article, he confessed that he now felt like he was in 'no-man's land'. Lawrence of Jamaica had become Lawrence of nowhere. His siblings were bona fide 'Jamericans', having migrated to the US in the 1970s in search of work. Miami, close enough to Jamaica that he could monitor his parents, was an obvious choice for relocation. It would also give him a vantage point to assess the political temperature in Jamaica, so that he could, in his own words, 'feel his way' back to an eventual return. In addition he would not be far from his two sons, from a previous marriage, who were already at school in Kingston.

The initial plan was to stay for six months in Florida; although Rowe was banned from playing, he was keen to coach back in his native land and 'give back' to the game he loved. But Violet continued to harbour fears about their reception. It put a strain on their marriage. 'I wanted to return but she wasn't keen,' Rowe says. 'She was worried about what would happen in Jamaica and she said she liked living in Miami. We weren't as visible there. We weren't sure what would happen. We weren't turning over much financially in Miami. I wasn't a permanent resident – there was nothing for me to do. Violet had to leave her job with Air Jamaica. It was tough.' They divorced in the early 1990s.

Meanwhile, time hadn't softened attitudes where it counted – among Jamaica's cricketing elite. The strength of feeling against the rebels in cricket officialdom was evident at the 1984 Jamaica Cricket Association (JCA) annual general meeting when a motion was tabled by a member of Rowe's old club, Kensington, to allow the five Jamaican rebels back into the Senior Cup. Only three of more than 50 people present gave their support.

According to Rowe, it was a different story on the street. 'In my old neighbourhood of Waltham Park Road, everything was alright,' Rowe says. 'No problems. My father was extremely popular. The only things they would say would be behind his back.'

It was the tours' legacy of shattered friendships that took its greatest toll on Rowe, a naturally social man. It made him distrustful and wary of his former colleagues in a way that he wasn't before.

Franz Botek was a giant of Jamaican business and cricket. Managing director of the Jamaica Telephone Company, he served as treasurer of the WICBC, acquiring several important sponsorships that secured the future of the sport in the region.

To Rowe, he was a father figure. Described by Tony Becca, the doyen of Caribbean cricket writing, as a 'godfather to many young sportsmen', Botek acted as a sounding board for the graceful batsman, dispensing invaluable moral and financial advice from early on in his career.

'He was what you'd call a "big boy" in Jamaica, but he never talked down to you or looked down on you,' Rowe says. 'If I was going to sign a contract, he was the guy who would look it over. When I went on a West Indies tour, he'd be the first person I'd see when I got back home. He even came to Australia to watch us play.'

He also tried to talk Rowe out of going to South Africa, acting as the intermediary during Michael Manley's unsuccessful attempts to contact the Jamaica captain in the final days before he left for the republic.

During one of his reconnaissance trips to Jamaica in the early days after South Africa, Rowe tried to contact his old friend. The Wimbledon tennis final was on and Botek had one of the few satellite dishes in Kingston that could receive the game. 'I asked him if I could come and watch the match,' Rowe says. 'And he said to me, "You want to speak with Carol," his wife. I found it strange. That had never happened before. So, when she came on to the phone, I said, "Who's at the house?" She said, "Allan Rae, and all the people on the board." I said, "Okay," and hung up. I didn't think much of him after that. I didn't think he was my friend. To see that those guys were at his house – I am his friend, these are not his friends – it was like a betrayal.'

Wary and suspicious, Rowe felt his allies were deserting him. 'Some of his friends who were friends with me said I was taking it the wrong way, that he was in a spot. I said that's nonsense. If he said to me, listen, I have a few people I've invited here already and I don't know how you feel to be among them and I don't know if you would be comfortable among them, I would have said okay. I would not have put him in that position. I'll see you another time. It was painful. We never reconciled.'

From Miami, where he'd bought property and opened a successful vacuum seal business with the money earned from South Africa, Rowe began to harbour a deep sense of grievance about the way the West Indian authorities treated him and his rebel team-mates. It grated that the English rebel tourists only received a three-year ban and in particular that Graham Gooch and John Emburey were permitted to play on the English tour of the Caribbean in 1986, less than two years after representing Western Province in the Currie Cup. It seemed there was one rule for white cricketers and another for everyone else. 'I thought there was no way they could get around Gooch and Emburey. They played against us in South Africa. How can you ban us for life and have these guys coming here? That's when I came to the conclusion that all of this was a farce,' Rowe says.

For four years Tony Becca had tried to lure Rowe from his Miami eyrie with the promise of headlining the annual Milo/Melbourne Cricket festival at the famous Derrymore Road ground in New Kingston. The club president could rely on Holding and Courtney Walsh, two of Melbourne's favourite sons, and he also had the services of Andy Roberts, Joel Garner and Jeff Dujon, but in Becca's eyes none of these greats came close to matching Rowe's star power. 'He was so loved in Jamaica, I knew that the people would come to see him, but he always had an excuse for not coming,' Becca said.

In 1994, the now 45-year-old Rowe changed his mind. If he'd had any fears that the public's love affair with him had soured, they were quickly allayed. 'Batting stylist heads star cast' boomed the match preview headline in *The Gleaner*. 'The ground was filled with people,' Becca said. 'He made 14 runs, and when he got out people got up and left the ground.'

'Rowe's timing was off key on a number of occasions,' *The Gleaner* reporter wrote. 'But to the thousands who came specifically to see him, it hardly mattered, as they saw him in the flesh.'

Two days later, Becca received a phone call from Michael Manley, now ill with prostate cancer. 'He asked me how Lawrence was. He wanted to know how he was going. He loved Lawrence, but he was so disappointed with him going to SA.'

Rowe maintains he always respected Manley's views, but says, like all politicians, the former prime minister's principles could be jettisoned when politically expedient. He says Jamaica's failure to follow Guyana's boycott of the 1976 Olympic Games demonstrated Manley's inability to match his anti-apartheid rhetoric with action. African nations pulled out in protest at New Zealand's rugby union tour of South Africa, and Guyana, under vocal Prime Minister Forbes Burnham, followed suit. 'Why didn't Jamaica pull out? Sprinter Donald Quarrie. Manley wanted to see him win gold at the Olympics. That's what suited him at the time,' says Rowe.

In his defence, Manley, the leading non-aligned figure in the fight against apartheid, said Jamaica's decision to participate in the Games was based on the fact that no one in New Zealand's Montreal squad had actually been to South Africa.

In Jamaica, apart from occasional historical references to the rebels in the press – and a petty newspaper debate blaming his 'pretty' batsmanship for the island's lack of gritty run-gatherers – Rowe's name faded from public consciousness. When in 2004 he was named alongside Holding, Dujon, Headley and Walsh as one of the country's top five cricketers of the past 75 years at a ceremony in Kingston's Pegasus Hotel, it seemed he'd been pardoned. Glowing with the belated acceptance of his peers, Rowe felt emboldened enough to declare that he could even have been one of the West Indies' top five save for the injuries that dogged his career. Seven years later he would find out that acceptance had its limits.

* * *

The North Street campus of Kingston College, the alma mater of Michael Holding and Marlon Samuels, is about 200 yards from Sabina Park. When Test matches are held at the ground, excited college schoolboys can hear the cheers and jeers. It makes focusing on history lessons difficult. Like a lot of his classmates, Delano Franklyn would sneak off to the stadium to catch a glimpse of the West Indies in action. In 1972, aged 14, he was there to witness Rowe's historic double century and century on Test debut. It changed his life. 'I was transfixed in my seat. I had never seen a more technically competent batsman, someone so comfortable at the wicket. He was cricket personified. When Lawrence Rowe walked to the wicket, you became a different person. You felt what it was to be a real fan of cricket. He made it the kind of sport it ought to be. I grew up loving Lawrence Rowe.' So enraptured was Franklyn by Rowe's ability to conjure shapes with his Gray-Nicholls bat that others could only dream of, he invented a word, 'Lawrencetonian', to describe it.

Delano Franklyn, practising attorney at law, former PNP minister of state and chief advisor to prime ministers, is also Rowe's biggest nemesis, one of the men he blames for triggering the most embarrassing incident in his life. In 1983, when it was reported that Rowe was to lead a rebel team to South Africa, Franklyn was crestfallen. In his eyes, his hero had let him down. 'I was rocked,' he says. 'And the blow became more decisive when it turned out he was captain and instrumental in recruiting others.'

A protege of Michael Manley, he was aware of his country's proud history of confronting apartheid on the world stage. 'It is something we have always been against and we expected our idols to adhere to what we considered understood by any reasonable human being.' He poured scorn on Rowe's argument that by playing in South Africa blacks would feel better about themselves if they saw men of their own race beating their white masters on the cricket field. 'If I am feeling pain and I say to you, "Don't touch my hand because it is going to increase my pain," who are you to tell me that if you touch my hand it's going to make me feel better? So, when the leadership of the ANC said to the rebel team and leadership in Jamaica, "Don't come," then don't come. Because, on the contrary, what the apartheid government is trying to do is to transmit to the world that despite apartheid being here, we are able to host and let into our country some of the best cricketers out there. It is assisting the process of apartheid, not dismantling it.'

In 2011, Lyndel 'Mud' Wright had just ascended to the job as president of the JCA. The former Shell Shield all-rounder and brother of West Indies legend Collie Smith had grown up playing cricket with Rowe. They were close friends, and as one of his first moves as president he proposed the idea of honouring Rowe, Courtney Walsh and Michael Holding by having parts of Sabina Park named after them. Holding would get the southern end, Walsh the northern end and Rowe the players' pavilion. On paper, it seemed like a popular decision, and in Rowe's case it would finally put a line under 27 years of recrimination and bitterness. 'Lawrence of Jamaica' was back.

Former Jamaica Labour Party Prime Minister Edward Seaga, Michael Manley's bitter adversary, was one of those who applauded the move. 'I don't have a problem with Rowe being honoured ... because so many other people who have done far worse than him have been forgiven.'

But from the beginning there were murmurs of discontent, misgivings from cricket people worried that Rowe's name etched on the players' pavilion would reopen old wounds. Tony Becca, a Rowe supporter, was sceptical. 'I spoke to Lyndel and said hold on a while, you have to get the people in this society onside before you do it, and maybe have a vote on it. He said he would get back to me, but I never heard back from him.'

Kingston Cricket Club owns Sabina Park. Together with the JCA, they administer the ground. Douglas Beckford sat on the board as a Kingston CC member when the pavilion-naming proposal was rammed through. He says the board favoured an alternative solution that would have let cricket fans decide the pavilion's name. 'Lawrence Rowe was not the only one worthy of consideration. Throw it open to the public or members of the organisation. Why not call it the Allan Rae, Jeff Dujon, Jackie Hendricks, Gerry Alexander, Collie Smith or Frank Worrell pavilion?' But he maintains that Wright overrode them because he had the backing of the powerful JCA. 'We said we don't think you should go ahead with this. I think we had forgiven Lawrence; we just weren't prepared to elevate him.'

Wright, clearly still uncomfortable with how the saga would play out, is unwilling to speak on the matter, other than to reaffirm that 'the decision was taken by the whole of the board'.

A lawyer for the JCA, Franklyn was also a close friend of Wright's. Given his stance on the rebel tours it was no surprise he wasn't in favour of honouring Rowe, but he was 'prepared to accept an apology and see how we take it from there'.

It was the apology, which was a condition of receiving the award, which became the sticking point. Initially thrilled, Rowe began to have reservations. Flying into Kingston from Miami, he spent a long night arguing with Wright about having to say sorry for events that occurred 28 years ago. 'I did not want to apologise. I have nothing to apologise for. I said, "You invite me here and I did not know this was going to come up. I'll go back to Miami. You don't have to put my name up. No hard feelings."'

According to Rowe, Wright spent five hours that evening trying to convince him to swallow his pride and apologise. 'He said to me, "I will have to resign. We have been friends since we were 13." I thought, if I don't do it, I'll force him to lose his job, so I said, "I will sleep on it."'

The next day Rowe relented, but he'd decided he wouldn't read a JCA-approved apology; instead, he would deliver one in his own words. But in the car ride to Sabina Park for the ceremony, which was arranged to take place at lunch during the first Test against India, Rowe was already having second thoughts. He confided in his wife, Audrey. 'I told her, "I think I'm making a big mistake." Even as I started to walk over to the main pavilion I did not want to go. The world press was there, and they were saying why now? I was saying some things that were pure lies because the board were honouring me – it was only fair for me to bury the hatchet and apologise. When I was done, one of the board members said I handled myself superbly.'

Afterwards, Rowe, resplendent in charcoal grey suit, red shirt and bright green tie, posed for photos under the sign that now bore his name. 'It's good to be back,' he told the press, 'and after making my apology formal, I hope that the people in the region who I offended forgive me. After all that took place in the past, it is an honour and privilege to be recognised in this way.'

Jamaica's prodigal son had returned to the fold. Wright was also happy, and relieved, telling *The Gleaner* that despite Rowe's 'error in judgement' in leading the rebels to South Africa, the honour was appropriate because of the 'sterling contribution to the game he has made in this region'.

Rowe's rehabilitation lasted barely a day. That evening, he gave an interview to the *Beyond the Headlines* programme on RJR, one of Kingston's most popular radio stations, with political journalist Dionne Jackson Miller. At the time, Delano Franklyn was driving home from his Crossroads office in midtown Kingston but he was so shocked by what he heard that he had to pull over. 'Rowe said, "I did nothing wrong." He'd apologised to appease those who might not have been in support of him.'

Franklyn was particularly incensed that Rowe had invoked the name of Paul Bogle, a 19th-century national hero who was executed after leading a rebellion against British rule. 'He said, "Look at some of our national heroes, they were seen as crooks. Look at Paul Bogle and what he did, and he became a national hero, so in 40 or 50 years, I may also be looked at as a national hero."' Franklyn phoned Wright to tell him he'd withdrawn his support and would be campaigning for the removal of Rowe's name from the pavilion. Wright was stunned.

Rowe, who began to feel the blowback from his interview the following day at the Test at Sabina Park, now thinks the radio interview was a set-up. 'I was going to stop the interview; she was all about taking me down,' he says now. 'She kept on saying, "Why are you apologising now?"'

He maintains he never reneged on his apology – an apology he never wanted to give – in the interview. Instead, he says he made it clear that 28 years ago he thought the South Africa tours were right, but with the benefit of hindsight that was no longer the case. He also said that history would be the real judge of his actions.

Franklyn wasn't persuaded. He wrote a series of articles in *The Gleaner* and the *Jamaica Observer* turning up the heat on Wright and the JCA to take down Rowe's name. It lit the blue touchpaper for a divisive public debate, as momentum built for the JCA to take action.

Rowe tried to talk Wright out of it. 'There was a backlash on him. He said sponsors weren't coming on board because some of the people on the companies didn't like that I was honoured. But that is a short-term thing. I said all you have to do is weather the storm.'

Wright was caught in a classic Shakespearean bind – torn between the demands of two dear friends he admired and respected. 'I remember one afternoon, when we met with guys who went through the Boys' Town club, which Lyndel has had years of association with,' Franklyn says. 'We would drink and socialise. But he was completely quiet. And I could see that here is a man burdened and caught in the crossfire.'

Three months later when Wright called Rowe in Miami to break the news that the JCA was rescinding his honour on the basis of what he'd said in the radio interview, Rowe was aghast. 'I asked him if he had heard the interview. He told me no. Franklyn had been writing these articles demeaning me and he didn't stand up and let the people know what was happening. I bent over backwards to deal with the conditions he wanted. I did not ask for this. He totally destroyed me. He went back on everything. We don't even talk now.'

For Franklyn, slaying his childhood hero was bittersweet. 'I went through a lot of emotions and a lot of wrangling coming to the position I did. I understand the gut-wrenching feelings Rowe was going through. But ultimately it was the principle and what was obtained in relation to the greater good.'

An interview Rowe did with sportscaster Orville Higgins on daytime radio days after his name was erased from the pavilion brought home to Franklyn how much pain and torment the former great was in. 'I heard the hurt, because after 28 years he did not ask for this thing. If Lawrence had not given the interview, we would not be talking about this now. If Lawrence Rowe were to walk in right now, I would not be the one to say don't join us. On the contrary, I would be the one to say join us.'

Rowe was devastated by the saga. He felt that his reputation had been destroyed by the JCA. He initiated legal proceedings against the board, declaring, 'I want the JCA to give me back my character. They have totally defamed me. My earning power throughout the world has been damaged. They have destroyed me at age 62.'

Once again Franklyn, as the JCA lawyer, was the roadblock between Rowe and validation. When Rowe found out that his own legal representative had previously worked with Franklyn, he was so enraged that he forfeited his J$90,000 deposit. It seemed as if the whole of Jamaica was conspiring against him. 'Nothing has upset me more than what happened,' Rowe says. 'It was a total mess, which embarrassed me. It was a miserable time in my life.'

Yet letters to the editor showed sympathy for Rowe's plight; one pointed out that reggae artist Jimmy Cliff performed in South Africa in 1979 and was subsequently awarded the Order of Merit, Jamaica's third-highest honour. Others were dismayed at what they saw as an inability to forgive, a meanness of spirit in the Jamaica character. His critics labelled him the 'consummate creature of convenience' and worse.

After the naming fiasco, Rowe retreated to Miami and the vacuum seal business that has sustained him and his family for nearly three decades, vowing not to let feelings of resentment destroy him. Instead, as if to prove that he was better than the calculating villain depicted in certain sections of the Jamaican press, he set up the Lawrence Rowe Legendary Cricket Foundation, a three-pronged charity that helps impoverished schoolchildren in Miami and Kingston, promotes black history and assists West Indian cricketers who have fallen on hard times. A few years ago, US$6,000 was raised for ex-West Indian paceman Patrick Patterson through a banquet and exhibition match, which attracted legends Sir Garfield Sobers and Brian Lara. Plans were afoot to assist fellow rebel Richard Austin, but the drug-addicted former Test all-rounder died before they could be acted on.

Rowe bristles at any suggestion that he's seeking a form of redemption through the foundation. 'I don't want to redeem myself from anything. As far as South Africa goes, I don't see there is anything I have done wrong.'

Over the past 36 years, the anonymity of Miami, far from Kingston's barrage of verbal beamers and bumpers, must have seemed like a form of paradise to Rowe. Outwardly at least it has treated him well. His skin is as smooth and unblemished as his batsmanship – he looks at least a decade younger than his 71 years. Untucked blue-and-black gingham shirt, dark slacks and black leather loafers suggest a man comfortable with his place in the world. He's quick to laugh and, surprisingly, given his history of feuds, even quicker to praise. Yet the casual, avuncular facade also conceals the scars of a fight that seems to have no end.

Instead of forced exile, he knows that if he'd resisted Bacher's advances, he could have been a national hero. Not a Paul Bogle hero, but a Michael Holding or Courtney Walsh hero, perhaps working in commentary or in coaching the national side, in the shadow of a pavilion that all his countrymen were proud to call by his name.

'Yes, I've thought about it,' he says. Yet his regret isn't so much about having perhaps chosen the wrong path at critical junctures in his life; rather, it's regret that officials and politicians didn't give him the opportunities he thinks he deserved. 'I know Jackie Hendricks, who was president of the board, was trying to get me back to coach, but every time it got close, the South Africa thing came up.'

In 2007, he was invited to Jamaica as a TV analyst for the ICC World Cup, but it only served to highlight what he'd missed out on. 'I believe I could have been a world commentator,' he says. 'But one of the biggest regrets I have is the club ban. I wanted Kensington to fight it. They couldn't have beaten us. It was restraint of trade. But that's why I didn't fight to come back to Jamaica, because I wasn't able to give to the younger kids playing at the club level. And I think the West Indies lost out.'

There's also the friendship carnage. Rowe occasionally lapses into calling Michael Holding 'Mikey', as if they are still good buddies, but they are no longer close. He puts some of the acrimony from former players down to envy, not the rebel tours. 'I believe that these guys were so jealous of what I was. A lot of people describe me in Jamaica as what Usain Bolt is now. Few of us reach that level, that kind of iconic level from the public. Mikey never got that. I don't know why.'

Do the fractured friendships keep him awake at night? 'Never,' he says. Indeed, Rowe is never less than sure of himself. But when doubt encroaches, he turns to God for solace. His foundation is linked to the Gospel Light Church, and in those dark nights of the soul in hotel rooms far, far from home, he would call on his faith to sustain him. He also carries these words of Nelson Mandela with him. 'Sport is more powerful than governments in breaking down racial barriers. It laughs in the face of all types of discrimination.' He can almost recall them by heart. They bolster him when critics' slings and arrows threaten.

The great irony, of course, was that South Africa, once a pariah state, is now embraced by the world, while Rowe, one embraced by his people, has for many years been the pariah. Over time, those attitudes have softened, especially among the younger generation. Perhaps as Kingston Cricket Club board member Douglas Beckford said, 'Jamaica has forgiven the rebels, but they will never honour them.'

Either way, Rowe has no regrets. 'I had such a strong belief in the cause, and I honestly believe that is why I got through it,' he says, as he climbs back into his white Range Rover and a life of exile. 'The only person who can convince me that is not so is Jesus Christ. If he comes down to me and says, "You are wrong," I will apologise.'

Herbert Chang

'He thought he was the best in the world'

TRIFLUOPERAZINE IS an anti-psychotic drug. Herbert Chang takes one tablet twice a day. A side effect is drowsiness, which means Chang often sleeps in the morning, and when he wakes up his speech is a little slurred. He spends most of the rest of the day wandering up and down Fourth Street in Greenwich Town, a ghetto area of south-west Kingston close to the Caribbean Sea, where he lives with seven other relatives in a partly repaired concrete-brick house.

Sometimes he stops at a shop to buy a bottle of Pepsi Cola – he usually drinks three or four of them a day – before slowly making his way past stray dogs and busted car parts back to the family home. Across the pot-holed road, the cream-coloured façade of the Apostolic Faith Church encourages worshippers to bathe in 'the light of Jesus'. In his more lucid moments, Herbert Chang must wonder whether that light shines on him anymore.

Google-searching images of 'Herbert Chang cricketer' is an unsettling exercise. In one, a heavily pixilated black-and-white picture of a young man in a terry towelling bucket hat stares aimlessly at the viewer. It could be a 'wanted' photograph. Then there are the so-called biographies; second-hand accounts of his life, based for the most part on hearsay, that describe Jamaica's only West Indies batsman of Chinese heritage as 'living the life of a destitute', 'mentally deranged' and even 'standing listlessly in a dark alley' – another victim of the so-called South African rebel curse.

In cyberspace, Chang is a strange and forbidding character. In reality, he's a 67-year-old man living with a psychological disorder and the tragedy of a wasted life. He's not crazy. He's not incoherent. But he's also no longer the 'cocky little fucker' who, Jeff Dujon says, taunted and destroyed the Caribbean's most ferocious bowlers with displays of batting bravado that belied his diminutive stature. The 5ft 5in slugger who shirt-fronted Joel Garner, all 6ft 8in of him, with the words: 'I hear they call you Big Bird, well I'm gonna clip your wings today, Big Bird.'

Patrick Gibson says his half-brother's breakdown was gradual. He recalls the excessive and pointless flights to Miami, sometimes more than five a month. Chang's sister Hyacinth Bell remembers him 'travelling, travelling, travelling' without a purpose. It was as if in the surreal comfort of an aeroplane, divorced from society's constant demands, he could escape the problems troubling him.

There's little in Chang's childhood to suggest the mental turmoil that would follow. The Chinese presence in Jamaica, especially in the retail trades, is well established. His father Gilbert's family ran ice cream parlours and grocery stores in west Kingston. Gilbert was also an effective medium-pace bowler for Railway in the Senior Cup, and Chang's brother Franchot played football to a high level.

His mother, Veronica Chavennes, is of French-Caribbean heritage. From an early age he lived with her and his half-siblings in the house on Fourth Street – a not uncommon situation in the West Indies, where mixed families are often the most convenient way of bringing up children. Hyacinth says his attendance at Greenwich All Age School was only distinguished by his devotion to 'cricket, cricket, cricket'.

The first mention of Chang in the nation's leading newspaper, *The Gleaner*, describes an 'outstanding young batsman' who richly deserves his call-up for the inaugural West Indies youth tour of England in 1970.

Three years later, following a defiant 64 in his third first-class match, against a Dennis Lillee-led Australian attack, sportswriter Jack Anderson anointed the pugnacious left-hander and a certain Michael Holding as the future of Jamaican cricket.

However, it was during the regional Shell Shield competition that the legend of Chang the fearless competitor and belligerent sledger emerged. The targets of his pitch chat were always the most lethal bowlers in world cricket, the men he had to get on top of if he was to move up the West Indies pecking order. He took a special delight in scoring heavily against Barbados, where the wicket, buttressed by coral limestone bedrock, was hard and fast. In April 1980, he faced down the fearsome four-prong attack of Malcolm Marshall, Joel Garner, Wayne Daniel and Sylvester Clarke, men who blasted out 713 Test batsmen between them. Fast-bowling behemoths with frightening reputations.

'He never feared anyone,' says Maurice Foster, Chang's first Jamaican captain. 'He was never intimidated by names. He felt he could score runs against anyone.'

In the first innings of that Shield match, Chang slammed a nine-boundary 50, as his team-mates floundered, 'viciously hooking, pulling and cutting anything short from the speedsters' according to *The Gleaner*'s correspondent. Garner took 6-37.

Requiring 301 in the second innings just to make Barbados bat again, Chang at number four smashed 132, a lone hand, as Jamaica crumbled to 295 all out. But it was the way Chang marked his century that lives in the memory of those who were at Kensington Oval. Jeff Dujon batted at number five. 'Changie played a short-arm jab through midwicket to bring up his 100,' he says. 'Then he took off his gloves and put them down on the wicket. He stood there – it was funny – he's just a short guy. Then he goes, "Well, what are you going to bowl to me now?" I'm just looking at him thinking this guy's a confident little fucker.' He then turned to each of the pace greats and gave them verbals one by one, reminding them that their efforts weren't quite good enough to dislodge Herbert Samuel Chang.

When the Barbados quicks peppered him with bouncers, he would question their intelligence, pointing out that the stumps weren't above his head, and that if they couldn't get him out when they bowled a regular length either, they may as well head back to the dressing room.

Not even the doyen of Caribbean pace, Andy Roberts, was exempt from Chang's gamesmanship. Team-mate Mark Neita, five years Chang's junior, was impressed by his elder's unrelenting self-belief. 'We played against Combined Islands in St Kitts in 1981, and before the match started, Changie was telling everyone how he was going to "kill Andy Roberts with lick", which is a Jamaican way of saying he was going to hit him all over the park, and score a century. When Roberts was passing the dressing room, Changie said, "Morning, Mr Roberts, I will see you out there," and Andy just waved back. When it came to bat, Andy got him out for a duck twice. But you had to admire he never took a step back.'

Probably the most audacious of his targets was Clive Lloyd, whose power and influence at the time was such that he wasn't so much the father of West Indies cricket as the godfather. Fielding at short leg at Bourda in a Shell Shield game, Chang was unimpressed by the Guyanese's momentary lack of timing at the crease. 'What kind of shot was that from the West Indies captain?' he needled. 'You can't even hit a full toss.'

Fortunately, when he did get the call-up to be the 173rd West Indian cap, Lloyd was contracted to WSC. As in Australia, the Caribbean was decimated by player defections to Kerry Packer's professional troupe, and the WICBC was desperate to fill the breach left by Richards, Greenidge, Rowe et al.

A consistent scorer at Shell Shield level, Chang got his chance on the 1978/79 tour of India under the captaincy of Alvin Kallicharran. He'd been controversially denied a first cap earlier in the year against Bob Simpson's Australians on his home ground of Sabina Park when Faoud Bacchus was preferred as a replacement for opener Alvin Greenidge, who was ill.

But in the fourth of the six-Test series at Madras, the selectors decided to play an extra batsman, much to the dismay of a young Malcolm Marshall, who was dropped to make way for Chang. Marshall's ire was heightened when the wicket turned out to be one of the fastest in Indian history, provoking the unlikely scenario of a bumper war between the West Indies pacemen Sylvester Clarke and Norbert Phillip and Indian seamers Kapil Dev and Karsan Ghavri. It was so slippery that Sunil Gavaskar told Reuters that he'd 'never seen a faster pitch and wouldn't want to'.

The greentop's unpredictable bounce meant that left-armer Ghavri – fast-medium at best – was able to extract nasty lift off a good length. Chang was one of his victims in the second innings, out hit wicket reeling from a ball that struck him on the head off a top edge. Jamaicans, reared on the batsmen-maiming antics of Michael Holding and Patrick Patterson, call body blows 'ledda'. This was serious 'ledda'.

'I slipped,' Chang says now, his memory undimmed by the passage of time. 'I got a lick from the ball. If I stayed in with Larry Gomes ...'

His captain, Kallicharran, was less circumspect: 'It was dangerous,' he says. 'He stepped on the wicket – he was so fucking scared!'

Some commentators say there was blood on the crease. It was a cruel and unusual method for a Test debutant to be dismissed – Chang had made just two runs to go with his six in the first innings – but he wasn't the only one to cop 'ledda'; Chauhan and Vengsarkar also had their faces pasted.

Patrick Gibson suspects that head knock, along with others Chang may have endured in a mostly helmetless cricket career, contributed to his brother's later psychological problems. Chang isn't so sure. What is certain is that he would never play for the West Indies again. Not that it bothered him. 'Boasie' is a Jamaican word meaning someone who carries themselves in a brash and showy fashion. Gibson says it perfectly encapsulates his brother in the late 1970s and early 1980s.

At that time, Greenwich Town was a breeding ground for roots reggae and dub music. Young artistes flocked to the area from the country hoping to absorb the vibe and get spotted by local producers. They would congregate on a stretch of footpath known as 'Corner Stone' on Sixth Street, shooting the breeze and drinking beer. Chang, the flashy local sporting hero, fitted in easily. Always well groomed, he would chug on a Heineken, his favourite brew, but never get more than three-quarters of the way down the bottle – there was no cachet in the dregs.

One of his best friends was Bertram Brown, who operated the Freedom Sounds studio around the corner from him at 14 East Avenue, where urban reggae icons Earl Zero and Prince Alla had cut vinyl. In the heady, experimental days of the 1970s it was common practice – and financially smart – to record a bunch of tracks over a few days with the house band Soul Syndicate providing backing. If a singer or instrumentalist was needed, he could be quickly recruited from the Corner Stone crowd. It kept things raw and real.

It's how Chang, who had a reputation as a smooth dancer, came to lay down lyrics and vocals on 'Coming of Jah', a gentle Rasta track, which, in the spirit of the day, aspired to 'free the children of Israel' and was later given dub treatment by the legendary King Tubby. The 1978 record is now a collector's item.

This was Chang in his pomp. This was what only the coolest of Test cricketers were invited to do. 'In those days, people used to look up to Herbert Chang,' Hyacinth Bell says. 'But now,' she adds sorrowfully, 'he is shit.'

It's a withering assessment, but her brother's days in the cricket sun weren't quite over yet. He continued to score heavily for Jamaica, always saving his best for the bumper boys of Barbados, and as he moved into his late 20s, became something of a mentor for younger players, despite a hard-earned reputation for hogging the strike. 'He had a talent for taking a single off the last ball of the over,' Dujon says. 'So, you'd be batting with him and you wouldn't get a whole lot of strike. He used to get to you after a while.'

Neita made his Jamaica debut in 1978. Talk of Chang's idiosyncrasies draws a wry smile. 'He was very encouraging to me,' he says. 'I remember we went to Guyana to play against Colin Croft. It was my first year of playing. Croft had removed the first half of the batting. He said, "Come on, keep your eye on the ball," and that kind of stuff. They brought on a spinner, and the first two balls he bowled to me I hit for four. And I saw Changie making a face. The next ball I hit for four again, and he quickly came down the wicket and said to me, "Churchill," he used to call me by my middle name, "if you beat up this man's ball, they will bring back Croft. No hit him more fours!" And let me tell you, he bowled just the one over and Croft was back on us. Changie wasn't happy.'

Chang goes so far as to say he had an 'agreement' with the WICBC to 'train the men up' to Test level. Clive Lloyd says he didn't. He insists he harboured no great desire to play international cricket and much preferred passing on the finer points of batting, and sledging, to up and coming youngsters such as Marlon Tucker and the Gordon brothers.

His famed feistiness also played out in the dressing room. Kensington Cricket Club, at Rollington Town on Kingston's east side, has supplied many West Indies cricketers since its inception in 1877 as St Andrews Juniors. During the late 1970s, it was home to Lawrence Rowe, Basil 'Shotgun' Williams, Richard Austin and Chang. All had Test experience, and all had egos to match. 'They were great players but could never win anything as a team because they were always fighting each other about tactics,' Neita says. 'Before they got on the field it would be war between them. Cussing, running people off the field ...'

Chang and his captain Rowe didn't always get on. The triple centurion and supreme stylist played by the rules, headstrong Chang was his own man. *The Gleaner* of 21 July 1978 reports Chang as being dropped by Rowe from the Kensington Senior

Cup side 'for failure to faithfully attend practice sessions' and maintaining a 'disinterested stance in the question of his practising regularly'.

Similar tensions were on display in the Jamaica side. Chang and Austin, both natural raconteurs, tended to dominate the dressing room with their tales of cricket conquests past. 'They were the funniest people,' Neita remembers. 'They always had good stories to tell.'

They also enjoyed niggling each other. If Austin was slated to open and Chang thought his friend out of his depth against the new-ball bowler, Chang would pad up and badger skipper Rowe to let him front the innings.

Batting order, bowling changes and field placements were often the subject of epic argument. In the 1981/82 Shell Shield things came to a head when Chang and Austin tried to stage a leadership coup before the match against Barbados at Kensington Oval. 'We had our run-ins from time to time on the field,' Rowe says. 'They probably thought I was too tough about certain things with them. They wanted Jeffrey Dujon to take over.' Rowe laughs. In light of how Chang and Austin's lives turned out it seems almost preposterous to think they could have dethroned a national sporting hero. 'I remember giving a warning. I said when the team is selected and I'm captain, I will deal with whoever I'm supposed to deal with. But I was never known to be a person who could keep up that kind of thing. I was able to work with you even if you weren't with me; I respected your ability on the field and how you can play. Chang could be quite militant. He thought he was the best in the world. He was an extremely confident and gritty man – a fine player.'

He was Jamaica's finest that season, his last full campaign in first-class cricket, belting 426 runs at 47.33; not enough to trade the dark blue of Jamaica for West Indian maroon, but enough to show he could still mix it with the best.

Chang was now almost 30. He could retire from first-class cricket knowing he was at the top of his game. There were commercial interests to pursue; he ran a betting shop, which employed two of his half-sisters, and he had business investments in California where his uncle lived. He also owned property in Portmore on the south coast and picked up work when he needed it at the West Indies Pulp and Paper on East Bell Road just minutes from Greenwich Town.

Then there were the children he'd sired – five of them – Princess, Donna, Herbert, Damien and Orville, to three 'baby mothers', some in 'visiting relationships', where Chang, as many men in the Caribbean do, lived apart from his partner.

He did, however, play the first Shell Shield match of 1982/83 against Trinidad, compiling a typically gutsy 64, a knock that led to *The Gleaner*'s correspondent labelling him as 'evergreen'.

By this stage, three of his Jamaica team-mates, Rowe, Austin and Everton Mattis, were already in South Africa, representing a rebel West Indies XI against the Springboks in a tour branded 'humiliating' to black people by former Jamaican Prime Minister and leader of the opposition Michael Manley. But it was clear the rebel side was short of a quality batsman. Chang had accepted he would never play for the West Indies again. A final payout reputed to be in excess of US$80,000 would make all the hard work and sacrifice of the past decade seem worthwhile.

But the perception remained that he was the 'evergreen' batsman, a stalwart of the national cricket side. Surely he wouldn't turn against the sporting and political establishment ... That's certainly what Allan Rae, the president of the WICBC thought. As speculation swirled about Chang's connections to South Africa, a notorious conversation took place between the two towards the end of the Trinidad match.

Rae: 'Mr Chang, there is a rumour that you are going to South Africa to play cricket. If this is not true, let us know, and we will assist you in scotching it.'

Chang: 'Mr Rae, I have no contract to play in South Africa.'

Rae: 'I did not ask you if you have a contract. Are you going to South Africa?'

Chang: 'Me? Going to South Africa? No, sir!'

A day later, barely out of his creams, Chang was on a plane to New York, having answered Lawrence Rowe's SOS call to join the rebels in South Africa.

* * *

It's a dry and dusty Wednesday afternoon in Greenwich Town, and Herbert Chang is sitting on the edge of an unused garden bed inside the gates of the Apostolic Faith Church across the road from his family's house. In the gutter, a couple of malnourished cats are playing with an empty plastic bottle of Coke.

Chang wears a baggy white T-shirt, burgundy-coloured shorts and leather sandals, all bought by his sister Hyacinth, who finances his wellbeing from her base in New York. His eyes have a milky quality, the legacy of decades of prescription drug use, and his voice is soft, the words occasionally garbled. It's clearly not the combative Chang of yesteryear, but neither is it the 'lost' man even his ex-team-mates have prepared me for.

Every ten minutes or so he asks, 'What else you want to know?' The effort of socialising obviously tires him and there's a sense of irritation, but his cricket memory is still sharp.

So how did he justify lying to Allan Rae? 'I didn't have the contract when I said that,' he says. One can only assume he received and signed it very quickly.

Was he worried about being banned from playing first-class cricket for life? 'No. Cricket was what I had played all the time. I'd finished. I thought I would stop at 30. Not really sad.'

Was he bothered by apartheid in South Africa? 'It's not what I believe. I wanted to see what kind of cricket they play in South Africa. They were good enough in the '60s. They were a champion side.'

Chang arrived in Johannesburg two days after the first 'Test', a cruisy five-wicket win for the Springboks. He missed the second and final 'Test', but played in four of the six ODIs, collecting scores of 23, 33, 5 and 0. 'I never performed as well as I would have liked,' he says.

Like a lot of the rebel batsmen he had trouble handling the left-arm bowling of Stephen Jefferies. It's one of the reasons Ali Bacher never invited him back for the return tour nine months later. Not for the first time, Faoud Bacchus would get the nod over him. 'They wanted to try some other players,' Chang says, without any hint of disappointment.

'What else you want to know?'

What happened next is the missing piece in the Herbert Chang jigsaw. The piece that explains why Chang is who he is today. The rumours, and there are many, centre around the huge payment he was meant to have received from South Africa – 60 times an average Jamaican's annual wage – and the woman he planned to marry. Most suggest that Chang was sending the money back to her in Kingston and she pocketed it for herself, before fleeing to Canada with their two children and shacking up with another guy. Chang is then said to have followed her to Canada, demanded she hand over the money, turned violent when she didn't, received a restraining order and finally deportation. The stress and anguish of the affair is said to have pushed Chang over the edge.

There's no question that Chang was careful with his money. Some say he was tight. Jeffrey Dujon remembers Chang batting with his wallet lodged in his back pocket. Terrence Corke, a coach at Kingston Cricket Club, and a former Jamaica team-mate, says Chang was a 'cash up front kind of guy'. 'He didn't take any chances with money,' Corke says. 'When we would go to the bar, he wouldn't run a tab. If there were six or seven of us there, he would ask each of us what we were drinking. Then he would go to the bar and order that, get the price and pay his bill instantly so you couldn't pad his bill or anything like that.'

Patrick Gibson agrees that his brother was frugal. He also thinks it's fanciful to suggest Chang would ever sign over his earnings to anyone. 'He wouldn't give it all to his girlfriend,' he says. 'He was good with his money. It doesn't make sense. I heard she had the money, but I don't think it happened that way because she's broke. He was a discreet person. Nobody knew his business. He would come home and eat and that was all we knew. Then he would go and play cricket. We didn't even know he'd gone to South Africa until we read it in the paper.'

Hyacinth says the family thought the money had been wired to the mother of his two daughters in Canada. But she told them she got nothing, and she was upset that Chang didn't give her anything. Bell also confirms that Chang did travel to Canada and had an altercation with the mother that resulted in him being deported.

So, where did the money go? Chang says it could be in the bank. 'I didn't spend any of the money,' he says. 'The bank has it. It's in Barclays Bank. They controlled the money.' Somewhere in Chang's mind, lost in the chaos of a psychological breakdown, is the answer.

Patrick Gibson is convinced that the tour organisers dudded his brother, but team manager Gregory Armstrong is adamant everyone was paid in full. Chang, with his reputation as a miser, would have been the last person anyone would have wanted to swindle.

There's little doubt that the combined trauma of girlfriend break-up and substantial financial loss had devastating effects on Chang's mental health. 'I think he was embarrassed about it,' Gibson says. 'He doesn't like to talk about it because it seems to trigger things. It brings back certain things.'

There's also a history of mental illness on the Chang side of the family. His grandmother and one of his uncles spent time at Bellevue, the psychiatric hospital in downtown Kingston. Chang would follow them there.

In the months after he returned to Kingston from Canada, the first symptoms of psychosis became apparent. Although he'd lost his job at West Indies Pulp and Paper because of the anti-rebel sentiment that had swamped some parts of the island, he was still travelling to Miami and California for business. Or so it seemed. The extraordinarily high number of international flights he took suggested something else was at play, and his friends in Miami reported that he wasn't sleeping.

'He was talking to himself and walking back and forward up the street,' Hyacinth Bell says. 'He wasn't dressing the way he used to or washing himself. You just knew he was sick. I normally go home [to Kingston] once a year and when I went home there was a big change.'

Bell then took it on herself to see that Chang had proper medical care, but his characteristic stubbornness made things more difficult than need be. 'He didn't want to see the doctor; he didn't want to go to the mental hospital. That's how he is for a long time. I had to pay people to do all kinds of things to admit him to Bellevue, get him treatment. Even if I say, "Let's go do this," he says, "I'm okay, I'm okay." He is a big man. I can't fight him.'

In the ensuing years, Chang removed himself totally from the cricket fraternity and became something of a recluse as he dealt with his problems. Of his former team-mates, only Richard Austin, who had his own issues with drug addiction and mental deterioration, regularly visited Chang. 'It was like two mad men talking,' Bell says. His children were nowhere to be seen.

Dujon says he saw Chang more than a decade ago. 'He was just standing, leaning on a fence, staring into space. I tried to talk to him, and he didn't even know me.'

There were other 'sightings'. One newspaper article had Chang asking a cricket official who'd driven into Greenwich Town which end he was going to bowl at. None mentioned that he had a roof over his head, and he was being cared for by his family.

Over time, Chang became just another detail on the Fourth Street streetscape; the eccentric old guy who hangs out the front of the shop drinking Pepsi Cola. Jamaican netballer Althea Byfield passes him every day on her way to work and study. She had no idea the 'loner who keeps to himself' was a Test cricketer. It's unlikely any of his neighbours do either.

* * *

As the humid Kingston afternoon winds down, so does Chang's conversation window. So, what really triggered his breakdown? 'No, no, no,' he wails. 'Years ago … sick, not sound mind … see a psychiatrist.' His voice splinters into sadness. It's clear, as Gibson warned, and understandable that he has difficulty confronting past demons.

Is he happy? 'I'm alright. I see the doctor every month. Yes, it could be worse. I'm not complaining.'

Does he believe in God? 'Yea, mon! God is good at all times.' He laughs. 'What else you want to know?'

In his 2006 biography, Ali Bacher regrets the SACU's decision not to invite Chang and Austin back for the second tour of South Africa. He says the players felt 'let down because they had made the initial sacrifice' and even though they were paid for the second tours in full, in light of the hardships they experienced later on, he and Pamensky should have been more accommodating.

But it's not certain whether such a move would have changed anything for either man. In Austin's case, it may have only delayed the inevitable. While Chang's woes were more difficult to predict, another ten weeks in South Africa, where he'd only been a fringe player, was probably not going to be life-changing.

It's a sobering thought, when towards the end of our conversation, Chang's answers become terser and more impatient. He reluctantly signs a leather-bound autograph book I've been collecting signatures of the rebel tourists in, and quickly kiboshes a return visit the next day. 'Don't come back tomorrow. I may be going to the country.'

He isn't, but as a form of sign-off he's happy to mime a cut, one of his favourite shots, for video. Momentarily, in the forecourt of the Apostolic Faith Church, it's 1980 again, and Jamaica's cocksure little left-hander is rising to meet a searing Joel Garner 'heat rock' outside off stump. His right foot lifts a few inches off the ground, bodyweight transfers to the left. Perfectly balanced, his hands swing an imaginary bat towards gully, wrists rolling over slightly at the point of contact, eyes following the ball all the way to the boundary.

But it's the post-shot swagger that affords an authentic glimpse into Chang's past. The rocking from side to side as he saunters off, satisfied with the efficacy of his stroke. He could be at Kensington Oval or Sabina Park lapping up the applause. Trifluoperazine is just another unpronounceable word.

He shakes my hand. 'Good luck with your book.'

Past a brown shipping container and the sound of his brother hammering renovations, Chang ambles the length of Fourth Street again. He will return, like he's gathering runs in a long, slow game only he can see. A long, slow game with no end in sight.

Alvin Kallicharran

'I only face cricket balls, not bowlers'

IT SHOULD have been his crowning glory. The award of a British Empire Medal in the Queen's New Year's Honours List. Recognition of his magnificent contribution to cricket and charity from the kingdom that ruled his homeland for 152 years. A right royal 'stuff you' to all those critics who'd ever cast doubt on the feisty Guyanese's achievements. But as proud as he is, Alvin Kallicharran, the former West Indies captain and crisp accumulator of 4,399 Test runs, is beset by insecurity – and a mood inclined towards defiance.

'Why would the Queen have given me an award if I'd done something wrong? You tell me that.' The 'wrong' Kallicharran alludes to is his once-forbidden relationship with apartheid South Africa.

The first brown cricketer to break the bar on contact with the republic, Kallicharran was a key figure in the rebel tours: a barrier-buster to some, traitor to others. He also feels he's been wronged. By a biased cricket fraternity that never gave him the acclaim his stellar record deserves. By the sport's establishment that repaid his loyalty with a life ban.

Christianity is the circuit-breaker. It enables him to forgive those he thinks have maligned him. He attends services and Bible class at his local Presbyterian church in Raleigh, North Carolina. But he's no puritan.

He invites me to meet him at the Fox & Hound Sports Tavern across the road from the apartment building where he lives with his wife in Raleigh's plush North Hills. It's 11am. He obviously thinks because I'm an Australian I have a lager appetite akin to Don Bradman's batting average. It will not be the first time I disappoint him.

Bandy-legged and slow moving thanks to a temporary sciatica problem, he has the deliberate, swaying gait of a gunslinger. He's clad in the bright red and blue polyester uniform of the Alvin Kallicharran School of Cricket. He's also a wily conversationalist. Considered answers are followed by long pauses, as if he's taking guard for the next delivery from one of thousands of faceless bowlers. Because to him they were anonymous.

'I only face cricket balls, not bowlers,' he says drily. 'It was a great venture you took to come all the way from Australia, to come this far,' he adds. 'You know how God designs things. I am a strong believer. I hope your book does well. People in the Caribbean must read it.'

Kallicharran has just flown in from Montana, where he was spending time with his biographer Robert Caine. 'God sent Robert, who is a good Christian,' he says of their divinely attuned relationship. But if God were seeing the ball clearly, he would surely have stationed this West Indian batting legend in a more favourable locale where the experience and know-how of over 20 years in first-class cricket could be passed on to greater numbers of children. Instead, the dual World Cup winner is living in the cricket no-man's land of North Carolina, amid the Confederate statues and monuments to white supremacy.

But Kallicharran has never been afraid to push back new frontiers. In South Africa, where similarly sinister structures were buttressed by the letter of the law, he spent years spreading the gospel of colour-blind cricket to a curious but sheltered white population. His 32,000 first-class runs spanned the globe, each one like a dollar in the bank, insurance against a return to the grinding poverty of his boyhood.

The theme of the book he co-wrote with Caine is how he rose beyond that bare-bones existence; how anyone can. How having to cut and bundle sugar cane as a 12-year-old developed Kallicharran's ability to focus for long periods – there's little room for error wielding a machete. How having to live with ten siblings in a zinc-roofed wooden shack fostered a sense of teamwork and acceptance of difference. And how communal spirit in the tight East Indian neighbourhood of Guyana's Port Mourant laid the platform for him to pursue his cricket dream.

* * *

Anand James went to school with Kallicharran in the 1950s and 1960s, first at St Joseph's Anglican and later Corentyne Comprehensive. His parents sold the rotting market vegetables that the Kallicharrans used to feed their pigs. James remembers him as a 'hustler'. 'He was smart and very energetic and if he can get five cents from you, he is happy,' he says.

In their underarm cricket games, which featured home-made wooden balls wrapped in elastic rubber bands and unpredictable bounce, Kallicharran learned to see the ball early and play late. His supernatural talent made him a popular choice when the boys placed bets on the outcome. 'But he didn't make a lot of money because he didn't have money to put in,' James says.

Kallicharran had other ways of making a few bucks. 'Five cents was a decent amount in those days,' James says. 'Alvin told my mum that all of us did some damage in the classroom at school, and they were collecting a cent from all the students to fix it up. So, he got a cent from me and my brother. We knew he was pulling one, but we allowed him to anyway. He was a teaser.'

Port Mourant has had a huge influence on Guyanese affairs, way out of proportion to its small size. Its favourite sons include one-time President Cheddi Jagan, and cricketers Joe Solomon, Basil Butcher and Rohan Kanhai. Kanhai's house was en route from school to home. Visible through a window was a mounted stuffed tiger's head, a present from the president of India in appreciation of the flamboyant right-hander's batting heroics. The boys would always stop to gawk at the exotic beast, but Kallicharran saw it in a different light. To him it wasn't a relic from his ancient homeland, it was a motivational tool. 'Bengali Tiger!' he would cry out, before confiding to his friend, 'Anand, one day I will go to play in India.'

India is also his heritage. His mother's family is from Chennai and, despite his admirable 'cricket knows no colour' ethos, his fate is in some way tied to the marginalisation of East Indians in Guyana and the Caribbean. Historically, his people have inhabited rural areas, first as indentured labourers and later as sugar cane workers, separated in culture and geography from their Afro-Caribbean countrymen in the cities and towns. When local hero Jagan was ousted as Guyana's premier in 1964, it ushered in 28 years of sometimes corrupt Afro-centric government, further accentuating the nation's divisions. And from the Indo-Guyanese cricket perspective, the Afro-Caribbean Clive Lloyd was a beneficiary.

When he was dropped from the West Indies Test team in 1973, Guyana's Prime Minister Forbes Burnham personally intervened to have him reinstated. No such intervention was forthcoming from up high when a similar fate befell Kallicharran just eight years later.

Cultural studies professor Walter Persaud grew up in Guyana. He says the marginalisation of East Indians led to frustration and destructive behaviours. 'There is a kind of internal violence. You see it in the sugar plantations, where even the cricketers went from the field to the rum shop, and they would not leave there till they were absolutely drunk. There is a bitterness about their experience. This underdog mentality. Kalli comes out of that culture.'

If there was a culturally transmitted bitterness about the plight of the Indo-Caribbean people, Kallicharran suppressed it during his long career. To television viewers he was the epitome of the smiling, happy-go-lucky calypso cricketer. In an Australian

TV advertisement for aftershave lotion he was so damn happy-go-lucky that he could even afford himself a giggle at a Dennis Lillee bouncer that threatened to decapitate him. Of course, it was a caricature. He knew he was the underdog – and in a West Indies side heaving with macho Afro-Caribbean athleticism and 'black power' connotations, he had to try that little bit harder to keep his place. In the dressing room, taunts of 'you Indian boys are too weak' acted as a spur for Kallicharran to train and play harder.

Throughout the 1970s, he was the mainstay of the West Indies batting line-up. Lloyd, Richards and Greenidge got most of the plaudits, but the 5ft 5in craftsman got most of the runs. His decade-topping haul of 4,071 to the end of the 1979/80 tour of Australia came at the impressive average of 49.65. Admittedly, WSC prevented that iconic trio from playing as many Tests as him, but that's not the point, according to Kallicharran. He held the side together through thick and thin and he feels he never got the acclaim the others did.

Former West Indies wicketkeeper Jeff Dujon certainly thinks he was due for it. 'If there was one man to bat for my life, it would be Alvin Kallicharran. He was a tough little fucker.'

Bobby Simpson, who faced off against him as Australian captain, is another unabashed fan. 'Alvin was up there with the best as a cricketer. He deserves just as much praise as Viv Richards and the other West Indies greats of his era.'

Dennis Lillee was savaged by Kallicharran in a 1975 World Cup pool game. He cut and pulled 34 off ten consecutive balls from the Australian paceman. 'It was one of the great one-day innings,' Lillee says. 'He rode his luck. Most of the great players are going to take you on and at some stage they're going to get you. That's cricket.'

Lillee's captain, Ian Chappell, wasn't as sanguine in his assessment. 'Dennis went berserk and bowled him bouncer after bouncer but the game was gone at that stage and I thought I'll let him go. I said to Dennis afterwards, "Mate, next time you're gonna go berserk, at least let me know and I can give you a bit of protection.'"

Yet despite their admiration for his heroics – Chappell says Kallicharran was the best player of spin bowling in the West Indies side – neither is willing to place him in the pantheon of Caribbean batting greats. Temperament was his downfall, they say. 'I think you could ruffle him a bit,' Lillee says. 'He would get pissed off from time to time, but nothing seemed to bother the other guys. That was the chink in his armour.'

Chappell agrees. 'I remember in 1972 when we played Warwickshire, and someone bowled him a bouncer and he ducked out of the way of it and stood up and practised the hook shot. Rodney [Marsh] said something like, "Don't just practise it, mate, why don't you play it." He tried to hit the next ball out of the ground, and it went straight up in the air and someone caught it.'

Understandably, it burns Kallicharran up that the rest of the world doesn't necessarily see his feats of batting resilience through the lens of greatness.

Half an hour and two convivial morning beers later, amid the sports bar darkness and phalanx of TV screens broadcasting college basketball games that never end, he makes a heartfelt request for me to source testimonials from Australian cricketers for his book. Kallicharran can be a thirsty man. His thirst for validation is unquenchable.

* * *

In 1978, Kallicharran became West Indies captain. The hustler and outsider from the sugar cane fields of Guyana had risen to the pinnacle of Caribbean cricket. It wasn't a pretty ascension, but these weren't pretty times. The ugly spectacle of the cricket world tearing itself apart over the unstoppable rise of professionalism and Kerry Packer's WSC had split the West Indies side in two. Contractual argy-bargy with his county side Warwickshire and Australian sports entrepreneur David Lord had forced Kallicharran to renege on a WSC deal. So, when Lloyd pulled his Packer team-mates from the Test side in protest at the WICBC's sacking of Deryck Murray, Desmond Haynes and Richard Austin, his Guyanese countryman was the only senior player left standing.

With six Test debutants under his command, and public sentiment firmly in favour of Lloyd's mercenaries, it was a baptism of fire – and thunderbolts – for the new skipper. One of Jeff Thomson's crashed off the inside of Kallicharran's bat into the stumps before the captain had scored.

But Kallicharran proved a shrewd captain, marshalling his young, second-string side to an even share of the remaining three Tests as the West Indies regained the Frank Worrell Trophy. His rival captain, Bobby Simpson, was impressed by Kallicharran's capacity to mould his side in spite of the off-field tensions swirling around him. 'We admired him,' Simpson says. 'But he was always worried about what was going on politically.' He says the Australian dressing room became a refuge for Kallicharran to momentarily escape the pressures of captaincy. 'He got on exceptionally well with our boys. In many ways, he was more than happy to be around the people he knew from the Australian team.'

Thomson and beefy Australian middle-order batsman Gary Cosier were friends with Kallicharran from his stint with Queensland the previous season. If the captaincy was troubling Kallicharran, Cosier wasn't aware of it. 'He was a deep thinker about the game, but always a really nice, gentle kind of guy and he was always laughing. I remember in one of the Tests, he was running, and he dropped his bat and he had to keep on running to make it to the crease. So, I went in from cover and picked up his bat and shoved it down the back of my pants and went back to cover. He took a minute or so to work out where his bat was. We had a big laugh about it. I wouldn't have done that to anyone I didn't think was my friend. I felt he was comfortable being captain. He was an excellent strategist.'

India in 1979 would prove to be Kallicharran's Waterloo. The intrepid hustler from a far-flung colonial outpost led a doomed three-and-a-half-month campaign with a motley bunch of past-it veterans, low-ranking recruits and rookies on cricket's most inhospitable terrain.

It was, as tearaway young paceman Malcolm Marshall wrote in his autobiography, a 'difficult and demanding tour'. The cricket was grinding, with six Tests and 19 matches marred by slow, turning wickets and political unrest – Indira Gandhi was imprisoned during their stay, sparking riots and the cancellation of the final day of the second Test in Bangalore. There was also the threat of strike action when players found out the financially strapped WICBC was planning to allow the high-profile WSC rebels back to play in the World Cup later that year, jeopardising their own positions.

Kallicharran had to manage their frustrations. His own form was superlative: 538 Test runs at 59.78 but the jury was out on his captaincy, even though the final result, a 1-0 series loss, was an indication of how closely the teams were matched.

Marshall, whose views were coloured by fierce ambition, and the sobering fact that he was only selected for three Tests, found his first West Indies leader lacking in 'leadership and inspiration'. While acknowledging that Kallicharran had few resources to draw upon, he felt they were used poorly. This assessment was echoed in a Caribbean News Agency (CANA) report, which declared: 'Kallicharran earned a reputation here as a remote moody figure who was often curt with the local press and showed little flair or imagination on the field.'

It was a harsh call. Rambunctious opener Faoud Bacchus stroked a monumental 250 against Kapil Dev, Chandrasekhar and Venkataraghavan in Kanpur. His memory of Kallicharran's leadership is much more favourable. 'You have to remember in that particular tour ... they just picked up a bunch of guys and said, "Here, go play a Test series in India." Clive Lloyd had the best opening attack in the world. Alvin didn't have that. I think

Kalli did the best he could have at that time. In terms of judging him, it's ridiculous. There was no appreciation.'

The lack of appreciation seems to irk Kallicharran more than anything we speak about. After completion of the marathon tour, which ended with one-day games in Sri Lanka, he was informed that Clive Lloyd would be reinstated as captain. There was no offer of the vice-captaincy, no recognition of loyalty. They didn't even read his report.

'I wasn't treated well as captain from day one,' Kallicharran says. 'What transpired was so sad. The secretary said Clive Lloyd has been reinstated as captain of West Indies cricket. And he said, "Are you available?"' Kallicharran still can't believe his audacity, 'Are you available! – to come to the World Cup?'

Although they are friends, there's no doubt the situation strained Kallicharran's relationship with Lloyd at the time. 'It was hard,' Kallicharran says. 'Everyone was in behind him, so it was a no-go. Clive said nothing to me.'

During the 1979/80 tour of Australia, Kallicharran wasn't even offered the captaincy in inconsequential regional matches when Lloyd was resting. 'I got the message. During a country game, a senior player told me that Clive Lloyd said Viv Richards was going to be the captain. Deryck Murray and the manager came to me in my room and said, "Sorry, we don't know what's happening."'

Vice-captain Murray, Lloyd's well-respected counsel, was aware that Kallicharran was disillusioned. 'There was talk at the time of an accommodation being made, and there were promises made to certain people,' Murray says. 'But he obviously had expectations. Alvin has described that scenario to me. He was disappointed. Everyone in the side knew that but it wasn't personal because I don't think he held it personally against Clive or me as vice-captain, but he was hurt. It didn't affect the team dynamic.'

On the surface, it didn't. Kallicharran averaged 50.5 in the three-Test series, including 106 in Adelaide, as the West Indies retained the Frank Worrell Trophy by a 2-0 margin over Greg Chappell's Australians. But some team-mates noticed the jovial left-hander wasn't the source of easy dressing room laughter he once was. The smile was still there, but the heart wasn't. It's not to suggest Kallicharran wasn't trying – 'I always gave my all,' he says – but his poor treatment by the board had scratched some of the gloss off representing the West Indies.

If runs are the determinant of a batsman's mental state, the next year of Test cricket suggests that Kallicharran's off-field disenchantment was affecting his batting. His preceding mountain of runs had been struck at a hall of fame-like average of nearly 50; his 1980 haul at a measly 19, but he was still in credit with the selectors. He was an ex-West Indies captain after all.

Andy Roberts was no respecter of reputations. Just ask Stephen Camacho, Majid Khan, David Hookes and Peter Toohey, who all had their faces and careers reconfigured by the paceman's bone-cracking short ball. In 1981 Kallicharran was the incumbent number five, and despite his run of poor form, first choice for the opening Test against the touring English. Then Roberts struck, breaking a bone in Kallicharran's right hand in a Shell Shield game in St Vincent. It kept him out for the entire series. It also ended his Test career.

When the squad for the 1981/82 tour of Australia was announced later that year his name was missing from the 16-man contingent, replaced by 21-year-old Trinidadian Gus Logie. Clive Lloyd voiced his disappointment publicly that both Kallicharran and Lawrence Rowe had been omitted, but said they were still good enough to force their way back into the team.

'One bad series and they nail you,' Kallicharran says, referring to his 1980 form slump. 'I've always done well in Australia. My average was 40. And that's among the top. Later on [after the tour], I was made to know that I was on standby for the WI team to go to Australia. Had they told me anything about it? Nothing.'

In Port Mourant and other East Indian enclaves across the Caribbean there was a feeling he was a victim of something more sinister: the black power movement that was becoming synonymous with the West Indies side. Viv Richards's public identification with Rastafari's Back to Africa movement did nothing to assuage their concerns, nor did subsequent media references to series victories as 'blackwashes'. Despite an estimated 20 per cent of the population of the English-speaking Caribbean tracing their roots to the subcontinent, no man of Asian descent would represent the West Indies in the 12 years following Faoud Bacchus's axing a year later.

Such was Kallicharran's disenchantment with the board that the 66-Test veteran could see no way back to representing the West Indies again. He was still contracted to Warwickshire but now had nothing to do in the northern winter – and there was a substantial dent in his bank balance. For a man who'd grown up with a work or perish ethic, a 'hustler', it was anathema.

It was, on one level, hardly surprising then that a month later, after several conversations with his friend Clive Rice, that he accepted Dr Ali Bacher's deal to play with provincial powerhouse Transvaal in South Africa's Currie Cup, a contract reported to be worth US$65,000 over two years. It was a trailblazing move. He was the first foreign cricketer to play in the outlier country but the WICBC was quick to respond, barring him from future West Indies selection.

Despite the outrage from anti-apartheid activists – his son Rohan says his family received death threats at their English home in Birmingham but Kallicharran denies this – there was sympathy for his decision from fellow players. Jack Bannister, the secretary of England's Professional Cricketers' Association, summed up the prevailing sentiment: 'Kallicharran got no marks for the sacrifice he made in the days of Kerry Packer. He forfeited the chance to play for Packer out of loyalty to the West Indies. I don't think anyone can blame him if he decides to go to South Africa for the winter.'

In newspaper reports, Kallicharran said his mission was to 'promote mixed cricket' and coach junior boys of all races. He was lauded by Transvaal's white fans, but other racial demographics weren't as enthusiastic. At Wanderers in a game before Christmas, he was bombarded with jeers from upset Indian and mixed-race spectators, calling him 'white man's stooge' and 'racist pig'. At one point, he asked to be moved to a different position on the field to avoid their abuse. 'I'm here to play cricket, not to be the target of politically motivated demonstrations,' he told reporters. 'I was disgusted by the behaviour of these people. I earn my living from playing and coaching cricket. I don't think anybody has the right to stop me from doing this. I am a professional cricketer.'

Even his club side, Kohinoor Crescents, from the Johannesburg Indian township of Lenasia, withdrew from the multiracial Transvaal Cricket League due to pressure from non-white political bodies unwilling to support desegregated sport while apartheid dominated all other aspects of daily life. But despite the political turbulence, Kallicharran was a hit on the field with Transvaal, eking out 484 runs at 53.77. 'South African domestic cricket, apart from Test cricket, is the hardest cricket I played in,' he says now. 'The reason for that is that they were out of Test cricket, so domestic cricket was their Test match cricket. There was a hunger and the bowlers were at you for four days.'

The West Indies ban served only to increase Kallicharran's own insatiable appetite for runs, topping the county run-scoring list with Warwickshire in 1982 and earning a gong as one of *Wisden's* five cricketers of the year.

Kallicharran maintains he had nothing to do with the organisation of the West Indian rebel tours, but he certainly gave them his blessing. 'Nothing would give me greater pleasure,' he wrote in a newspaper column for the *Johannesburg Star* in March 1982. Residing in South Africa for another summer with Transvaal, he was an easy fit for the rogue squad, adding instant credibility and an insider's knowledge of local conditions. And unlike his rebel team-mates, he was spared the outrage from Caribbean governments. In his native land, former Test team-mate Roy Fredericks, now a minister in Forbes Burnham's Afro-centric government, insisted the rebels were no longer fit to 'live among us'.

Kallicharran wasn't scared by his hyperbole. 'He was a token. It was from the government. We were very close until he died.'

The arrival of the rebels took the spotlight off Kallicharran, who was regularly portrayed in the South African press as 'ready-smiling' and 'bubbling', enabling him to focus on enjoying his cricket and his role as vice-captain to Lawrence Rowe. He sees his team-mates as missionaries who shook the pillars of apartheid. 'The highlight was to bring people together. To see a black team in South Africa for the first time. They loved it, the enjoyment of the brand of cricket we played.'

But as the second tour became mired in sponsorship problems and tensions between the SACU and the tourists over gate receipts and bonuses, Kallicharran began to feel the strain. Relations between himself and Bacher soured.

'Kalli's smile is lost to South Africa' the *Rand Daily Mail* headline sobbed. The accompanying photograph showed a smile-free Kallicharran, clad only in a bath towel, staring listlessly at the camera. The story detailed his decision to resign the vice-captaincy, quit Transvaal and return home to England. It also noted that his smile had turned to a frown and that Bacher had talked him around to at least finishing his season with the provincial side. 'It's very sad,' Kallicharran is quoted as saying. 'Deep inside, we knew the English had the best hotels [when they had toured in 1981/82] and they were paid more money,' he says. 'We were filling up the grounds. We made more money for South African cricket.'

Kallicharran started the 1983/84 'Test' series with 103 but his form tapered off as the marathon tour ground to a close. Post-tour, back at Edgbaston, he took out the disappointment of the premature end to his West Indies career on county bowlers, racking up a tower of runs and leading *The Guardian* cricket correspondent Paul Fitzpatrick to write: 'This has been another astonishing season for the outlawed West Indian. It is hard to believe there is a better technician around at present or a sweeter timer of the ball.'

Runs kept Kallicharran grounded and diverted his mind from off-field controversies. 'I scored them, and everything went away,' he says. 'That's how I dealt with being banned. That was my punching bag, my emotional release.'

The WICBC was aware that the man they had blackballed for life was in career-best form. They also knew none of Kallicharran's successors had been good enough to lock down his old middle-order spot. Even Gus Logie was having only intermittent success. According to Kallicharran, a desperate WICBC official approached him with a proposition: apologise for playing in South Africa and the ban will be lifted. He wasn't persuaded. 'I said no, because if I apologised, that said I'm guilty. I had nothing to be guilty about. If I were to make an apology and WI cricket didn't pick me, who would look a fool?'

Despite his previous intention to quit, Kallicharran continued to represent Transvaal in the county off-season, pitting his skills against rebel team-mates Sylvester Clarke, Collis King, Faoud Bacchus, Emmerson Trotman, Ezra Moseley, Franklyn Stephenson and Hartley Alleyne in the Currie Cup. He sees their decision to play on in South Africa as a positive legacy of the rebel tours, raising standards and preparing the Springboks for a return to Test cricket.

It also continued the exposure of white crowds to black sportsmen. But life in the apartheid republic could be rocky. There was a story he'd been kicked out of a burger bar because of his skin colour. And the slow pace of reform in South Africa meant the threat of violence was never far away.

Ian Chappell remembers Kallicharran telling him a disturbing anecdote during a charity match in England in 1997, about his time in South Africa. 'It was the last game I ever played in,' Chappell says. 'I hadn't seen Alvin since I'd played against him. He came up to me with this big grin on his face, and he said, "Lillee and Thomson are nothing." I said,

"What the hell are you talking about, Alvin?" He told me this story about how he was driving with a mate in a Mercedes through Soweto and they got pulled up. And he said, "I had a gun pointed at both sides of my head. After that, Lillee and Thomson were nothing." I said, "Okay, Alvin. I understand where you're coming from.'"

* * *

The nagging question of where he ranked in the honour roll of West Indies greats continued to dog Kallicharran, or at least his entourage. Professor Walter Persaud met Kallicharran at a Bangkok sixes tournament in the 1990s. He was shocked by what he saw. 'He was with a few other guys who were all drunk. I said to them I'd just seen a new Indo-Guyanese character who is going to be one of the greatest ever – Chanderpaul.'

It wasn't Kallicharran, but his inebriated friends who immediately set Persaud straight. 'No, you don't know. This man Kalli is the greatest,' they roared time and time again. When he did speak with Kallicharran, now in his mid-forties, the former great told him he was attempting to get branded cricket hats made in India. 'He was trying to make some money, which said to me that this guy's a great Test cricketer, but is he struggling selling hats? I felt sad for him.' There was no reason to. In his many long innings, Kallicharran had experienced hit and miss periods and soldiered on. This was no different.

When he returned to Guyana for the first time since the rebel tours, it was to attend his mother's funeral. Forbes Burnham had been dead almost a decade and the People's National Congress was no longer in power. Instead, Cheddi Jagan had assumed the presidency. Kallicharran says the government now wanted to honour him with the Golden Arrow of Achievement, the fourth-highest award in the Order of Service of Guyana, a sure sign that his homeland had excused his South African transgressions. But the process was bungled by an insensitive government minister and he never received it.

'When I was at my mother's funeral, there was a telephone call. The minister of home affairs. I spoke to him. He said, "Seeing as you're in Guyana, we'd like to present you with your award." I said, "I'm at a fucking funeral, my mother died, and you want me to celebrate an award." I never got it. At that time, for me, awards were meaningless. It's how you treat somebody. What does it mean if you don't treat somebody properly? So, I never bothered with it.'

But the British Empire Medal clearly does mean something to him. A few months after our meeting I telephoned him to offer congratulations. At first, he was cagey and stand-offish. 'I have been thinking some very dark thoughts about you,' he said. 'You promised me some things and you didn't deliver.' The 'things' he was referring to were the testimonials from Australian cricketers he wanted for his book. I told him that I had been busy writing this book. He was sympathetic. 'I am a good Christian,' he said. 'We can start again.'

I felt relieved. No one wants to let down a famous Test cricketer. I promised to find him the glowing career references he wanted. He repeated his belief that the Queen wouldn't have honoured him if he wasn't a man of integrity. 'We brought black cricket to the forefront in South Africa.' He wondered whether the news had received much publicity in Australia and asked me to spread it far and wide.

A few days later, while researching, I stumbled across a column from *The Age* newspaper written by Bobby Simpson in 1980. Headlined 'Tiny Kalli stands tall among Windies giants', Simpson praises Kallicharran's 'underplayed' contribution to West Indies cricket and brackets him alongside the greats. 'With his superb technique and unselfish attitude, Kallicharran is the ideal foil to his more explosive team-mates. His timing is exquisite and, whereas the more robust Richards explodes on the ball, Kallicharran caresses it to the boundary.'

I made a screen grab and sent it to Kallicharran via WhatsApp. He was pleased ... very pleased, and I was pleased that he was pleased. 'Love u,' he texted. 'U should share this with world'.

We spoke later and revisited the question of his place in West Indies history. I assured him that Simpson is one of the most significant figures in post-war Australian cricket and his opinion carries a lot of weight. He told me that, as a youth, he idolised Simpson and his batting partner Bill Lawry.

But it seems there can never be enough validation. I interviewed Simpson face to face, Rodney Hogg, Gary Cosier, Dennis Lillee and Ian Chappell. I passed on their appraisals. They all rate him highly; some say he sits at the top of the batting greats ladder, while others say he's nestled on the rung below.

'I was as good as them,' Kallicharran says. By them, he means Richards, Greenidge, Kanhai, Haynes and Lloyd.

Ultimately, there's a fair case to be made for the hustler from Port Mourant to be included by critics in the pantheon of West Indian batsmen. Perhaps the taint of South Africa has denied him that inclusion and, down the track, history will be kinder to him and, most importantly, he will be garlanded with the same respect as Lloyd et al. But it's a debate, by its very nature, that can never be fully resolved.

In his quieter, more reflective moments, Kallicharran knows this. 'I always think about the future,' he says. 'The future looks good. I try not to think negative. I know what I have achieved. I know I gave it the best of everything, and the regrets are nil, because I realise that even if I came back today, I don't think I'd be a better player.'

Faoud Bacchus

'Am I gonna kill a kid for a pair of shoes?'

HE BATTED in an ice hockey helmet, didn't drink and didn't come from a ghetto. Even his name, the impressively long Sheik Faoud Ahamul Fasiel Bacchus, had none of the Anglo pretensions of his team-mates. A man of Muslim heritage in a West Indies side that put its faith in rum and fast women, Faoud Bacchus could easily have been an outsider. But such was his cheerful demeanour that the diminutive Guyanese right-hander was a popular figure in a dressing room dripping with machismo.

The problem was he never attained the levels of consistency that his Duncan Fearnley bat promised. There was the epic 250 against Kapil Dev, Venkataraghavan and Chandrasekhar on an uncovered Kanpur wicket in 1979, a few brisk half-centuries, but little else to gloat about on his Test CV. Yet he could have been Gordon Greenidge's opening partner bar a nick or two.

Some said he couldn't handle the pace of Jeff Thomson, while others said he was too impetuous. Bacchus is just happy to have played in what he considers 'the best team ever'. 'That team was not easy to make,' he says. 'I don't know why I was selected. I was told they saw something in me that was supposed to be good, but I never fulfilled it.'

Now comfortably ensconced in Orlando, Florida, accounting at a car salvage yard, he speaks with a benign detachment about a cricket career that feels a lifetime ago. 'It's funny,' he says, 'no one I've ever played with has kept in touch with me. It's strange.'

Like many of the rebel tourists, he has found a contented niche in the great vastness of the US, just far enough from the Caribbean madding crowd. But in one significant facet he differed from the other rebels. At least that was the perception in West Indies cricket circles. 'He came from a wealthy background,' wrote Malcolm Marshall in his autobiography, the implication being that cricket for Bacchus was more of a hobby than a profession. The truth was far more nuanced.

'I was married to a rich girl,' Bacchus says. 'Her dad was wealthy, not her. But even after we were married, I wasn't in his business and I was still playing cricket. But when I went home, I was using his cars. Georgetown is pretty small – two square miles. He had there, four, five cars, so I would just jump in any one of them and drive. So to those guys I was wealthy, but it wasn't me.'

One of six children, his father and uncles were butchers from Peters Hall on the southern outskirts of the Guyanese capital. His dad, he says, was a 'harsh' man whose notion of fatherhood entailed drinking quart bottles of rum and steering well clear of his sons and daughters.

Bacchus's cricket evolved on the dusty Peters Hall streets, where the tin ball would dart unpredictably off the tarmac, unwittingly sharpening his reflexes in the process. His friends likened him to the obdurate Australian opener Ian Redpath, because they couldn't get him out, but Guyanese legend Rohan Kanhai was the man he wanted to emulate. 'He was our hero,' Bacchus says of the Indo-Caribbean great.

Bar that momentous 250, Bacchus never acquired the descriptor 'great', but his journey to the Test side was certainly one of the more circuitous in West Indies history. Joe Solomon, the man who created history by throwing down Ian Meckiff's stumps in the first ever tied Test, had earmarked Bacchus as a future West Indian, having seen him bat in the under-19 British American Tobacco Tournament in 1970. But after his father died when Bacchus was in his teens, he and his mother emigrated to Toronto, Canada, to join his older sister. To maintain his Canadian citizenship, Bacchus was forced to remain in Canada for six months of every year.

The standard of cricket was rubbish. 'It was in no way comparable to Guyana,' Bacchus says. 'You were playing on matting in public parks, the grounds were not sorted for practice and you only played on weekends.'

To keep fit he played squash and did so very well. His West Indian team-mate Jeff Dujon says Bacchus was unbeatable on court.

Every November Bacchus would return to Georgetown to press his claim for Shell Shield selection. A debut first-class match against international opposition, the touring 1973 Australians, exposed him to the dark arts of gamesmanship. 'I remember Greg Chappell at slip saying as I'm about to bat, "Kill this little motherfucker!" We'd never had that before, but it sure made you more determined.' Bacchus compiled 36 not out and 31 in that match, a match his hero, Rohan Kanhai, sat out to give the 19-year-old his first taste of the big time.

Meeting and playing with Kanhai was an exercise in the perils of hero worship. 'Rohan was a harsh person as captain. If you did something wrong, he'd really look at you, whereas Clive Lloyd would tell you never mind, it's gone.'

Over the next four years Bacchus promised a lot but rarely delivered. A reputation for not valuing his wicket developed. Guyanese cricket commentator Reds Perreira says Bacchus had all the shots but the wrong temperament. 'He was a very good attacking player but was too impetuous. He played strokes too early and lost his wicket too early.' And unlike his contemporaries he couldn't spend the off-season in England honing his footwork on seaming wickets.

Looking back, Bacchus can see that the demands of maintaining a dual existence in Canada and Guyana stymied his batting. 'Playing in England would have tightened me up,' he says. 'Playing in the West Indies the ball didn't do too much. In the first eight to ten overs you may get something, but after a while it's waxy and soft. In England I would have been contracted and performance would have been part of the deal, and failures would not have been tolerated.'

The retirement of heavy-scoring opener Roy Fredericks in 1978 had left a gap at the top of the West Indies order to partner Gordon Greenidge. However, Greenidge was also absent for the start of the upcoming one-day series against Bob Simpson's Australians as he was in England to be with his wife, who was expecting their first child. Bacchus was among the candidates to open the batting, in competition with Barbadian Desmond Haynes, and Jamaican Richard Austin.

Bacchus had alternated between number five and opener for Guyana. In some ways it was a reflection on the paucity of quality new-ball batsmen in the Caribbean – Bacchus's record up to this point was hardly stellar – but 102 against Jamaica early in the Shell Shield forced the selectors to take notice of the pint-sized Guyanese. The first one-day game against Australia at the Recreation Ground in St John's, Antigua, was the scene of the shootout for the vacant opener's role. Austin and Haynes opened. Bacchus was listed at number five.

But not even representing the West Indies could tone down Bacchus's attacking instincts. 'Haynes got dropped first ball,' he remembers, 'then he made 148 batting like a king, and Austin got six or eight.'

Blond all-rounder Trevor Laughlin was only in the Australian side because of the mass defection of Test players to WSC, but his nagging right-arm medium pace had accounted for Alvin Kallicharran. The West Indies were beginning to wobble at 78/3, but if the 15,000 spectators packed into the Recreation Ground's quaint timber stands expected caution and consolidation from the debutant, they were sorely mistaken.

Laughlin's first-ball bouncer was met with a characteristically aggressive response, as Bacchus's hook shot sailed over the advertising hoardings. A statement six on his first ball in international cricket. Except that the force of the ball had tipped him off balance, and he fell on his stumps.

'I made zero,' Bacchus says without a trace of regret. 'So, the first-team replacement was Haynes. That was the type of cricket I played. Everybody tells me I was playing T20 cricket when I was playing Test and regular cricket.' Austin also made the Test side as a utility all-rounder.

But fortune was to favour Bacchus later in the series when the WSC-contracted West Indies players pulled out en masse in protest at the omission, ironically enough, of Austin and Haynes from the third Test side because of their links with Packer's rebel organisation. Jamaican Basil 'Shotgun' Williams and Barbadian Alvin Greenidge were elevated to the opening roles but, for the fourth Test, middle order batsman Irvine Shillingford was dropped, and Bacchus wore the West Indies' navy blue home cap for the first time. Disappointing scores of 9, 7, 5 and 21 ensued but such was the talent drain following the West Indies WSC exodus that he was still called up for the three-and-a-half month tour of India and Sri Lanka.

A gruelling campaign that extinguished many Test careers, Bacchus was one of few to enhance his reputation. The 250 in Kanpur, the textile and leather capital of India, was the single most important innings of his first-class tenure. It added ballast to a career that was teetering at the mercy of the winds of professionalism and lack of self-belief. It was a memo to WSC West Indians that he could bat. It was also a millstone.

Opening with Alvin Greenidge in pursuit of India's grinding 644, a series-winning total amassed over three days, Bacchus motored to 204 not out at the end of day four. The CANA correspondent observed that Bacchus 'played with confidence and without inhibition ... and dispelled any doubts about his ability to play a long innings.' When bad light halted proceedings he'd clubbed 26 boundaries and was within striking distance of Rohan Kanhai's India–West Indies record of 256. But the next day was washed out and, because of India's policy of not covering the wicket, when play resumed after lunch on day six – the final Test was allotted an extra day – the Green Park pitch was still damp.

On 250, his hero's record beckoning, Bacchus swept Venkataraghavan to the boundary. But just as in Antigua a year before, he committed batting hara-kiri, slipping on to the stumps as he completed the stroke. Momentarily defeated, he sat on the muddy pitch in a state of disbelief. 'They thought they were going to get us all out,' Bacchus says of the Indian bowlers on that last day. 'They would just pitch the ball and it would be in your face. My boots were caked in mud from the wetness of the wicket and running up and down the pitch. So, when I played the sweep shot at 250, I ended up off balance because I had no grip.'

Despite his disappointment, Bacchus could point to having registered the highest ever Test score at Green Park and a partnership of 160 with keeper David Murray that remains a ground record for the fifth wicket. He'd also earned the selectors' faith and forbearance for the next couple of years. A double centurion could expect a higher tolerance for failure. The flipside was there was now more pressure on him to perform.

The puzzling thing is, then, how did a batsman who pummelled 250 against India's finest finish with a poor average of 26 in Test cricket, a mere trivia night curiosity and historical footnote? A man who shares with Wasim Akram the dubious distinction of the lowest Test average for a batsman who scored 250 or more in one innings.

It's complicated. There was, as he acknowledges, the lack of county cricket polish, but there were also the hierarchical machinations of dressing room politics. Certainly, he was a positive influence in the pavilion. 'What I try to do is make the atmosphere a little light,' he says.

His Guyana team-mate, Mark Harper, brother of West Indian off-spinner Roger, remembers a playful presence. 'He was a great guy to have around. He would come past and flick you on the ear, things like that. Always smiling.'

But his aggressive batting style alienated the men who counted. Not for the first time, powerful selector Clyde Walcott was the bane of a West Indian cricketer's life. 'He came into the dressing room after a one-day game against Barbados when I'd scored 81 and kept on playing my shots,' Bacchus says. He said, "Son, batting is like driving a car. In the morning, you start it and warm it up, then you go into first gear, second gear, third gear and fourth. You don't reverse." In other words, you don't play the cut shot until you are past 50. But that wasn't my style. Any time you get out early that's behind your mind. These are the guys that control your life. If you don't please them, you're out of the team.'

He started second-guessing himself. 'If you went and played a shot and got caught, that's your natural style, but they came and told you you've got to save your wicket, so you start doing that.'

There was also a tricky pecking order to negotiate. Lloyd, Richards and Kallicharran were household names who commanded instant respect. If they didn't want to bat with an hour to go before stumps, they damn well didn't. 'When we toured England in 1980, we would often bowl them out and have an hour and a half to bat,' Bacchus says. 'Haynes and Greenidge would open, and about 40 minutes before close of play Viv would take his pads off. He's not going to admit it but that's what he did. Alvin Kallicharran was next, and he would take his pads off with half an hour to go, and I am next in, so if a wicket falls, I have to go in. Now when I get in, I'm blocking, which is against my natural instinct. Then the next day the bowlers are fresh against you. A lot of my career, that's what happened.'

It didn't help that he was constantly shunted up and down the batting list depending on Greenidge's health and availability. There was also a perception he was uncomfortable against extreme pace. 'He wasn't as good with fast bowlers,' Jeff Dujon says. 'He would be jumping around. He didn't like it.'

Footage of a peroxided Jeff Thomson making Bacchus hop all over the crease during the 1981/82 West Indies tour of Australia makes for uncomfortable viewing. But he wasn't alone there, and he wasn't alone in not wanting to get hit. In the early days of helmets, a perspex visor was the only barrier separating a batsman from a crushing facial injury. But the tendency for the perspex to fog up in the heat meant most of the game's elite unscrewed them from their helmets before batting. It was courting danger.

Bacchus drew on his experience of living in Canada to find a solution. He observed that ice hockey players were unfazed when struck on the helmet by pucks that weigh more than cricket balls, so he adapted one for batting use by cutting off two of the grilles to ensure that his view to the bowler was unimpeded. He credits it with saving him from serious injury while fielding at short leg during a Shell Shield match in Guyana against Jamaica. 'Derek Kallicharran was bowling spin and Herbert Chang was batting. He got a full toss and hit it at the helmet. There was this great "pow" noise. But nothing happened. I was not dazed, I was normal.'

Bacchus's close-in fielding was brilliant. A seemingly effortless catch to dismiss Kim Hughes off Joel Garner at silly mid-on from a full-blooded flick off the pads was just one example of his natural talent for snaffling sharp chances. Quick reflexes in the field gave him the edge over batting rivals and kept him in the one-day reckoning when his form in the middle wavered.

Leading into the 1983 World Cup in England, Bacchus hadn't played Test cricket for the West Indies since what he concedes was a disastrous tour of Australia the previous year. His 19 appearances had yielded just 782 runs but the same impulsiveness that seemed to limit his Test career was considered something of an asset in one-day cricket. He was selected for all the pool matches as West Indies marched to a third World Cup final in a row. In the game against Zimbabwe, he and Haynes, who had long since won the shootout for the vacant opener's role, shared an unbeaten stand of 172. Greenidge had been rested with a stiff neck.

The 1983 Prudential World Cup Final against India had a sense of inevitability about it. West Indies were huge favourites to seal a hat-trick of titles, and Bacchus, batting at number five, was destined to etch his name in history. So certain were they of victory, the Westmoreland Hotel across the road from Lord's was booked as a celebration venue.

It had all started so well. India, 50-1 outsiders at the beginning of the tournament, could muster only 183 as an ageing Andy Roberts showed he was still a potent force in international cricket, hustling figures of 3-32. Caribbean fans waved 'The Cup is Ours' banners in anticipation. But their batting idols failed to deliver. Greenidge shouldered arms to Balwinder Sandhu and was bowled for 0, and Viv Richards top-edged a pull aimed at Father Time into the hands of Kapil Dev.

Entering at number six with the Windies teetering at 66/4, Bacchus attempted his best impersonation of a mature innings builder but nicked a ball he didn't have to play at and departed for just 8. Clive Lloyd, who limped into the match with a groin injury, hobbled about with a runner, before holing out to cover.

Recriminations for the 43-run loss were immediate. The dressing room descended into a heated blame game. Bowlers accused batsmen of not pulling their weight; batsmen ludicrously suggested that bowlers should have skittled India for less. 'I remember Michael Holding sitting in the pavilion, angry and grabbing his hair. All the bowlers were angry,' Bacchus says.

A pointed Andy Roberts comment about fitness was misconstrued as a jibe by Clive Lloyd, and the veteran captain resigned later that night, only to be talked out of it later. 'Clive played the game on one leg,' Bacchus says. 'We felt he wanted to go out as a hero, but he should not have played. He could only field at slip or short extra cover. His muscles were strapped up. In that game everything went wrong.'

It was a sentiment echoed by *The Guardian*'s cricket writer, Matthew Engel: 'If the same personnel could be reassembled in the same circumstances another 50 times, India would not win again.'

The ramifications for Bacchus's career were huge. He felt he was made a scapegoat for the upset loss, which dented pride in the Caribbean. 'They didn't actually say it, but it was acted out. I felt they looked at you as if you were one of the reasons, if not the reason why we lost.'

Of course, Bacchus wasn't solely to blame for the West Indies' shambolic batting performance, but his age, 29, and precarious hold on the number six spot meant he was more vulnerable to the selectors' axe. His worst fears were realised when the tour to India was announced six weeks later in August and his name was missing from the 16-man squad, replaced by Gus Logie and Richardson. What made it hard for Bacchus to accept, he says, was that he was told in an unofficial capacity that he would be chosen for the tour. His previous stellar form on the subcontinent had also been overlooked.

Tony Becca, the doyen of Caribbean cricket reporting, wrote: 'Bacchus has already had more than a fair share of opportunities to be a regular member of the team, but he is such a fine player to spin, that one wonders if the selectors have not chosen the wrong time to remove him.'

But he wasn't totally out of the picture. The WICBC offered him the captaincy of a West Indies A side tour of Zimbabwe. It was small consolation. 'My fee was going to be $20 a day for the tour,' Bacchus laughs. He declined the invitation. He sensed his West Indies career was over. 'I thought, once you're out of the West Indies, you're out because that team in those days was not an easy team to get into. I was left out of the team to tour India where I had done my best.'

Bacchus had been quoted in the press earlier that year about his rumoured involvement in the first rebel West Indies tour of South Africa. He wasn't interested. 'I have no intention of doing anything which could embarrass my country or isolate me from West Indies cricket,' he said. It's a statement he now denies making, but with a West Indies future no longer applicable post-World Cup, it was certainly an attractive option.

SACU board member Ali Bacher was desperate for new recruits to spruce up the second tour squad and meet the demanding expectations of the South African cricket-loving public, who had watched the first tour in record numbers. On a spying mission to England during the World Cup, Bacher earmarked Bacchus and Larry Gomes as potential recruits. But Gomes made the India tour, and the Trinidad cricket establishment supported him with financial incentives when they heard he was being targeted.

Living in Canada, Bacchus had no such support. He'd taken up a short-term coaching deal with Amstelveen VRA in Holland when he got the call from Bacher. The SACU paid for his flight to London. For Bacchus, their meeting at a park in the British capital's business district was a no-brainer. He had a wife and young daughter to think of, and the offer of over US$150,000 for three years was irresistible.

The only sticking point was Bacher's insistence that Bacchus pay tour manager Gregory Armstrong a ten per cent agent's fee. Bacchus refused, pointing out that unlike the first tour recruits, Armstrong hadn't hired him. The former South African Test captain was forced to relent. Bacchus was too big a prize.

The politics of the tour were of little consequence to Bacchus. He was aware of the opposition from black consciousness groups but his journey as a professional cricketer was coming to an end and he had to try to set himself up for the future. 'There was apartheid, but I didn't feel it because we weren't treated any differently as blacks or whites,' he says. 'I didn't go for political reasons. Ali Bacher promised me, "You will be secure; you will get your money and you will play cricket." I didn't look at it as being pioneers. I just went because I was given a lucrative offer and I grabbed it.'

Landing in Johannesburg with all-rounder Bernard Julien and batsman Everton Mattis, Bacchus, sporting longer, curlier hair, cut a relaxed figure. He immediately impressed with his level of fitness. At a pre-net workout in Johannesburg run by Highlands Park football coach Jimmy Williams, Bacchus's agility caught the eye. 'He has a wonderful range of movement,' the noted taskmaster observed.

In the first National Panasonic 'Test' at Durban, he opened with Emmerson Trotman on what appeared to be a lifeless Kingsmead pitch. But on 19, burly Garth Le Roux's good-length ball rose unexpectedly, cannoning into Bacchus's right hand as he launched a defensive prod. His index finger was a bloody mess. The dislocated middle joint had dropped at the knuckle so that it was hanging underneath the palm. South African captain Peter Kirsten tried to push it back into shape. Le Roux blanched.

'He saw blood and he was gone. He's a chicken,' Bacchus says. The upshot was five stitches and a month out of cricket. He missed the rest of the Yellow Pages ODI series and two 'Tests'. But he didn't let it get him down.

In a colour piece for the *Rand Daily Mail*, Rodney Hartman wrote that teetotaller and non-smoker Bacchus 'proves an impish companion, always looking for a joke and teasing anyone who crosses his path. In serious conversation, however, he reveals a deep insight into world affairs. He knows what he is about, and he knows a lot about other people's customs as well.'

His return to the crease for the must-win fourth 'Test' more than justified Bacher's decision to sign him. Struggling to come up with adjectives to describe his 'truly breathtaking batsmanship', the *Rand Daily Mail*'s correspondent labelled Bacchus's second innings 76 as a 'wirlwindie', as he flayed new-ball bowlers Kenny Watson and Rupert Hanley to set up a 2-1 West Indies series win.

On the tour, Bacchus revelled in the hospitality of his hosts. 'We were treated so well,' he says. He was befriended by a Malay family in Rylands, Cape Town, who cooked him exotic meals when he was sick of hotel fare, but in spite of the across-the-board generosity, he knew the daily grind of apartheid was a grim reality for many South Africans. 'When you're living in Guyana or Canada you don't know what's happening in Africa. Nobody would cover it on the news. But when you're there you see poverty. It's the same way at home in Guyana; people hustling to make a living that are not educated and going to different places looking for work.'

He scoffs at suggestions made by Franklyn Stephenson and more strident team-mates that the rebels were missionaries diligently unlocking white and black mindsets. 'How people come up with these statements I don't know. He went to play cricket. He could not liberate them all of a sudden by going.'

As part of his contract with the SACU, Bacchus played another two seasons in the republic with Western Province, Border and the Impalas. With the threat of violent crime increasing as political tensions rose, Bacchus made the difficult decision to buy a handgun. In Cape Town, he almost used it. He's glad he didn't.

After a long afternoon run, he'd placed his track shoes outside the front door of the flat he was staying in. A black youth approached him. 'He came into the backyard and wanted to sell me something,' Bacchus says. But then he scarpered with the pair of trainers. Bacchus quickly fetched his revolver. 'I had the gun and I watched the kid. I said to myself am I gonna kill a kid for a pair of shoes? I let it go.'

Back in Canada, Bacchus set about maximising his rebel earnings. Returning to Guyana was never an option. 'I was told President Forbes Burnham got up in parliament and said he was disappointed that "our son has left for South Africa".'

Instead, he chose to relocate to Orlando with his wife and three daughters. But what did Orlando, the amusement park capital of the world, have to offer that Canada didn't? Anonymity and a closer proximity to the Caribbean where he'd successfully invested in a trawler business with former Guyanese team-mate Timur Mohamed. He'd experienced little ill feeling in Toronto regarding the rebel tours. 'There were people saying they wouldn't play alongside you, but they did.' But America enabled him to wipe the slate clean cricket-wise.

Still fit in his forties, he captained the national team in the 1997 and 2001 ICC Trophy. But it wasn't something that made his heart swell with pride. 'It was a step down. You're playing with a bunch of guys that didn't reach country or first-class level. And they're coming in with this American attitude: everything is on paper; this is what we have to do. But they can't do it.'

He also coached them, but the huge expanse of the country made organising training camps a logistical nightmare in a land where cricket is a minor sport. 'I coached but how can you coach? They pick a team and give you a team, then they have one weekend of coaching. What is coaching in one weekend?'

These days he lives alone. He drives a tan Toyota Sienna minivan to work at the car body shop where he sorts out the paperwork on repaired vehicles. Unlike many of his rebel brethren, he's not discontent with his lot in life; he has no axe to grind. But he's not indifferent to their tales of woe. Rather, he sees them as an inevitable consequence of financially illiterate young men given fantastic sums of cash. 'Everyone saw it as quick money and not the ramifications. It was good for the guys who used their money well and bad for those who blew it, because now they've gone back to worse than they were before.'

Bacchus didn't blow his. He has the freedom that some of his old team-mates can only dream of. 'I have no hassles. I do whatever I want whenever I want, how I want. If I want to go home now and sleep, I can. That's the convenience I have with the job I'm doing with these guys. I can leave when I want. I could go to Trinidad now if I want. It pays all my bills. I don't want to be rich.'

Richard Austin

'The coke, it helps me forget'

ON 14 March 2015, the pews of the byzantine-revival Holy Trinity Cathedral in Kingston, were stuffed with the heavyweights of Jamaican cricket and society: ex-Test players, administrators and ministers of government. The man they had come to pay tribute to, Richard Austin, had, in death at least, been forgiven the sins of life. But as one eloquent speaker after another recalled Austin's tragic slide from West Indies all-rounder to shoeless street beggar, it became apparent that many of those well-dressed orators were seeking their own kind of salvation – forgiveness for the way Austin, whose primary sin was playing cricket in apartheid South Africa, had been treated by his countrymen. It was a reminder, the presiding priest said, that 'we are all mere sinners, here to help each other in love to make it home to God'.

In many ways, the phases of Austin's life hold a mirror to Jamaica's own expedient moral consciousness. As a young, elite-level sportsman from the ghetto area of Jones Town, he was feted for transcending a poor background, a rare example of social mobility in a nation dogged by the remnants of slavery; as a former Test cricketer he was shunned and scorned for visiting a country that practised a modern form of slavery; and finally, as a middle-aged vagrant, he was tolerated and humoured, the target of both earnest sympathy and benign neglect.

Years earlier, in 2003, sitting in a gutter next to Tastee, a pastry chain restaurant in the commercial district of Kingston known as Crossroads, Austin, then 48, began to tell me his story. Wiry and weather-beaten, eyes bloodshot with the effects of rum and cocaine, his conversation veered between the tragic and comic as he first asked me to call his 'good friend' Kerry Packer. 'I can come to Australia and play for Sydney or NSW,' he rasped, while politely refusing a swig of rum from one of the gang of drifters he was running with. 'Kerry Packer to me was like a gift in the cap.'

Then he addressed his cocaine habit. 'When you live on the street, you live with street people. If you want to party, then sometimes I have to do it [cocaine].' The truth was he didn't have to flounder on the streets. He part-owned a house and car in the uptown suburb of Mona, which was looked after by his brother Oliver. It was as if the gutter, where no man dare judge another, was the only place he felt at home.

He acknowledged that old Jamaican cricket friends had tried to help him, but he complained that the money he got from coaching jobs was barely enough to cover his laundry expenses. 'I hope you can get through to Kerry Packer and WSC and see if you can do something for me,' he cried, as he disappeared into the night, clutching the J$2,000 dollars his friends had wrangled out of me as payment for chatting. It was the kind of delusional conversation that Austin would have time and time again in his final years as a disjointed life meandered to its inevitable conclusion.

Packer, the brusque media freebooter, was at the centre of many of Austin's highs and lows, flooding him with the kind of money the son of a poor Coronation Market trader could only dream of.

Yet despite growing up at a time when deadly violence between warring political tribes was rife in west Kingston, there was, outwardly at least, little to suggest the turmoil that would plague Austin in later life. At All Saints Primary School and later St Andrew Technical High School (STATHS) in Trench

Town, Austin nurtured a reputation as one of Jamaica's finest young athletes. His first mention in *The Gleaner* newspaper, as a 16-year-old, wasn't for feats of willow or leather, but as a table tennis player whose 'attacking' mindset and 'crisp drives' won rave reviews. He was also a promising footballer with a hard-running style that helped propel Arnett Gardens to a national championship in 1977.

'He was a talented sportsman and probably all-round the most talented cricketer I played against,' Jeff Dujon, his Jamaica team-mate, says. Austin could bat as opener or in the middle order, bowl off spin and seam, and keep wicket to a standard some said was almost the equal of Dujon. In his pomp, enthusiasts labelled him a potential 'right-handed Gary Sobers', critics a 'Woolworths Gary Sobers'.

At STATHS, under the tutelage of influential coach Roy McLean, he was feted for his sporting achievements, representing Jamaica in the Benson and Hedges Youth Series in 1973 and 1974. But schoolmate and former Jamaica batsman Terrence Corke says the growing fame never affected him. 'He was level-headed. There was nothing to say what might happen to him later. He always did his work. But anything he did in sport, there was a crowd around him. He was the life of the party, always making people laugh.'

He was also developing the tactical acumen that would impress cricket devotees up until his death and, like his friend Herbert Chang, an uncanny and annoying ability to monopolise the strike. 'He would pinch the strike all day,' Corke says of the man he knew affectionately as 'Danny Germs', the nickname Austin collected as a child, a moniker that would become hauntingly apposite as his life unfolded. 'I remember we were opening in a school match and Danny and I put on 109 and I got 52. And how did I get 52? Danny would bat four or five balls every over and he would give me one or two, so I had to hit ten boundaries. When Danny batted, he scored two, two, two, two and a one. I thought he had a calculator in his head.'

Austin's rocky home life in Clarence Lane off Jones Town, watching his father slowly drink himself to death, couldn't divert from what seemed an inexorable rise to the apex of West Indies cricket. He graduated from STATHS with qualifications in electrical installation and slotted straight into the Kensington Cricket Club Senior Cup team, a side bristling with the once-in-a-generation talent of Lawrence Rowe, Basil Williams, Desmond Lewis and Chang.

Former West Indies Test opener Easton 'Bull' McMorris is 19 years Austin's senior. He was a selector and manager of the national side, and in 1975 captained Austin, Chang and Michael Holding on a seven-match tour of Bermuda, which was then pushing for Shell Shield status. He remembers Austin's pugnacious, recalcitrant streak and forceful opinions at team meetings. 'He always wanted to try something different, to experiment. If he was supposed to bowl a little seam for you, he would want to bowl off break and the other way around. He didn't want the easy path. We loved opinions coming in, but Richard said too much.'

Rowe, Austin's Kensington, Jamaica and rebel captain sometimes wished his talented all-rounder would hold his tongue. 'He and Changie were very similar. They would taunt you and things because they thought they were that good. It goes without saying we had our differences on the field because Danny was that kind of personality. But it never went too far. It always ended up with a smile and him saying, 'Hardcore, Yagga, hardcore! This is hardcore cricket we are playing!'

McMorris recalls the difficulties of finding Austin in crime-ridden Jones Town. 'I remember once we were taking the squad to the country and we were going to leave about five o'clock in the morning and I was picking up Changie, Austin and the fellas along the way. Richard said, "You cannot come where I live. I meet you on the main road." I never knew where he lived but I got an impression it was dangerous.'

Austin made his Shell Shield debut in 1975, aged 20, scoring 0 and 74 and posting figures of 3-34, including the wickets of West Indies Test men Bernard Julien and Deryck Murray. It was a fine first-up effort, as much a triumph for his community as himself. In the same way local musicians U-Roy and The Skatalites were lauded for beating the poverty trap, Austin also found himself the centre of adulation in west Kingston.

McMorris says the entourage that came to surround him ultimately sullied his development as a cricketer. 'It was the wrong crowd, and when you have that crowd around you, you know what it means: you are the king and the greatest in the world. How is he going to grow if he feels he is the greatest? You can't grow up anywhere.'

Nevertheless, his star continued to soar – the scalps of Majid Khan, Javed Miandad, Zaheer Abbas and Asif Iqbal in a six-wicket haul against the touring 1977 Pakistan side; a record Jamaica second-wicket partnership of 308 with captain Maurice Foster. Unsurprisingly, the politicians lined up to capitalise on his popularity.

Tony Spaulding was the minister for housing in the PNP government of Michael Manley. Dubbed the 'Trench Town Rock', he built thousands of homes for low-income earners in the down-at-heel constituency of South St Andrew, but also encouraged a form of political cleansing that alienated many constituents and led to the growth of the notorious and violent garrison culture.

Maurice Foster believes the powerful Spaulding played an important role as a mentor to Austin in the absence of his father, helping anchor him amid the growing fanfare. 'He almost literally adopted Richard,' Foster says. 'He would come down to games and give him packets of money and look after him.' When their relationship soured after South Africa, Foster says Austin lost an important advocate. 'I think that was it for Richard. It was almost like when Mike Tyson lost his coach Cus D'Amato.'

It was common knowledge that Austin, like many of his team-mates, enjoyed smoking the 'chalice', but his casual marijuana use and consumption of Heineken, the flash Jamaican cricketer's beer of choice were not, in 1978 at least, at a level to bring him into conflict with management.

That year proved to be a watershed for the lanky, gregarious all-rounder. Although he'd bowled off spin in practice sessions, Austin was primarily considered a seamer. Against Trinidad at Queen's Park, his captain Foster had boldly declared Jamaica's second innings at 340/7, setting a target of 313, but he lacked a spinner to take advantage of the deteriorating fourth-day pitch. 'I had seen Richard bowling in the nets with such bounce, turn and control,' Foster says, 'and I remember calling him over and saying you're on from this end, bowling off spin.'

It was a masterstroke. Austin routed the Trinis, furnishing him figures of 8-71 as Jamaica ground out victory by 96 runs. Match stats of 12-116 and 88 and 56 opening the innings catapulted him into the mix for the West Indies' home series against Bob Simpson's Australians. With Roy Fredericks having recently announced his retirement from Test cricket and Gordon Greenidge unavailable, two vacant opening spots appeared for the first Guinness Trophy ODI at the Recreation Ground in Antigua. Recognising his superior all-round ability, the selectors chose Austin over Basil Williams and Barbados's Alvin Greenidge at the top of the order, alongside fellow debutant Desmond Haynes. That he made only 8 – caught Simpson bowled Wayne Clark – and was spanked for 13 runs in his only over, went virtually unnoticed in the excitement of another crushing West Indies victory.

Test honours followed; his first yielded only two runs and a catch as Garner, Roberts and Croft brutalised Australia, but his second in Barbados had more far-reaching consequences.

Once again, his contribution with the bat was modest, 20 from number six, and his solitary over in Test cricket cost five runs, but it was his effort in the field that showcased Austin's intermittent but electrifying talent. On the second day, Australian left-hander Graham Yallop had braved the jeers that accompanied his decision to wear a white crash helmet to the crease – a Test cricket first – to motor to 47, when he clipped Colin Croft sweetly off his toes. According to *The Gleaner*, it was a 'full-blooded shot that seemed a certain boundary as it passed backward square. But Richard Austin flung himself hard right to take an extraordinary one-handed catch that must go down in Test history as one of the greatest.' The doyen of Caribbean commentators, Tony Cozier, wrote that it was impossible to describe how good the catch was, and a story grew that captain Clive Lloyd, thinking the ball must have passed Austin all the way to the boundary, demanded his fledgling all-rounder fetch it, only for Austin to pull it, magician-like, from his pocket with the words 'ball, sir?'

That night, Austin Robertson, Kerry Packer's WSC scouting agent, met with West Indies players at Bridgetown's Caribee Hotel in an exchange that would transform Austin's life forever. Robertson had been tasked with beefing up the West Indies squad for the next season of World Series Cricket, and Austin, along with Haynes and Croft, were on his hit list. An offer in the region of US$20,000 for two years plus a share of prize money was tabled, and Austin, who had been paid just US$74 for the Test match, had no hesitation in accepting. It was the 'gift in the cap' that Austin would reminisce about when his life had spiralled out of control.

But when the WICBC got wind of their defection to the Packer troupe, and subsequent unavailability to tour India at the end of the year, they reacted by dropping Austin, Haynes and players' rep Deryck Murray from the third Test side in Guyana. Captain Clive Lloyd was furious. He sensed that the board was playing political games designed to entrench their power, and he and the other six Packer men withdrew from the remainder of the series.

Austin, of course, had no idea it would turn out to be the last time he represented the official West Indies side; his growing international profile had secured him a contract with the Church Cricket Club in the Lancashire League, and at 24 he was poised for a long and bountiful career.

But outsiders noticed his approach to the game verged on casual. 'He was different; I got on well with him, but he lived for the moment,' says former Australian captain Greg Chappell. 'He was more laid back than the most laid-back West Indians. You could say he was Joe Cool before it had even been invented.'

Chappell and Australia experienced the full force of Austin's all-round arsenal in the third Supertest at VFL Park, Melbourne, in January 1979. The Jamaican snared 4-85, out-bowling Garner, Roberts and Croft, and scored 77. At the other end for most of his innings, Lawrence Rowe was in the midst of shaping a sublime 175. Rowe remembers Austin in his element as he signalled the batting stylist for a mid-pitch conference. 'Yagga, you can imagine them boys back home listening to us batting so well together,' he laughed.

Austin felt like he belonged. He also formed an unlikely alliance with Viv Richards. 'They became very good friends,' Rowe says. 'Richard was always telling Viv, not in a bad way, boasting about how many things he could do in a match. "I'm a medium-pacer, off-spinner, opening batsman, a number six batsman and me can keep, you know." Viv would laugh.'

But it was a message the Master Blaster slowly absorbed. Austin had deputised as wicketkeeper for Deryck Murray in the International Cup ODI series when the vice-captain was sidelined with a shoulder injury and had acquitted himself well as opener alongside Gordon Greenidge. A loss in the first of the best of five one-day final series had loosened their grip on the AU$35,000 prize pool and the West Indies were looking at ways to strengthen their batting. One solution was to bring in all-rounder Collis King, who was capable of batting pyrotechnics beyond the capacity of Murray, now back in the side, and persist with Austin as keeper. According to Rowe, Austin sold the idea to Richards, who sold it to Lloyd. The Windies duly romped home in the second encounter but, understandably, the veteran Murray wanted his job back. Rowe says it was Richards who insisted Austin keep his place. The West Indies seized the series 3-1. Austin, a part-time keeper, had done in a few weeks what acclaimed gloveman David Murray had failed to do in seven years: unseat the venerable Deryck Murray.

His consistent opening stands with Greenidge had been critical to the West Indies' winning charge. It didn't seem to matter that his form tapered off when the Australian XI visited the Caribbean for five Supertests and a slew of ODIs. The expectation was that he would be selected for the Prudential World Cup in England in 1979. However, in a spirit of reconciliation, establishment youngsters Malcolm Marshall and Faoud Bacchus were given the nod over Austin, filling out a squad that was top-heavy with WSC players.

Perhaps Austin's off-field behaviour had also thwarted his chances. Rumours of his marijuana use were rife on the tour Down Under, and back in the Caribbean he quickly earned a reputation as a spendthrift. Flush with Packer dollars, patrons at nightclubs such as Skateland and Epiphany in New Kingston became the beneficiaries of Austin's rampant generosity. 'He'd see people he knew and ask, "What are you drinking?" You'd say a beer and he would bring you a whole case of beer. He would shout the whole bar,' Dujon says. Austin was inexperienced with handling large sums of money and it showed.

Patrick Terrelonge had been instrumental in convincing Kerry Packer to bring WSC to the Caribbean. A software consultant and keen cricket fan, he'd cold-called the redoubtable Australian with a bold plan to spread the gospel, and Packer, conscious of giving back to the region that had contributed so much to his television extravaganza, was happy to oblige. Terrelonge was also in charge of paying the West Indies players. When the money was sent back to the Caribbean he looked after the disbursements. Most of the players had their money sent to sports marketer IMG, where it was invested. Not Austin.

'I remember Austin coming into my office and asking me if his money had come in and I said, "It should be in the bank next week,"' Terrelonge says. 'This particular tranche was for US$16,000. He came back later, and the money had come in. I said, "Would you like to put it in the bank or send it to IMG?" where most of the other guys, the wise ones, had sent it. They looked after the accounts of lots of big sportsmen. He said to me, "Mr Terrelonge, how much does a BMW cost?" I said, "I think about $8,000." He said, "Send the money down to the BMW dealer." I said, "Are you sure that's what you want to do?" He said yes. "What would you like to do with the other $8,000?" He said, "I'll buy two then." I tried to dissuade him, but he eventually did it.'

Dujon says Austin's problem was a lack of education in financial matters. 'He'd seen more money than he'd ever seen in his life and he figured it couldn't finish.' He recalls Austin's turbulent relationship with cars. 'He bought the BMW, put gas in it, but never knew it needed oil and water, and he drove and drove and drove it and drove it and one day it just seized up and that was it. Then he started renting cars and he got banned by every rental agency in Jamaica because he destroyed them. I remember seeing him sitting on the sidewalk next to the highway, his car a total wreck, waiting for the recovery truck to come.'

Austin had also started experimenting with cocaine. His younger brother Oliver, then still at high school, walked in on his famous sibling racking up lines at the new family home in Mona, a purchase Austin had contributed to, in a middle-class area of Kingston. 'I asked him what it was, and he told me. It was later on that I learned what it really was. The good thing was he even encouraged me to stay away from it. I think it was being rich and famous that got to his head and he couldn't deal with the pressure.'

Austin's cricket suffered. Still a lynchpin of the Jamaica side, and respected for his ability to analyse a game – Corke says he could almost tell you what a bowler was going to bowl before he bowled – his match-winning feats were becoming rarer.

Jamaica selector Leonard Chambers observed a drop-off in intensity and a blasé approach to training sessions. 'He never showed the application he should have. He never showed the commitment. It created the wrath of people at club and national level. It was unfortunate because when you listened to him talking about cricket, it was an education.'

As a respected mentor of Jamaican cricket and an admirer of Austin's talent, Chambers felt a duty of care to the wayward young all-rounder, but his carefully administered advice fell on deaf ears. 'I had a chat with him, and I told him there are certain things you should avoid doing. There was a suspicion he was smoking weed and, later on, heavier stuff. But he listened to me and that was it. He was such a humble young person but got carried away. He was in the limelight. Lawrence Rowe was the darling of our kids, but Austin was just behind Lawrence and Michael Holding.'

Chambers wasn't the only one who tried to help him. Molly Biggenot-Austin, a bank clerk, was introduced to Austin at a nightclub in 1980. They quickly fell in love. 'Richard was awesome. He was always smiling and having fun,' she says. 'That's what drew me to him.' Although a non-drinker, she also loved to party. They would hang out with Austin's cricket buddy, Herbert Chang, 'chit-chatting and carrying on' in Maxville Avenue, west Kingston, the home of the famous reggae recording studio Channel One.

Biggenot-Austin lived with her family in Washington Gardens in the north-west of the city. Austin was supplementing his cricket income with coaching work at the Institute of Sport and the plan was to buy a house together. For a while at least, she seemed to curb Austin's excesses. 'When he worked at the Institute of Sport, he used to come straight to the bank and hand me a cheque, and say give me what you don't want out of it, and pay the rest to the house we were saving for.' They married the following year and bore a son, Ricardo.

Although he was no longer in the mix for West Indies selection, in 1982 Austin was still good enough to be offered the job of club professional at the Enfield Cricket Club in the Lancashire League. Biggenot-Austin visited him in England during his six-month tenure. 'I saw Buckingham Palace and it was so exciting,' she says. 'He could have continued getting overseas jobs. Cricket was his life.'

When the offer came via Lawrence Rowe to tour South Africa in early 1983, Austin had no idea how much that cricketing life meant to him, how deeply embedded its ritualised certainties were. But astronomical-for-the-time money in the region of US$100,000 was irresistible to a man with a family to raise and a hedonistic lifestyle to finance.

'I told him he wasn't to go,' says Biggenot-Austin. 'Him say, "But I want to make a better family life." And I said, "No, I don't need you to make a better family life. I can do with whatever you are getting from the Institute of Sport," plus I worked at the bank. I'm not saying it was the greatest pay at that time, but I could survive. But the money was too sweet. I don't say I don't like money, but I'm not going to sell my soul for money and that's what he did.'

She wasn't the only one urging him not to go. The hostility from the political and media class was summed up by the Minister of Youth and Community Service, Errol Anderson: 'Let me go on the record as hoping those Jamaicans who put their feet on South African soil and compete in sports there, will never be allowed to enjoy their "blood money" in Jamaica.' His words would prove prophetic.

When Austin arrived at Jan Smuts Airport in Johannesburg with fellow Jamaican Everton Mattis, he looked every inch the professional sportsman in a navy Enfield Cricket Club jumper and light-coloured slacks. There was little to hint of the angst and apprehension he was feeling on the inside. En route, at Heathrow Airport, he'd pleaded with the tour's critics, declaring 'I cannot feed my family on principles' to a *Daily Mirror* reporter.

It was Austin, clutching a Duncan Fearnley bat, who, along with Alvin Greenidge, strode to the Newlands wicket for the history-making first West Indian innings in South Africa. He was soon out lbw to Adrian Kuiper for nought, but the 16,000-capacity Cape Town crowd still got to witness Austin's signature magic – an airborne catch to dismiss Western Province's Graham Gooch, which turned the match in the rebels' favour.

Off the field, to the amusement of team-mates, Austin went on a wild goose chase searching for long-lost relatives, descendants of his father's eldest brother Harry, who was rumoured to have married a Cape Town woman.

During an occasionally stressful tour he was a regular source of entertainment. 'He talked a lot and was quite funny, so the guys used to get him to talk. He was a character,' Nevis all-rounder Derick Parry remembers.

But there was also concern for his reckless behaviour. Fast bowler Ray Wynter says that at a meeting of the Jamaican squad members in his Johannesburg hotel room, captain Lawrence Rowe zeroed in on Austin's wayward spending. 'He said to Richard, "You can't do what you did with Kerry Packer's money," and Richard said, "No, skip, me much smarter now."'

Parry recalls Austin turning up late for a game with a black eye. 'He went wandering into the town, started arguing with some guys and got beaten up. He came just as we were about to start but missed the warm-up. Normally he wasn't violent, he was making jokes.'

In the first 'Test' at Wanderers in Johannesburg, Austin showed admirable restraint of character in compiling 93 over almost five hours against South Africa's formidable pace attack of Garth Le Roux, Vintcent van der Bijl and Stephen Jefferies, but it was his only performance of note on the 12-match tour. With SACU president Ali Bacher looking to freshen up the appeal of the West Indies squad for the second tour ten months later, the decision was made to dump Austin along with his Jamaican team-mates Chang and Wynter. That a bag of marijuana was reportedly found in his suitcase didn't help Austin's cause.

Back home in Jamaica, the subject of the rebel tours continued to stir emotions. Unlike WSC, which had media support and was portrayed as a just battle against a backward-looking establishment, the rebels were viewed in newspaper reports as soulless mercenaries aiding the cause of apartheid.

Apart from a lifelong Test cricket ban, Austin was also shut out of the Senior Cup and stripped of his job as a coach with the Institute of Sport. He had buckets of money, but nothing to do. With unemployment running at 26.4 per cent and the brand damage associated with employing a 'blood money' cricketer, there were no businesses willing to stick their neck out to hire him.

Without the lifeblood of cricket, his tendency towards self-destruction exploded. His wife copped the brunt of it. Their plan to buy a house together disintegrated – a casualty of Austin's growing cocaine addiction. 'I could have got a loan for the house ... lawyers wanted him to bring the money to them so we could buy the house, but he took the money behind my back and invested it in coke. I think it was the rejection – he didn't know how to deal with that. He wanted something to null the pain.'

During the day, while Molly Biggenot-Austin was at work, Austin would booze and ingest drugs with his old nightclub friends, often not returning until the early hours of the morning, stoned and drunk. When husband and wife did catch up, Austin was regularly consumed with jealousy. It was an emotion that could bring out an even uglier side.

Jamaica batsman Mark Neita says his team-mate was well-known for 'putting his hand on his better half'. It reached absurd proportions during a Shell Shield match against Guyana when the police arrived at Sabina Park to arrest Austin for beating up his then girlfriend the night before. Neita says, 'We had won the toss and Danny was opening the batting when the police came. So, they said, "Look, the moment he gets out, we will take him away." But he batted and batted because he knew the police were after him. He batted straight to lunch, and he batted after lunch and made 118. Eventually the policeman left. When I asked him about it, Danny's explanation was that he thought she was cheating. There were a lot of moments like that.'

Biggenot-Austin says his violent behaviour ultimately tore them apart. 'I remember one time Ricardo was sick and I had to carry him to the doctors. My girlfriend was going to take me, but it was too late, so I went back home. He knocked me out on the floor, and I could not believe it. My hand was broken. He thought I was going out to look at men, but I had my son with me trying to get a drive to the hospital. He was jealous. In his mind, according to him I was too pretty, so he never wanted no one to get me. It was so stupid. That was what the coke was telling his mind to think ... because he wasn't like that before.'

In an effort to dry out, Austin decamped to New York. But the separation from home proved too hard to deal with. He was soon back in Jamaica, and into his old habits. Increasingly desperate, Molly forked out J$10,000 for Austin to see a psychiatrist but there was no change in his demeanour. 'All the clothes he bought for me when he went shopping, he destroyed them. He burnt them and cut them up. Oh Lord, the destruction. I had to run back to mum's. I had a rough life with him.' She left Austin in 1984.

The one-time Jones Town hero was on a downward spiral. Jamaican society turned a blind eye to his suffering and the suffering he was causing others. In their eyes, he'd brought racial shame to a proud people and the consequences were his and his alone to endure.

'Austin was totally ignored,' Foster says. 'From celebrity status to nothing.'

Clubs that once welcomed his patronage were now turning him away. Neita remembers the owner of an establishment where Austin had once shouted the bar champagne kicking him down the stairs 'because at the time he had lost it, and nobody wanted to be associated with him anymore'. It wasn't an isolated incident.

Rex Fennell, the JCA secretary, went so far as to say that the rebels had acted in a way that was akin to 'murdering your brother. It was like putting a knife into the back of the South African people.'

Jamaica has an honourable history of fighting racial inequality. Its successful slave revolts lit the fuse of liberation across the Caribbean. Understandably, bitterness dies hard in a land where any hint of skin colour prejudice provokes justifiable outrage. But at times it seemed that the reaction to Austin's plight bordered on spiteful; he'd reaped what he'd sown and now he was living his comeuppance. It touched on a dark current in the Jamaican psyche: the notion of 'bad mind', a tendency to resent the success of others. 'Dem nuh want see we prosper' – the flipside of which was a peculiar pleasure in their demise.

But as time wore on, the public spectre of Austin's ostracism, a troubled former Test cricketer living out his demons on the street in full view of the nation, began to elicit concern and even sympathy. In 1991, two years after a Test ban on the rebels was rescinded, the JCA lifted the prohibition on Jamaica's rebels playing in the Senior Cup. Fittingly, a Kensington member tabled the motion. It signalled the beginning of a long campaign to rehabilitate Austin.

Rowe, Wynter and Mattis were now living in America, and Chang was dealing with his own private mental hell in Greenwich Farm, but Austin, despite being ravaged by years of rough living – a bus shelter in Crossroads was one of his many 'homes' – could still mix it with the nation's best.

Former Jamaica batsman and Kensington team-mate Wayne Lewis remembers him stealing the show in his comeback match against Melbourne, aged 37. 'It was the biggest crowd in a long time; everyone came out because they wanted to see Richard play once more,' he said at Austin's funeral. 'And of course, he outdid us all; he made 50-odd and took five wickets.'

Austin was no longer strong enough to maintain the kind of physical intensity required to perform at the top every week, but his sharp cricket brain entranced his younger team-mates. Ex-West Indies opening batsman Wavell Hinds was a teenager at the time. At Austin's funeral, he remembered the tremendous impact the all-rounder had on youngsters at Kensington; how they would huddle around him for batting tips that their regular coaches couldn't provide. 'He told me, "If you want to score runs, young man, you have to be at the non-striker's end." I was baffled ... He then turned to my opening partner and told him the same thing. And he said, "If both of you try to bat at the non-striker's end, then you'll get six singles, three singles each, and the bowler won't have time to work you out, study you, and if you do that for the first two hours of play, then Kensington will be somewhere about 80 without loss."'

They formed a strong friendship based around the older man's quirks and demands. 'He was just an affectionate person,' Hinds eulogised. 'Even in my days playing for West Indies, Richard would meet me at Sabina Park ... and I knew I had to deliver all that he demanded ... lunch. I had to drop him at Crossroads irrespective of where I was going. He's gonna sit in the car and he's not going to move; I'd have to go to Arnett Gardens to watch football if that's what he wanted me to do.'

In between being feted by Test players, Austin was again falling between the cracks. In 1995 he was contracted to coach Kensington after they had enrolled him in a rehab programme. The club even appointed people to monitor his whereabouts, but once again he returned to the streets, and the lure of cocaine.

In 1999 he was convicted of illegal possession of a firearm and ammunition in Papine, near the University of West Indies campus. 'I only got the gun to protect myself, but I never used it,' he told *The Gleaner* newspaper. 'Some guys wanted to take away my $500 and it was to defend myself and my money. Right now, I make enough to eat so I couldn't allow anyone to come take it just like that.' He received a two-year suspended sentence.

Four years later, his younger brother Oliver made a public appeal for assistance. 'We can't blame anyone for his problem, but it would be nice if the government, for example, could have a programme to help him and others. Things like this mash up family life. He could be a motivational speaker. Who better to talk on issues like this but people who've been there? I give him everything he needs, except money. I encourage him to come home and make sure that I go out and get him. Our father was an alcoholic and that's what killed him. I don't want him to end up like that, but I can do so much and no more.' He even offered his brother use of the family Volvo in Mona.

Austin, also interviewed, pleaded to be given another chance at coaching. 'I'm not ashamed to say I need help. With my kind of problem, I need caring for ... I need help to clean up and a job to take care of myself and then, believe it or not, I can make a valuable contribution to cricket again. I'm friendly. I need to interact with people, so I leave my house every day. My job right now is begging. I don't really have to do this, but it is part of the territory. The coke, it helps me forget,' he added. 'It probably seems like I am a hopeless case, but I have potential.'

He complained that he didn't want to be shoved back into Patricia House, a New Kingston rehab facility, because it was 'depressing'. 'Give me a job, please, so I can take care of myself because situations like mine always end in tragedy.'

One of the key components of Austin's job as a beggar involved setting up camp near the Pegasus Hotel during international matches and catching the eye of officials or former players who would guardedly welcome the bedraggled and by now bone-thin street dweller into conversation. Tony Cozier recalled how impressed former England player and commentator Robin Jackman was by Austin's passion and insight into the game as they drank at the hotel bar late into the night.

Leonard Chambers says that at Test matches and cricket functions, which Austin had a curious knack of crashing, he was often seen holding court to eager groups of men and boys captivated by his gift for entertaining commentary. But there were also instances of him, high as a kite, causing a public nuisance. At Sabina Park, during a Test match, he had to be calmed down by police as he shrieked tearfully from the grandstand.

Regardless of his state of mind, he never seemed to lose his gift for mustering a laugh. Former England captain Mike Atherton recalled meeting him at a Texaco petrol station in the Crossroads area. 'Give my regards to the Queen when you see her,' Austin said to him. 'Yeah, give my best to the good lady.' Then he blew a kiss into the air.

Perhaps the saddest encounters Austin had were with his son, Ricardo, who, because of his father's itinerant lifestyle, grew up without knowing him. Ricardo, now in his late 20s, was working as a graphic designer at an ad agency in New Kingston. After a meal with his girlfriend at a local restaurant he opened the door to leave. Sitting on the step was his father, hands cupped in the begging position. Ricardo knew instantly who it was – he'd seen pictures of his dad in the newspaper – but the older man didn't recognise him. Ricardo was momentarily taken aback. 'I am your son,' he pleaded. There was a pause, and Austin murmured 'Bambino', the name he used to call him as a baby. It was the first time he'd seen him since he was a young boy.

In the few years Austin had left, Ricardo would look out for his father and give him money for food, in spite of his mother's protests that it would only be used for drugs. It was a common moral quandary everyone from politicians to lawyers, cricket administrators and ex-team-mates faced as they passed him on the street – a daily test of their good Samaritan credentials. 'People were always trying to help him and reform him,' says former Jamaica team-mate Ray Wynter. 'But there was nothing you could do for him.'

Perversely, by rebuffing those who tried to rehabilitate him, Austin was in his own way thumbing his nose at the society that had once rejected him; he was now rejecting them with the smidgeon of power he had left.

Wayne Lewis had been Austin's team-mate at Kensington in the Senior Cup in the early 1980s. In a side bristling with internationals, and egos, the young batsman, eight years Austin's junior, appreciated the Test player's approachability. 'A lot of those guys didn't care about the Senior Cup, because they had played for West Indies. I was frightened to bat with Herbert Chang because he was so demanding. He would always be telling me what I should be doing, and he was not interested in helping the younger players. He only cared about himself. Whereas Richard was selfish too, but he was friendly and so knowledgeable about the game.'

Lewis was also a product of the Jones Town ghetto. He'd watched Austin's descent from community hero to national eyesore with great sorrow – and a sense of shame. He felt he had to intervene. 'It got to the stage where he was smelly and on the streets, but no one would help him. I went to see my friend, whose father was in charge of the Institute of Sport. I was told they could do nothing for him – they could not give him government funds, because people would always bring up South Africa. They were afraid to touch it, but the government could have done something.'

Austin's last cricket hurrah was in a masters tournament with the Jamaica Panthers in 2009, aged 55. Nehemiah Perry, a former Windies off-spinner and organiser of the team, hoped Austin might 'find himself' by playing, and that by having him in the dressing room alongside his team-mates, which included Jeff Dujon, Jimmy Adams and Courtney Walsh, they would 'try to clean him up'. Austin, for his part, said he'd 'stopped smoking' and was 'taking care' of his health. 'I am a bit weak, but I think I am batting well and hope that I will get a game and be able to entertain the crowd.' Accompanying the story in *The Gleaner* was a photo of Austin holding a bat, his gaunt, sunken features casting a harrowing shadow.

In previous over-40s games he'd shown that he could still defy his worsening condition. Kingston Cricket Club's Denis

Robotham recalled a final against Kensington when Austin upstaged everyone. 'On the Friday night we were having a few drinks and we saw Danny Germs and we thought, here is our chance. So, we bought him about nine beers. When we turned up for the final on Saturday, Danny Germs was in the opponents' dressing room lying down. He hadn't bathed for three or four days and he wasn't looking good. So, we said mission accomplished. We won the toss and asked them to bat first. I was keeping. Danny Germs was opening with another West Indies Test player, Basil Williams. I could smell the liquor on him. The man made 95 and we lost the final ... and our money!'

The last time Albert Padmore saw Austin was at a Jamaican government function honouring West Indian players. The Bajan off-spinner had played with Austin on the 1978/79 WSC tour and accompanied him as team manager in South Africa. He was shocked by his friend's deterioration. 'Richard and I got together before the start of the event. He called me "Manage" because I was the manager on the South African tour. We were excited to see each other, and we started reminiscing, but he would zone in and out briefly. He was a shadow of the person I knew. There was nothing between the skin and bone.'

In his final years, Austin's behaviour became more unpredictable; at one point he even entered a talent competition staged by a fast food chain, wheezing through an Earth Wind & Fire tune. He was now the ultimate street entertainer, a figure of mirth and mercy.

* * *

Petunia Way in Mona is a neat assortment of well-kept houses, manicured lawns and footpaths, a far cry from the corrugated iron 'zinc' and crumbling gutters of Austin's Jones Town boyhood. There's no whiff of the violence or poverty crippling downtown Kingston. The flat-roofed, six-bedroom Austin family home is painted yellow ochre. It sits quietly behind a spiked metal fence and an imposing wrought iron front gate. Its only point of difference is the latticework of bars that protect the windows and front door – installed presumably to shield it from the corrupt ambitions of Richard Austin's drug-dealing friends.

Bobby Austin is tall like his older brother, but thick-set. He says the house was like a refuge for Austin because it was a place where he wasn't allowed to do drugs. It was his cocaine addiction and the freedom of living rough that kept drawing him back to the streets. 'When he was here, he was clean,' Bobby Austin says. 'He would sleep on the street because we don't have drugs here. At Crossroads I would find him after a few days. I would try to bring him, but him no wanna come sometimes so just leave him. I try all them things a whole heap of time to keep him off the street.'

For several years up until his death, Richard Austin experienced abdominal discomfort. Diagnosed with a hernia, he spent the last few months of his life in hospital as the pain intensified. According to Bobby Austin, doctors wanted to operate, but he insisted they wait because his brother's body was too weak from years of drug and alcohol abuse to survive major surgery. It was a battle Bobby Austin was never going to win. 'Him have operation. That kill him. He was in the ICU ward for a while with a big cylinder, breathing in and out with big hose. But he couldn't manage that.'

Richard Austin died on 6 February 2015 at Kingston Public Hospital in downtown, a mere forward-defensive from his primary school, All Saints. At Austin's Holy Trinity Roman Catholic Cathedral funeral, younger Jamaican team-mate Wayne Lewis spoke candidly about his feelings for the dead man, and gently chided those present for failing to offer the concerted care that may have turned his friend's life around.

'When Richard was going through his struggles and he would come to Sabina Park during first-class games or the Senior Cup, a lot of us would joke around and pick his brain from time to time, and we did what we could right there and allowed him to go his way rather than embracing him some more and try and fix the situation that he was going through. So, all of us basically let Richard down at some stage. From my personal point of view, I'm sorry that I didn't do much for Richard because I loved the man so much.'

But could any more have been done? Wasn't Austin the driver of his own colourful journey, the good and the bad? Austin himself was never in doubt where the blame lay for his downfall. 'The board did nothing for me because we went on the rebel tours,' he told me. 'The drugs help me to live. South Africa ...' his voice trailed off into mumbled sadness. 'South Africa.'

Alvin Greenidge

'A real proper gentleman'

TO RIVAL opening batsmen in 1970s Barbados it must have seemed like an unfair advantage to possess the Greenidge surname. Three unrelated Greenidges – Cuthbert Gordon, Geoffrey Alan and Alvin Ethelbert – won a call-up to the West Indies Test side during that turbulent decade. Cuthbert, better known to the cricket world by the slightly less grandfatherly name of Gordon, blazed into the history books as one of the greatest ever new-ball combatants. Geoffrey had a negligible impact in just five Tests but is best remembered as the last white man to represent in the maroon cap.[1] But Alvin, the elegant classicist who snuck in a few games while the big boys chased Packer dollars during WSC, slid into anonymity.

Alvin who? Almost. And that's the way he likes it. Private and reserved are the primary adjectives ex-team-mates pin on him.

At the historic Barbados Defence Force (BDF) headquarters overlooking the appropriately named Drill Hall Beach, Greenidge emerges from a morning meeting with team officials. He's BDF coach in the Barbados Cricket Association (BCA) competition. He's a large guy now – his gut rests gently over blue training shorts – but his batting muscles are intact. He agrees to mime

---

1   Australian-raised Brendan Nash made his Test debut in 2008 and is sometimes referred to as the last white man to play for the West Indies, but it was later reported that he was of mixed-race heritage.

an on-drive for video posterity; his round head follows top and bottom hand in almost balletic unison.

But he's reluctant to reveal anything about his career. It's not unexpected. During a year of frustrating WhatsApp messages and calls, he concedes that Jeff Thomson was quick – Greenidge encountered him on debut in 1978 – and that a year later it wasn't Venkataraghavan's flight that deceived him on an unpredictable Madras wicket, it was instead a bad shot that got him out.

He also says he has to obtain permission from someone at the BDF to talk about the rebel tours. It never comes. That someone is always on annual leave or business. Either Greenidge is genuinely reticent or he fears that talk of South Africa will dredge up ancient frictions that might endanger his job. Probably a bit of both.

Yet when they were youth players, keen judges rated him better than Gordon Greenidge's batting amigo Desmond Haynes. The flipside, team-mates say, was that he lacked the confidence and self-belief to convert that talent into Haynes-like greatness.

John Vanderpool, now resident in California, batted in Barbados youth squads with Greenidge in the mid-1970s. 'I think he was the best batsman of all of us,' he says of his Christ Church buddy. 'He could teach you to bat when you watched him. He was technically more correct. Very strong off the pads. But he is a reserved guy.'

In 1999, Greenidge broke the habit of a lifetime to speak with Barbados newspaper *The Nation* about his first Test match. That's the one where he found out how quick super-slinger Thomson was on a lifeless Bourda wicket.

His innings had begun with cavalier intent. 'There was little in the pitch to make Jeff Thomson venomous,' wrote the CANA reporter. 'And when he tried to dig one in for a fast riser to Greenidge the confident young Barbadian opener pivoted gracefully and hooked at chest height to the backward square leg fence.'

He raced to 56 not out at lunch, including ten boundaries. After the break, with the breeze flapping at his rump, Thomson returned in top gear from the northern end. Twice he tempted Greenidge outside off stump, but the young Bajan refused to nibble. The sixth ball he had no choice. It all but deconstructed his back-foot defensive prod, rapping him on the pads in front of the wicket. At least, that's how the reporter viewed it.

Unsurprisingly, Greenidge saw the lbw verdict differently. 'The decision I got in the first innings still, up to this day, has left me a bit upset,' he told *The Nation*. 'I was going well, and then I got a poor decision by umpire [Ralph] Gosein. I went to hit a ball from Thommo through the leg side and up went the finger. I went to whip the ball, and everyone knew it was high. The appeal was not even a confident one.'

It was a minor blip. At the end of the series, seasoned commentators offered their praise for the stylish newcomer. Tony Cozier wrote that Greenidge had a 'touch of class about him' and Henry Blofeld observed that he's a 'clean striker of the ball' who is 'well balanced' and 'loves nothing more than to use his long reach and come on to the front foot and drive'. He had the makings of a top-notch Greenidge.

With the bulk of the West Indies first team still contracted to WSC, his inclusion in the WICBC-sanctioned six-Test tour of India later that year was a foregone conclusion, but his form was much less certain. Footage from the Madras Test backs up Greenidge's assertion that he played down the wrong line to the wily Venkat, and a grand total of only 80 runs from four Tests enabled the belligerent Guyanese Faoud Bacchus and Jamaica's Basil 'Shotgun' Williams to surge ahead of him in the preferred opener stakes. Add in the possibility of the much-lauded Gordon Greenidge and Desmond Haynes combination returning to a reintegrated post-WSC side and Alvin Greenidge's opportunities to represent the West Indies appeared slim.

His demotion was confirmed as selection for the 1979 Barbados Shell Shield side played out. Greenidge was chosen as opener for three of the four matches, but when Gordon Greenidge and Haynes became available for the Trinidad clash at Kensington Oval, he was quietly nudged to number three in the order. Not even an insubordinate century could convince the cricket powers that he deserved another chance.

At 22, his Test career was over. He wouldn't be picked for the World Cup later that year – Bacchus was chosen as the back-up opener – nor would he touch down with the West Indies squad in Sydney for a three-Test match series in the southern hemisphere summer.

Greenidge, like a whole host of discarded Australian and West Indies players, was evaluating his future. Question marks over the validity of baggy green and maroon caps earned when the best players were barred from selection only added to the sense of insecurity.

In 1980, he was plucked from the obscurity of Dutch club cricket, where he was playing in the off-season with cousin, Emmerson Trotman, to field for an injury-depleted West Indies side in the Oval Test against England, but it was his last glimpse of the big time.

The runs continued to flow as an opener for Barbados, but he was always made to defer to the celebrated Gordon Greenidge–Desmond Haynes combination when they were available.

* * *

An invitation to join the rebels' South African adventure had obvious appeal for a man in Alvin Greenidge's position but detonating his Test aspirations at just 26 was no straightforward decision. He was one of several anxious players nursing a serious case of buyer's remorse as their flight landed at Jan Smuts Airport on 12 January 1983.

But it was Greenidge, sporting a red helmet and wielding a Gunn & Moore bat alongside Richard Austin in a white sun hat, who broke the Caribbean ban on sporting contact with South Africa. Amid a throng of appreciative boys and youths in caps, visors and bucket hats, they made their way to the Newlands wicket to begin the first tour match against Western Province. That they both recorded ducks – Greenidge nailed in front by tricky left-arm seamer Stephen Jefferies – was immaterial. History had been made.

The second 'Test' at Wanderers was Greenidge's high point in the republic. Despite contracting tonsillitis, experiencing double vision and being forced to retire, he returned late in the first innings to chisel a partnership of 34 with number 11 Ray Wynter – runs that ultimately proved the difference between the two sides. His second innings 48 was also punctuated with illness-related heroics as he and a grey-looking Collis King, who was suffering from leg cramps, added 71 to help post the South Africans a reasonable target.

Curiously, a report from the final match of the tour, a benefit game in the Free State mining town of Welkom, revealed Greenidge in a rare public display of good humour, as paceman Sylvester Clarke chased him about the Rovers Club pavilion with a cricket bat, and manager Albert Padmore intervened to halt what appeared to be a mock fight.

In the second rebel instalment, old nemesis Faoud Bacchus pilfered his spot at the top of the order, but a glut of injuries afforded him a start in the third 'Test' at Wanderers. Once again Greenidge proved a gritty customer, collapsing on the pitch after wearing a quicker ball from Rupert 'Spook' Hanley on the right knee, but recovering to score 43. Yet blond bomber Hanley has little memory of the delivery or Greenidge's feats with the willow, although he insists that he was 'stylish like all the other West Indies batsmen'.

It speaks to the perception that Greenidge lacked charisma and bravado; that he couldn't gain traction with the public or the people that counted; that he couldn't self-promote. 'He never had that character to carry it to another level like a Dessie Haynes,' says his friend John Vanderpool. 'Yet technically he was much sounder.'

Greenidge's final A-list knock was a powerful 68 off 87 balls at Wanderers against the might of Hanley, Clive Rice, Stephen

Jefferies and Kenny Watson. But the local press seemed just as keen to report that he'd won a diamond from a jewellery shop in Durban's West Walk arcade after buying a ring for his wife. He was 27.

Like many of the rebels, Greenidge viewed South Africa's Currie Cup in the context of career life support, but import restrictions and that terminal lack of box office appeal condemned him to a stint as club pro with Victoria Park Pirates in the Port Elizabeth club competition.

Aubrey Duff had represented the Springboks in football at right-back. An all-round sportsman, he was Greenidge's opening partner at the cemetery-bordered ground known as 'Tombstone Gulch'. For the neglected Barbadian it was a chance to emerge from the shadows of his more famous compadres. The anonymous Greenidge held centre stage, albeit a reduced one.

Personality-wise, there wasn't a lot more to see. Duff says Greenidge was a well-respected, model professional, but also a naturally introverted character, at odds with the hard-playing, hard-partying Caribbean stereotype nurtured by many of his team-mates. 'He was quiet and soft-spoken, a real proper gentleman,' Duff recalls. 'He fell out of favour with some of the West Indies guys because he wasn't like them. He was not a party animal. He wouldn't get involved. Whereas Ezra Moseley [who was contracted to the local Currie Cup franchise Eastern Province] was very vocal after a few drinks. But Alvin would be on his own having his cool drink. Of course, we'd pull him into the team ... and join him in. Once he got talking, he was a very interesting guy to listen to.'

Duff maintains that it was a source of irritation to Greenidge that he hadn't been able to lock in a provincial contract and remembers that they often talked about his desire to wear the West Indies maroon again.

In 1986, still only 29, the *Sunday Sun* reported that Greenidge was writing to the UN to have his name removed from a blacklist of sportsmen who had played in South Africa. Three years later, the ban was lifted, but he never represented at first-class level again.

In the 1999 *Nation* story, Greenidge is quoted as saying that he had no regrets about touring South Africa and was glad he 'helped with the development of young black cricketers, especially those in Soweto'. It has remained his last – and only – public utterance on the subject. The less that is known about the least-known Greenidge, it seems, the better.

Not even Gordon Greenidge, as of 2020 a Knight Commander of the Order of St Michael and St George, can shed more light on the man his batting heroics consigned to the boondocks of history. 'He was a capable enough batsman,' the top-ranking Greenidge says before conceding that his surname-sake might have been more successful in another era. But he's willing to speculate on Alvin Greenidge and his rebel brothers' mindset. 'There are some players who felt a bit of grief that they were not treated well when they returned to the Caribbean and they were hurt. They still do. That was disappointing.'

Emmerson Trotman

'He was like a battery that never ran flat'

HAL'S CAR Park Bar is doing a modest trade. Rum-throated karaoke singers croak lyrics that only tourists tolerate, and a few sunburned Brits dot the counter. Outside, the Gap burger man works from a grill attached to the back of a truck while bored taxi drivers spruik for business. This is the glitzy Barbados strip of St Lawrence Gap. On one of its off nights.

Emmerson Trotman, small and pugnacious, isn't having an off night. 'I'm not a struggler like them,' he boasts. And he's not. Coach of the Barbados Pride national cricket team, father of a top-tier Dutch soccer player, co-owner of this bar. He even has an agent.

The 'them' he's referring to are his former rebel team-mates. Guys such as the drug-dealing wicketkeeper David Murray, who occasionally stumbles into Hal's for a drink. Guys who squandered their South African booty. Guys who outscored Trotman but couldn't play the game of life.

'Trotters', 'Trotty' or 'ET', depending on which dressing room you shared with him, was a Barbados batting prodigy. Dial set permanently to attack, he out-stroked Jeff Dujon on a Young West Indies tour of England, debuted for Barbados before contemporary Desmond Haynes and smote a century off Colin Croft aged just 22. He could also keep wicket. But his belligerent blade was also his downfall; the more measured

Haynes quickly leapfrogged him in the pecking order – and in reputation.

Photo agency Getty Images owns an archived picture of the West Indies squad taken at Kensington Oval, Bridgetown, in 1981, and standing next to 12th man Malcolm Marshall, six down from Haynes, is Trotman, presumably selected as 13th man after a flurry of runs in the Shell Shield. But such is his anonymity in the wider world, the agency mistakenly labels him as Derick Parry, the Nevis off-spinner. Not that it bothers him. 'I'm a professional,' he says bluntly, in an accent that lies somewhere between the Caribbean and Enschede, Holland, where he has spent a large chunk of his life.

And a professional doesn't give information away for nothing. Especially not about his participation in the rebel tours. Yet by all accounts Trotman was a generous, open-hearted cricketer. He was also well-travelled.

At Border in the Castle Bowl competition, he earned a reputation as a flamboyant team man and fan favourite, helping steer the East London-based side into the top tier of South African cricket.

Ian Howell, later a Test cricket umpire, was Trotman's captain. 'He was small in stature, large in life,' Howell says. 'We could have called him Duracell because he was like a battery that never ran flat. He had so much positive energy and a great rapport with the supporters.'

He was also cocky. Seamer Brenden Fourie has Trotman the energetic wicketkeeper to thank for bagging a leg side catch that delivered him a hat-trick in his third game for Border. And teaching him to believe in himself. 'It wasn't in his nature to defend,' Fourie says. 'He was a confident guy who would back himself in any situation against any player. If Allan Donald was bowling to him, he was going to take him on; if it was Kepler Wessels batting, he was going to be in Kepler's ear.'

Burly paceman Kenny Watson played with Trotman at Border and against him for the Springboks on the rebel tours. He enjoyed the extrovert's presence, but he also sussed his weakness. In the third 'Test' at Johannesburg in 1984, South Africa had been bowled out just before lunch. The West Indies XI openers were forced to negotiate one over from Watson before heading back into the dressing room again. It was an unenviable task that seemed to mess with Trotman's head. 'I don't think he knew what to do,' Watson says. 'He was half stuck between attacking and surviving. With his mindset being attack, attack, he was in two minds and didn't move his feet.' Trotman duly tickled a Watson outswinger to Graeme Pollock at third slip. 'You had to do something with the ball to make him look weak. There was no use bowling line and length to him – he would get his eyes in line.'

But the jury was out on whether he was good enough to make the official West Indies side. 'There were better West Indies players around. We thought some of their rebel bowlers would have made the side, and Lawrence Rowe, he wasn't just a big basher, he knew how to build a big score. But Trotters wasn't really of the same league as Rowe,' says Watson.

However, unlike master craftsman Rowe, he was able to return to the island of his birth via a coaching job with the Dutch national side, and later to the summit of Barbados's coaching profession. Perhaps if he'd been a heavy hitter like Haynes, Greenidge or Garner the rebel condemnation would have been fiercer, but his low profile seemed to work in his favour.

Dressed in a red polo shirt, black trousers and running shoes, Trotman, still nimble and easy-moving at 65, bosses the bar like he once did Shell Shield trundlers. He kindly offers me a Banks beer, the watery local lager, and calls his agent to negotiate a deal for appearing in this book. It's somewhat ironic that the least widely known of all the rebels has an agent, but such has been his post-playing prosperity.

Kenny Watson isn't surprised that Trotman made a go of it where others failed. 'He was never going to fall on hard times;

he had a sense of maturity about what he was going to do. He would not just blow his money on rubbish.'

John Vanderpool opened the batting with Trotman at Barbados youth level in the mid-1970s. He says 'Trotty' was good enough to play for the West Indies but always had a broader focus that others lacked. 'Trotty was very, very serious about cricket and trained very hard but he was a very smart guy. Very sharp.'

In September 1981, West Indies selectors met to discuss the impending three-Test tour of Australia. Jamaican cricket columnist Jimmy Carnegie wrote that of all the uncapped batsmen on the selectors' radar, 26-year-old Trotman 'seems to me the most ready'. But chairman of selectors Clyde Walcott thought otherwise, preferring the diminutive Trinidadian Gus Logie as middle-order ballast. Significantly, Lawrence Rowe and his Jamaican colleague Everton Mattis were also passed over.

Sixteen months later, Trotman, Mattis and Rowe were in South Africa sticking up defiant middle fingers to Walcott, the WICBC establishment, world opinion and anyone who'd ever doubted their batting prowess.

Looking every inch the seasoned international traveller in aviator shades – chains dangling from his neck – Trotman was one of four rebels photographed for the front page of Johannesburg's *Rand Daily Mail* in the arrival hall at Jan Smuts Airport. But apart from injuring a finger keeping, in David Murray's absence, to Ezra Moseley in the tour opener and cracking up in laughter when Jamaican slinger Ray Wynter tumbled over in his follow-through at Wanderers, Trotman's modest contributions went unnoticed in the South African press.

Notwithstanding his soft dismissal to Watson in the third 'Test', Trotman's second tour was much more productive; 94 in an ODI at Newlands that showcased the tremendous power he could generate from a short backlift, and 77 in a record rebel opening stand with Faoud Bacchus that set up a West Indies series victory – and a contract with Border.

***

In interviews with Netherlands cricket and football websites, Trotman makes it clear that he feels more Dutch than Bajan. It's easy to see why. His wife and children hail from Enschede, and he has coached in Haarlem and Amsterdam since 1976. His 20-year-old son, the ambitiously titled Ryan Lara, has a cricket name but a football brain, having played on the left wing for Eredivisie club FC Twente and now Den Bosch.

Talk of Ryan's vocational progress adds spark to an increasingly empty conversation as negotiations with Trotman's agent grind to a halt over money and the vibe at Hal's Car Park Bar, like the stiff North Atlantic breeze, begins to cool.

'I am a professional,' Trotman repeats. It's a mantra that has served him well. The Barbados Pride mentor, king of attack, will play the defensive line tonight.

David Murray

'Tell your friend not to come to the pasture so high'

A SOUVENIR Barbados beach towel masquerades as a cover sheet. It hugs one half of the mattress, which lies flat on the unvarnished wooden floor. On the other side are CDs, a plastic Barry White case and a remote control. To the left of the mattress is a half-eaten bowl of noodles bisected by a plastic fork. Nearby, cigarette papers are spread thick with marijuana; rolled joints compete for space in a tiny gap between the edge of the mattress and the mouldy salmon-coloured wall.

In the entrance to the room, a chest of drawers props up an outmoded portable TV, along with a finished bottle of aftershave and various ointments. Affixed to the front of the top drawer is a Levi's jeans sticker indicating slim-fit 511 style and 29-inch waist measurement. That small waist measurement belongs to the diminutive, skeletal frame of David Murray, joint-holder of the West Indian wicketkeeping record for most dismissals in a Test match.

This is the man Malcolm Marshall described as the best, most agile keeper he played with, the only one he could rely on to snaffle every edge and half-chance off his bowling. The man Jeffrey Dujon says was a class above him behind the stumps. The man whose bedroom resembles a depressing scene from a men's refuge.

'I fucked up,' Murray confesses softly, shaking his greying deadlocks. It's a phrase he returns to often. Almost as often as 'I have no regrets'.

Painfully thin – his shoulder blades protrude through a V-neck yellow T-shirt – Murray spends most of his days wandering the tourist beaches near Bridgetown selling dope to what he calls the 'chosen few' before returning to the family home in Station Hill, four doors down from an old prison, where he lives with two aunties.

Some nights he ventures to St Lawrence Gap, a gaudy tourist strip, to sell to foreigners. But he maintains that the reports of him being a 'beach bum' are untrue, that he's not an 'out and out' dealer. He says he has cleaned himself up. He also says that his spartan lifestyle shouldn't be mistaken for an inability to take proper care of himself. 'I'm not depressed. I go to the beach; I listen to music. That keeps me company. And the BBC too. I like to know what's going on in the world, so when you go out you can communicate with people. Girls still like me, but I don't like too many girls anymore. They gotta be something special.'

Over the years, 'girls' have been very special to Murray, regularly supplying him with food and money to subsidise his hand-to-mouth existence. He says he has a current girlfriend based in New York who visits him from time to time to ensure he's okay.

His son, Ricky Hoyte, a one-time Barbados wicketkeeper like his father, also returns from his base in Bermuda to check on him. And he still sees his dad, batting legend Sir Everton Weekes. 'I look after myself, get some good rest, eat some good food and do some exercise walking to the beach,' Murray says, shrugging off the notion he's in any way derelict.

What he won't deny, however, is that he's an outcast. That people on the street often call him an 'honorary white' and worse. That he's still paying for pocketing apartheid-tainted money. It's a line of thought he likes to promote – probably because it makes his current situation seem more comprehensible.

The ritual of foreign media prying into his life, astounded that a former top-line Test wicketkeeper is living as a virtual destitute, is becoming familiar to Murray. Part of that ritual involves taking him out for dinner – and slipping him BDs$40 to find his way home.

Sitting in the outer garden area of Mojo bar and restaurant in Worthing on the south coast of the island, Murray, dreadlocked and with bloodshot eyes, resembles any number of ageing hippies or Rasta men. He also talks like them – frequently describing friends and foes alike as 'beautiful'. Apparently, I remind him of the brother of his ex-Australian wife Kerry, and he asks to see photos of my children. He seems at ease, his mind uncluttered. But the speed with which he wolfs down the 'catch of the day' – mahi mahi dolphin fish in a white wine cream sauce – suggests he has been hanging out for this meal for some time.

* * *

Sir Everton Weekes is the only Test cricketer to have scored five centuries in a row. He's also one of the only cricketers in the world to have a roundabout named after him. In Barbados, he's a national hero.

Murray didn't inherit his name because he was born out of wedlock, but he inherited the pressure that comes with being the son of a famous sportsman – even though he was brought up by his grandmother. He had all the trappings of a respectable, contented childhood. Anglican choirboy, keen cricketer, doting grandma. His younger brother Andy Weekes lived with his dad. His mum had moved to England. 'I was happy,' he says. 'But I was lonely. I had a little troubles.'

Murray began smoking marijuana at 13. 'It was a way of being with friends,' he says. Dope has been his constant companion for the past 56 years. Even on the cricket pitch. 'It was good meditation,' he laughs. 'You could concentrate for real. First ball you say, "Good luck to everybody", and then I'm on my own. The stronger it was, the more I would concentrate.'

On the 1979 tour of India he discovered hashish at a market in Bombay near the Gateway of India. It blew his mind, even more so, it would seem, than compiling 206 not out on the same tour, his highest first-class score, against East Zone in Jamshedpur. 'That innings was my best ... I would have a shower in the morning, get my muscles warm, then eat a piece and I would be high for the whole day. I recommend eating hashish,' he says, warming to the topic. 'People in India always have a chalice with hashish. There are a lot of pretty girls there, too. You've got to pinch yourself and say am I in the real world? Sometimes it [hashish] would be so strong I would forget women, that I had a date with them.'

Did his team-mates notice? Murray rubs his knuckles, a tic that often strikes when he's unsure of himself. 'No one said anything because they didn't know.'

Of course, they did know. 'There were others into it, but I don't want to disclose names. But I took the blame.'

In Australia in 1975/76, Murray admits that veteran off-spinner Lance Gibbs prevented management from sending him home after his drug consumption got out of hand. Later, he remembers Clive Lloyd got a message to him via Viv Richards – Murray and the Master Blaster were married to Antiguan sisters at the time – to 'tell your friend not to come to the pasture so high'.

Murray's final days in a maroon West Indies cap would end in a haze of marijuana fumes and recriminations.

In Michael Holding's biography, *Whispering Death*, the silky fast bowler describes Murray's keeping as 'high class', pointing to his 'soft hands' and smooth technique.

Deryck Murray says that his namesake was good but not consistent: 'He had moments where he was brilliant and moments when he wasn't.' The Trinidad keeper, seven years Murray's senior and vice-captain to Clive Lloyd, held a mortgage on the West Indies keeping position during the 1970s. On several overseas tours, David Murray was his deputy. It's still a source of great frustration. In many ways, Deryck was Murray's polar opposite – compact and tidy rather than silky, a good team man and players' advocate, he was secretary of the West Indies Players' Association, a stable hand in a side bursting with egos. But David Murray, despite his own regal cricketing pedigree, saw him as part of the West Indies establishment. 'His family controlled cricket here,' he says, without any real evidence.

'I don't know if I smoked less I would have played more. Deryck had something on them. He was educated at Cambridge. When Trinidadians talk to you, you are convinced. They are sweet talkers … they can mum a guy.' His voice fades away.

Even when David Murray got his chance behind the stumps at the relatively late age of 28 it was because Deryck had joined Kerry Packer's WSC. To him, it seemed his nemesis was still controlling his destiny.

The third Test against Australia in Georgetown, Guyana, in March 1978 was also giant Bajan paceman Sylvester Clarke's debut. 'I took a great catch off him, my first dismissal, down the leg side. I was standing a bit wide and Bobby Simpson gloved it. I always picked up the ball early – that's the secret,' he says, revelling in the technique so many team-mates admired.

The step up in quality was an eye-opener. 'Thommo [Jeff Thomson] bowled me a ball in Trinidad and it was the first ball that ever beat me for pace. And I thought I have to wake up.'

Despite a successful tour of India in 1978/79 with both bat and gloves – 261 runs at 29 and 18 dismissals in six Tests – when the World Series men returned to 'traditional' cricket, Murray had to make way for his great rival, who was now 36. 'He was past it,' Murray says. 'He played about four years over. The English papers made cartoons and jokes about him.'

By the end of the 1980/81 tours of Pakistan and England, in which Murray started as Deryck's understudy yet again, the selectors agreed with him. But his stint as number one custodian would last just ten Test matches.

It didn't help that his tenure was sandwiched between the venerable and highly respected Deryck Murray and Jeff Dujon, the greatest keeper-batsman in Caribbean history. Dujon toured Australia in 1981/82 as a middle-order stroke-player and back-up to Murray. Elegant in front of the wicket and acrobatic behind it, he can't praise Murray's glovework enough. 'Technically he was extremely good – great hands, the way he moved – he was a top-class keeper, no question.'

And, unlike Dujon, he didn't have to fling himself around the turf – he was always in position, thanks to nimble footwork. 'In terms of all-round keeping ability, and up to the stumps, I would never put myself in David's class. Standing up to the wicket, he made me look like Dolly Parton.'

During that Australian summer, Dujon would have a ringside seat to Murray's self-destruction.

The 1981/82 vintage West Indies had won a record-breaking 15 Test matches on the trot; there was possibly no greater side in the history of the game. Murray's position looked secure – as long as his drug contacts didn't run out.

The Camperdown Travelodge in inner-city Sydney played host to many international sporting teams in the 1980s and 1990s. When the West Indies stayed there for a warm-up match against New South Wales, Murray, the incumbent keeper, was rested so that Dujon could accustom his hands to the bruising pace of Clarke, Holding, Roberts and Croft. He was, however, like all squad members, still required to turn up for team meetings.

Dujon scored a century in that game, bolstering his credentials for a call-up to the first Test in Melbourne. He says Murray never made it to the team meetings because he was always too out of it. 'We couldn't find David. No one could. After one meeting, I went downstairs – a friend was coming to visit. David was standing at the entrance to the hotel, looking out, watching the cars go by. I said to him, "D, we had a team meeting," and he kept looking at the cars go by and said, "Yeahhhh, you know." He was as high as a kite. I could see it in his eyes. He'd forgot about the meeting, everything. He didn't really get chastised for that, but it was the first black mark against him.'

Gentle and peaceable, it was hard for anyone to get angry with 'Little D', even when his transgressions were so obvious. The days of micromanaging coaches and sports psychologists hovering over professional sportsmen were decades off, and the media were far more tolerant of off-field indulgences.

Drugs weren't Murray's sole indulgence. In *Marshall Arts*, Malcolm Marshall's autobiography, the champion paceman talks about the West Indian squad's insatiable lust for Australian women, a lust that was eagerly reciprocated. 'There were always plenty of bikini-clad women at cricket matches, and if they take a shine to you, they soon make themselves known when the opportunity arises. Aussie girls love West Indians, and I for one was not rude enough to deny their hospitality.'

Neither was Murray. Even team-mates from his youth cricket days recall a 'sweet mouth' and uncanny ability to connect with the opposite sex. Footage from the tour shows a bevy of beautiful Caucasian women loitering in and around the West Indies players' pavilion. Murray says a bar in Melbourne named Maddisons was a popular hunting ground. Not that he or his team-mates had to try very hard.

'One day I did an interview with a girl in Melbourne, a reporter, while we were practising,' he says. When he went to Maddisons later that night, she was sitting at the bar. 'I used to drink Cinzano Bianco vermouth and we got connected ... she took me back to her apartment. So when I would come into Melbourne you know you've got a little friend and you could have a you-know.'

The trouble was, Murray was already engaged to Adelaide woman Kerry McAleer, a 27-year-old university arts student. He'd first hooked up with her two years earlier on a previous West Indies tour, and she'd already travelled to Barbados, the plan being that she would finish her arts degree there at the Cave Hill Campus of the University of West Indies.

On this occasion he didn't get caught, but it was only a matter of time.

During a net session early in the tour, Murray, bowling off spin, broke the middle finger on his right hand attempting to catch a full-blooded drive off his captain Clive Lloyd. It made his feats in the first Test at Melbourne seem all the more extraordinary. His injured finger swollen and bandaged, Murray crouched behind the stumps to the legendary quartet of Holding, Garner, Roberts and Croft, snaffling five catches in the first innings (Laird, Wood, Chappell, Border and Alderman) and four in the second (Wood, Chappell, Marsh and Lillee), setting a West Indies wicketkeeping record of nine dismissals that has never been surpassed. What is even more extraordinary is that after just one more Test his career would be over for good. Arguably, even more than drug-taking and womanising, bad luck sealed his fate.

The congested 1981/82 Australian cricket calendar was organised so that Pakistan and the West Indies would compete in a one-day tri-series in between and around the Tests. That gave Murray a chance to repair his finger by sitting out the one-dayers leading up to the deciding third Test match beginning on 30 January in Adelaide. It was a decision with far-reaching consequences.

Dujon filled the breach in his absence. The Jamaican had performed well since his debut in Melbourne as a batsman, scoring a succession of neatly crafted 40s; the one-day series gave him the chance to succeed as a wicketkeeper. Lloyd's men triumphed in the Benson and Hedges World Series Cup with Dujon playing a key role.

The intention was still to play Murray in Adelaide – commentators agreed that he'd kept superbly in the first two Tests – but his finger hadn't fully healed and Dujon had demonstrated that he was more than competent in keeping wicket during the one-day series. Plus, his batting was superior – and he didn't have a drug problem that threatened to bring the whole tour into disrepute.

When tour manager Steve Camacho informed Murray of the decision to play Dujon, Murray, in his own quiet way, was furious. He was the incumbent and had stoically soldiered through the first two Tests with a broken finger. He was at the peak of his powers. He was a record-holder. 'I had rested my finger with the assurance I was going to play the third Test. I had already done two, I could have done three,' Murray says. But the lure of Dujon, six years his junior, at 25, and a batsman of rare quality, was irresistible. At that stage it was a one-off arrangement. Murray's reaction would ensure that it became permanent.

'He turned up to do 12th man duties in Adelaide without his gear,' Dujon says. 'The manager told him to go back and get his stuff and he refused. Camacho told him he was no longer a part of the tour and he was expelled. He was gone.'

Murray confirms Dujon's recall: 'Camacho told me to come out with the water cart and I told him no way. He fined me $1,000.'

Does he regret it now? 'I have no regrets,' he says, rubbing his knuckles.

He bears no animosity towards Dujon either. 'The more he kept, the more he improved. But the ball always caught him by surprise, so he had to dive. You have to pick up the line earlier. He took some fantastic catches – diving,' he laughs, as if his successor never quite mastered keeping's finer points.

A week later Murray married McAleer in an Adelaide wedding registry. It was a low-key affair – he wore an open-necked check shirt and fawn slacks, she a traditional bridal gown. No team-mates were invited. Whether that was because he felt estranged from them or he merely wanted a quiet reception, as he maintains, is hard to gauge. What is certain is that Murray knew where he stood in the pecking order. 'I thought my career was over after Adelaide.'

When Ali Bacher came calling, Murray, frustrated by the cricket establishment, newly married with a pregnant wife and always desperate for money to supply his drug habit, was fair game. The next West Indies Test series – a home campaign against India – wasn't until the following February.

But according to Murray, the WICBC, via Camacho, were still interested in him taking the gloves for the India series. He would be given a second chance. Living with Kerry in the Adelaide suburb of Glandore and coaching at the Glenelg cricket club, Murray says Camacho asked him to fly to Barbados to prepare for the 1982/83 season. Peter Short, president of the BCA, had other ideas.

During one game, the flamboyantly moustachioed army captain had famously headed off police at Kensington Oval by paying Murray's late child maintenance fees – his son Ricky was from a previous relationship – before they could wrench him from the pitch. He knew about Murray's foibles and, Murray says, he knew about his link to a possible rebel tour of South Africa. Aware of the government's vehement opposition to apartheid, Smart couldn't guarantee Murray's place in the side. 'It pissed me off,' Murray says. 'I represented Barbados to the fullest … for 13 years.'

Saying yes to Bacher's offer of US$125,000 was easy, despite the lifelong playing ban he knew he would cop. Murray had no job to fall back on. In between seasons, he did what he calls 'beach work' – a combination of 'swimming and playing frisbee with girlfriends and going to nightclubs'.

The hard part was convincing his family. Kerry was understandably against the tour, worried that Australian Prime Minister Malcolm Fraser, a fierce anti-apartheid campaigner, would prevent him re-entering the country. His father implored him not to go, telling him he could still resurrect his career with the West Indies.

There was also a pressing legal matter to deal with. On 4 December 1982 *The Age* newspaper reported that Murray appeared in Adelaide magistrates' court 'charged with having assaulted a policeman and resisted arrest'. Murray says it was a misunderstanding and the charges were dropped, but the sense of chaos and uncertainty enveloping him was unmistakable.

It was compounded by a bungled exit from Australia that left Murray wondering what he'd let himself in for. He was meant to meet West Indies opener Desmond Haynes, Malcolm Marshall and Hartley Alleyne at Perth and fly from there to Johannesburg. But when he arrived from Adelaide, his three Barbados countrymen were nowhere to be seen. They'd got cold feet at the last minute and decided not to tour. 'I said to the woman at the airline, "I'm not going" and turned back,' Murray says.

Barely back in Adelaide, the phone rang. It was Bacher. This time, he says, the rebels' heavy artillery of captain Lawrence Rowe and vice-captain Alvin Kallicharran were on the line. After missing out on current West Indies team members Haynes and Marshall, Murray was critical to the project's integrity. With him in the squad, Bacher could boast that the South African tourists had snared the Caribbean's finest wicketkeeper. Murray listened to their arguments, and under what he calls 'heavy bombardment', relented. 'I sacrificed a lot. With no regrets,' he says.

In the republic it was a different story. The other rebels had flown from the Caribbean and arrived at Jan Smuts Airport a day and, in some cases, two days earlier. Murray was alone. His memories of checking in to the Johannesburg Carlton Ritz still trouble him. 'The place is fucking paranoid, man,' he says, rubbing his knuckles. 'There was a black man at the front desk. He looked at me like "what are you doing here?" I was so afraid. That place had a feeling. I didn't sleep. I put on all the latches on my door. Early in the morning I was going to meet up with the guys, so I prayed for morning to come.'

The guys had already travelled to Cape Town for the first match of the tour against Western Province at Newlands. Richard Austin stood in for a still-jet-lagged Murray behind the stumps. Murray would debut against Border in the next fixture. The first ball he pouched from Sylvester Clarke was a catch. But he wasn't celebrating in the normal fashion. 'Lawrence Rowe said to me as a joke, "You can't play for the West Indies anymore." Only one delivery. It felt bad.' A tear rolled down his cheek. The enormity of what he'd done – the life ban, the uncertain future – was sinking in.

Rumbling in the background was the question of Murray's status in Australia, where he had only a temporary visa. Days after the rebels arrived in South Africa, Prime Minister Fraser slapped a ban on them entering the country. There would be no concession for Murray either, despite being married to an Australian citizen.

Knowing he wouldn't be able to see and support his wife after the tour, by which time she would have given birth to their child, only added to Murray's sense of unease. 'Of course, I don't support apartheid, but I don't get involved in the political side,' he told *The Age*. 'I just know how to keep wicket and bat a bit. It's hard to play cricket with all the stories coming out. I'm having sleepless nights.'

On the first day of the first 'Test' against South Africa at Newlands, Murray was uncharacteristically sloppy, conceding 18 byes. But the effect of the ban on Kerry was more serious. She went into contractions and was rushed to hospital.

Two days later she gave birth to a 3.2kg (7lb) daughter, Ebony. In the *Rand Daily Mail* there's a photograph of a beaming Murray in suit and tie clutching a picture of Ebony and Kerry. A proud dad, he proclaims, 'She's definitely a Murray', before expressing gratitude for his wife's labours.

He had another important reason to celebrate. Fraser had revoked the ban on him re-entering Australia on 'citizenship and compassionate grounds' after a public backlash.

'Thank heavens' was Kerry's response. 'I'm looking forward to seeing him back.'

Unlike the rest of the Caribbean, Barbados allowed its rebel cricketers to play for their club sides in between the tours, figuring the lifetime ban from all first-class cricket was punishment enough. It provoked the ire of regional cricket boards, who thought the BCA was being too soft, but when Murray, a member of the Spartan Cricket Club, returned to Barbados with Kerry after the first tour ended, he was more concerned with spending quality time with his wife and new daughter.

The lay-off did him wonders. Refreshed and free of citizenship dramas, Murray played his best cricket on the second tour, collecting a record ten catches in the deciding fourth 'Test' at Port Elizabeth, and impressing experts with his glovework. He was still using marijuana, as were others on the tour, but he seemed to have it under control.

Johnny Waite, the classy South African keeper of the 1950s and 1960s, was in awe. 'I rate him one of the best I've seen,' he told the *Rand Daily Mail*. 'Murray has beautiful hands; he moves so well, and he stands up so well. He also stops a lot of shots down the leg side without having to dive to field the ball. That is because his movement is so good. He moves into the right place. He seldom takes a catch with one hand. He also takes most of his deliveries waist high because he is standing up. He doesn't have to grovel on the ground. Some people are under the misguided impression that a wicketkeeper is good if he is diving all over the show.'

The young Guyanese batsman Monte Lynch fielded in the slips, next to Murray. 'People talk about Little D – I think he was one of the best keepers ever. He was magnificent. You couldn't hear the ball going into his gloves. Half the time you didn't know where the ball had gone. The ball just went into his gloves in a different way.'

Murray says he was offered the chance to prolong his career in South Africa 'but that place was so paranoid I didn't want to go back'.

He also says he felt guilt about touring but maintains that the rebels' entertaining brand of cricket attracted black fans to the games, but not necessarily in ways that would always have pleased Ali Bacher. Women, it seems, were more interested in the cricketers' bedroom prowess. 'Our boys had a lot of girls in South Africa,' Murray laughs. 'Some of the boys had kids – even twins. A lot of them are grown up now.'

Post-South Africa, there was little to suggest that Murray would self-destruct so profoundly. His lifelong passion for marijuana hadn't dimmed and he still had a West Indian cricketer's wandering eye for women, but he had a substantial fortune to spend on his family and, significantly, he didn't have to return to Barbados.

* * *

Sir David Simmons, chairman of the National Sports Council at the time, had played a major role in convincing Haynes and Marshall not to tour with the rebels, and was there to greet them at the Grantley Adams International Airport when they returned to Barbados after rejecting Bacher's money. In Caribbean stereotypes, Jamaicans are often portrayed as aggressive and opinionated, while Bajans are considered more reserved and equable. Simmons says there was a general understanding among Barbados society that the rebels had already paid the price: 'I think it would be inhumane having banned them then to seek to deny them the opportunity to reintegrate them back into society.' He says that if there was any ostracism, it was mild compared to what was happening in Jamaica.

But when Murray returned home to holiday during the Australian winter, he says there was a 'vibe' of rejection. 'I came home, and it was fucked up,' he says. 'They say things like "he sold his birthright". You can't play on certain pastures.'

In Australia, he bought a house in Glenelg, did odd coaching jobs and followed Kerry in her work as a forensic scientist to Darwin. It was there, coaching kids and playing with former Australian paceman Jeff Hammond at the East Darwin cricket club, that he made what he considers his biggest fuck-up. 'Me and my wife was tight. She was a beautiful woman. The club gave me the opportunity to coach in schools and I met a PE teacher. Very nice. She told me after the coaching to come and have a cup of coffee and things just went from there. Somebody saw us together – we used to go to the Darwin Hilton and have a little [laughs] … and somebody saw us. I fucked up you know. All Kerry wanted was honesty, which is fair.'

The fallout was severe. Murray returned to Barbados, estranged from his wife and distanced from his young daughter.

But the Barbados he encountered in the early 1990s was having its own difficulties. The economy was in recession. Sugar prices were down and tourist earnings had slumped. The government was forced to seek help from the International Monetary Fund.

Although Murray had put some of his money into renovating the family home in Station Hill, he'd blown most of it on 'jeeps, new cars and partying out'. The remaining loot was, he says, spent on helping neighbours struggling with the recession. Every Sunday morning, they would knock on his door begging for money for basic provisions such as cooking gas. The goodwill it generated is why, Murray says, he can still 'live among his people', even if he still sees himself as an outcast thanks to the rebel tours. His beef is more with the establishment and 'rich people', though he can't quite articulate how it is they have wronged him.

Hostility to the South African tourists in Barbados had long since run out of steam – the first post-apartheid Test between the West Indies and South Africa had taken place at Kensington Oval in 1992 – but Murray says there were, and still are lingering pockets of resentment. 'They don't forget. They are narrow-minded. I still cop it. "He is a traitor." I have no regrets.'

Impoverished and alienated from his family and the cricketing establishment, Murray turned to harder drugs such as cocaine, which was flooding into Barbados in huge quantities for the first time. 'Things went haywire,' he says.

Old friends became reluctant to see him. They knew he would hit them up for drug money. They were also shocked by his physical deterioration. His once boyish face was gaunt and hollow; his hair matted in dreadlocks.

Sir David Simmons knew Murray well. Everton Weekes had been his hero as a boy, and Murray had visited him in his chambers alongside his famous father. Back in the 1960s and 1970s it was to have documents signed. Now it was to beg Simmons for money. 'We always talked. It was painful. He wanted money for drugs. David was a personal disappointment to me.'

Friends say Everton Weekes became nervous about his son's visits, fearing Murray would steal from him to subsidise his habit. He asked Ricky Hoyte to make sure his dad was taking care of himself. However, Hoyte, a gifted keeper like his father, had his own problems. He'd debuted for Barbados in 1990 but garnered a reputation for waywardness, often going AWOL before matches and testing the patience of selectors. Hoyte's inability to crack the West Indies side – the unrelated Junior Murray from Grenada was the incumbent – only added to Murray's drug-fuelled paranoia, believing there was a conspiracy to deny his son a maroon cap because of his own South Africa links.

When Murray did get clean – or at least reduce his drug intake – it was because he was sick of feeling like crap. 'One morning I woke up and said to myself I'm done with that. I wasn't enjoying it. I didn't have to go to rehab,' he says proudly. 'I still smoke,' he adds, 'but not like before. I just need a little smoke and I'm high. You just got to smell it now. I'm cool, my brother. I am clean now,' he says, not for the first time.

He still hears from Kerry – 'She married again, she's rich' – whom he idolises, and Ebony visits from time to time.

The great tragedy for West Indies cricket is that the secrets of Murray's smooth glovework have been for the most part lost to future generations. The West Indies Players' Association has occasionally hooked him up for one-on-one coaching sessions with current stars. Murray says he recently spent time with Test gloveman Shane Dowrich – 'He stands too far back. You have to trust yourself and catch it on the up' – but Murray's scavenger lifestyle mitigates against any permanent position.

Unlike fellow rebels Ezra Moseley, Emmerson Trotman and Alvin Greenidge, who have all mentored at the highest levels of Barbados cricket, Murray has no official coaching qualifications. 'I didn't get offered a job. They are in the system. Fuck them.'

In the same contradictory breath he adds: 'They have a lot of respect for me.'

* * *

Later in the night, Murray promises to take me to see Collis King, who is back in town sorting out visa problems.

It's early Sunday evening and on the outskirts of Bridgetown a street preacher can be heard singing the praises of his Lord. But there's something edgy about Murray's demeanour. He's wearing the same yellow T-shirt, shorts and trainers, which dwarf his bony ankles, but he's not the cool 'clean' guy from the Mojo bar.

At the Stadium Road Bar & Restaurant (also known as Mike's Bar), a rum shack opposite the crumbling National Stadium, King is living up to his reputation as the great entertainer of West Indian cricket, reeling off rum-soaked anecdotes in the same cavalier fashion in which he dominated bowlers. Murray sits beside him at the outdoor table, his anxiety dimmed by several glasses of Mount Gay rum and tonic. He's clearly enjoying being close to a man who has shared much of his cricket journey, but little of the hardship.

King is a big guy. He can handle his alcohol. Murray can't. He's soon clutching his old team-mate's right hand, gibbering, 'I love you, man.'

It's obviously a heartfelt sentiment but after a dozen or so admissions, King gently takes Murray's hand and repositions it on the bench. An incomprehensible low-level burble is all Murray can manage for most of the rest of the night.

Later, Ricky Hoyte warns me that his father's real Achilles heel is alcohol.

The following afternoon I call Murray to see how he is. We hatch a plan to meet at Pirate's Cove beachside bar in central

Bridgetown then drive to see the elusive Alvin Greenidge at the BDF training ground. Pirate's Cove is a thatched palm-leaf and cane affair gazing across the Caribbean Sea – a textbook tourist set-up with hammocks and cheap Carib beer, the perfect spot for Murray to deal to his 'chosen few'.

Watching Murray discreetly work the small crowd of European and local buyers, it's clear he's on familiar sands. It's also clear he's not clean. He shoots glances at imagined enemies and, when he spots me, blurts out a desire to meet Mark Taylor because he's a 'beautiful person who stopped his score on 334 out of respect for Don Bradman'. It's the last coherent sentence he will utter all night.

I had planned to ask him about comments he reportedly made in South Africa claiming that apartheid wasn't so bad, comments Aboriginal activist Charlie Perkins said should have precluded him from being allowed back into Australia. But after drinking half a glass of red wine, he's too wasted to respond to anyone – a slurred mumble his only mode of communication. We will not be seeing Alvin Greenidge this evening.

Chefette is Barbados's home-grown 'broasted' chicken chain. Locals consider it superior to KFC, which has failed to penetrate the island. It's dinner time and it seems a reasonable bet that Murray will be happy to eat at one of their purple and gold-liveried restaurants throughout the capital. I can't leave him at the bar in his current condition.

'What would you like, Dave?' He looks at me like I've flushed his stash down the toilet.

'David!' he grunts, suddenly hostile to the abridged version of his name.

Chefette's clientele is mainly families and groups of flirting teenagers; that their country's greatest wicketkeeper is lurching among them, stoned and incoherent, is either too familiar a sight or simply not entertaining enough to be of concern. Murray scrapes together greens from the salad bar to take away.

In the hire car, I suggest driving him back to Station Hill, but he doesn't want to go home. There's also Emmerson Trotman's bar in St Lawrence Gap, but that holds no appeal either. We drive up and down Highway Seven, avoiding effluent spewing from manholes – the south coast was experiencing a huge sewage problem at the time – and tolerating each other's company. Murray seems happy mumbling to himself, but I have a plane to catch in the morning and there's a limit to the number of times we can span the highway without arousing suspicion.

Eventually, he convinces me to let him out near the gaudy entrance to St Lawrence Gap. It's 9pm. Despite fears for his safety, I stick BDs$50 in his hand and wish him well. He's played the game. Another foreign media representative seen off. One last reprimand for calling him Dave again, and he shuffles into the night.

* * *

David Murray is often held up as the poster boy for rebel ruination, but there are many more factors in his fall from grace. To outside observers his life seems shambolic, bordering on tragic. To Murray, for the most part, it's minimalist and low-key.

At the Barbados Legends Museum, opposite Kensington Oval, homage is paid to the nation's cricketers. The tiny island of just 167 square miles has produced more Test representatives per square mile than any other country. The museum's downstairs layout is divided into 'legends' – the Bajans who've played for the West Indies – and 'icons' – local greats of the game such as Garfield Sobers, Frank Worrell and Everton Weekes. Portraits of the living 'legends', photographed in suit and tie, adorn the walls, alongside a potted history of their achievements. Geoffrey Greenidge, the former Sussex opener is there, so is Murray's good friend Collis King. They appeared in 14 Tests between them. Murray played 19, but there's no portrait of him. Perhaps he was doing business at Accra beach the day the pictures were taken. Perhaps he doesn't own a suit. More likely, he's the eternal outsider who never quite fitted the Bajan cricket establishment's mould.

Collis King

'You're a jackass, you should have scored 200'

FORTIFIED BY five shots of Mount Gay rum, a bony middle-aged man wanders off. 'David, come here, you old goat,' Collis King yells into the warm Bridgetown night. 'Come here, man!' It's obvious that King, brawny, boisterous and seemingly oblivious to the effects of alcohol is the dominant figure in their friendship, a bond that dates back to their teenage years with Spartan Cricket Club in the late 1960s.

When David Murray, 19-Test wicketkeeper, meanders back to the old green bench at Mike's Bar, nine-Test all-rounder King slaps a broad, comforting hand on his pointy shoulder.

'I want a chaser,' Murray mumbles.

'The police will be chasing you,' King quips, explaining that rum followed by beer is known locally as a 'bicycle'.

King also dominated batting partnerships. Viv Richards was reduced to gum-chewing bystander as the Bajan swung a St Peters bat through planes, angles and Lord's orthodoxy in the 1979 World Cup Final.

Tonight, thanks in part to Sir John Gay Alleyne's 86 proof, he's in a world cup final-winning mood, slashing and flaying queries almost before they've left the questioner's hand. When he wants to make a point, words tumble out of his mouth like rapid gunfire with an explosion at the end of the sentence.

On accusations that he had to sign a document according him honorary white status in order to play in South Africa: 'Tell the world, I Collis Llewellyn Ezekiel Episcopal Jeroboam King tell you that is a blatant LIE!'

On the tour 'grasses', who would always report him for curfew breaches: 'I don't give a shit about them fellas. Them would go to sleep at 8 o'clock, come in, make 10. I'd go out till 2am and make 100, so who is the FOOL?'

When demonstrating his trusty back-foot technique for a mobile phone video: 'You can go back and go forward, you can't go forward then go back.' He stares demonically at the camera and barks, 'YOU GOT THAT?'

It's somewhat ironic that King, the maverick six-hitter, back-foot apostle and square cut aficionado, who glorified in destroying bowling attacks as much as batting manuals, is a stickler for method.

He coaches at St Leonard's Boys' Secondary School in Bridgetown's north, where he has had great success and was awarded a benefit match alongside Sir Garfield Sobers in 2015. In England, where he lives most of the year with his wife, he continues to smash batting records with Dunnington in the York and District Senior League aged 68. Well, he did, until the British government denied him, and continues to deny him re-entry because of a visa problem.

Yet distanced from the love of his wife, King still has the love of his people. His batting and bowling feats for the Searles plantation side in the Barbados Cricket League (BCL) and Young Men's Progressive Club (YMPC) in the BCL's big brother, the BCA, still arouse maximum reverence.

'He did things no one else could do,' says Eric Bynoe, a former YMPC team-mate. There was the time in the early 1970s when he convinced a disbelieving Bynoe that at 26/6 they both could chase down an improbable 354 against glamour club Wanderers. 'I said, are you joking? The tail starts with me.' He wasn't joking. In one over, he clubbed spinner Peter Short, president of the

BCA, for 34, as he charged to a match-winning double century with an awe-struck Bynoe at the other end. Then there was the bludgeoning 154 on a Maple pitch described as a 'vegetable garden'. And the 268 in a day against St Catherine's. It was as if he could will victories through the power of his personality, and the ability to make team-mates believe in themselves.

The off-field roistering and capacity to back it up the next day, rum-lashed and sleep-dashed, only cemented his legend. 'Collis is a hero to the people,' says Roddy Estwick, former Barbados paceman and half-brother of Sylvester Clarke. 'They love him. The man in the street identifies with him. We all do. He would give us younger cricketers pocket money and look after us.'

Mike's Bar is around the corner from the spearmint-green coloured house in Bush Hall where King lives when in Bridgetown. He bought the timber dwelling with his South Africa earnings in the 1980s on the advice of his dad, Glennis Powlett.

If King was a beast at the wicket, his father was most definitely lord of the beast. 'A hard taskmaster, 260 pounds of pure muscle,' King says of the man who fathered 21 children. The man who wouldn't tolerate failure in his most talented sporting son. It's said that King scored so heavily as a youth because of fear of the punishment his dad, a self-taught sugar plantation engineer, would mete out if he didn't.

And as captain of Searles in the BCL, a side replete with King and many of his brothers, there was no escaping his father's wrath. 'In 1962 I was 11 years and 11 months when I played my first game for them,' King says. I was in short pants and the pads were too big for me, and he said to me, "Go and open the innings."'

Sheltering under a coconut tree behind square leg, his father didn't care. He wanted to see what his son was made of. It didn't matter that the bowler, DeCoursey Pile, was a 6ft 8in monster, who could make the two-piece Swingmaster General ball dance at terrifying speed.

'I walked towards the non-striker's end and he [King's father] called to me: "When I say open, I mean face the first ball." Jesus Christ! All I could see was this giant.'

From the boundary, wags in the crowd yelled, 'You send David to kill Goliath. Cut his throat!'

King, terrified, looked to his old man for support. 'Yes, I'm here son,' he bawled. 'Stand your ground!'

The first ball, King says, was a 'ripsnorter – it came across my face and I smelt the varnish on it'. The next he flicked off his oversized pads. His relief was boosted by the sight of Deighton Powlett, a family relative who'd watched King bat since he was eight years old. He was so impressed by the boy's bravery that he'd run on to the field and given him $5.

He did the same for the next two deliveries, which King square cut and turned on the leg side. The schoolboy was $15 richer. He was beginning to like this playing with the adults caper. 'I was working out all the things a boy could buy – sugar cakes, nuts, sweeties ...'

Glennis Powlett wasn't enthused. 'That's too much money for one young man, I'll take that,' he snapped at his crestfallen son.

In his childhood, King loved his father in spite of his toughness. Now he loves him because of it. 'He was right,' he says. 'He only made $7.50 a week. This was when we used East Caribbean dollars. What was I going to do with $15? He beat me when I was 18 for making a gun barrel at his work, and I ain't got a problem with that, because he could have lost his job. I loved my father for the way he brought me up.' His voice wavers. 'We never had to buy meat. My father had ducks, sheep, goats, chicken, turkeys. God bless him.'

Mike's easy-listening menu has stalled on the Bee Gees' 'Too Much Heaven'. David Murray is pouring four shots of rum into a tall glass. 'It looks more like kiss my arse than rum,' King laughs. He tastes it and exhales. 'I can live with that!' Then he roars his approval. Collis the party hound is back.

But he still wears his heart on his T-shirt, along with a Barbados flag and the words 'A special Barbadian captured my heart/Neville Stephen King 11.10.1942 – 15.02.2017' emblazoned on his chest. 'This is my brother,' King says, stretching the shirt so all the print is visible. 'He was 74 when he died. I can die happy with a good heart.'

'You gotta live, man,' Murray mutters.

If there's a premier league for living, King has always been at the top of the ladder. But in his youth, his fearsome father was keen to ensure pleasure and partying were offset by discipline and dedication. He was also intent on his son receiving a fair go.

In the highly segregated world of 1960s Barbados cricket, the two oldest clubs, Wanderers and Pickwick, were the sole preserve of whites, while teams such as Spartan and Empire catered to various classes of the majority black population.

In the latter half of the decade, Spartan's Queen's Park dressing room was plump with West Indian and Barbados representatives David Holford, Peter Lashley, Tony Howard, Nolan Clarke, Valance Connell and David Murray – and as the alma mater of Clyde Walcott, it carried prestige in the black community.

Glennis Powlett wasn't intimidated. When he found out that 17-year-old King was being forced to bat at number eight or nine every week because of Spartan's star-saturated line-up, he parked his battered old Triumph 500 at the side of the ground and elbowed his way up the players' pavilion. King saw him coming. 'Oh Lord, the old man. I said to David, "This is shit."'

In front of King's illustrious team-mates, Powlett laid out his son's cricket future in no uncertain terms. 'Collis, this is your last game for Spartan. Do you understand that?' he bellowed.

'Yes, dad,' Collis replied.

'Right, just as long as you understand,' and Powlett turned and walked out.

Playing for YMPC next season, King blasted 120 in his first innings. It wasn't enough for Powlett, who had been watching from the gate of the Beckles Street 'pasture' since before the beginning of play. 'You're a jackass, you should have scored 200,' he snapped as his son walked off to cheers and applause from everybody else.

Hardened by his father's tough love, King was never going to be a soft touch in international cricket. Certainly not against the part-time antics of ludicrous Geoffrey Boycott in a cap, a lumpen Graham Gooch and wild-haired Wayne Larkins. Not that it would have mattered who was bowling that balmy June day in London NW8. 'I worked around him while the fire raged,' Viv Richards said of his match-winning 1979 World Cup Final partnership with King.

Batting first, the West Indies were teetering at 99/4 when King arrived at a seaming Lord's wicket that Chris Old and Mike Hendrick had just about made their own. In England, where his form had been patchy at county level with Glamorgan, and where his WSC heroics had gone unnoticed – a 98-ball fourth Supertest 110 earlier that year against Australia at Bourda had earned him man of the match honours – there was an expectation that the inconsistent King would be another minor statistic on the host nation's drive towards an elusive world title.

But no son of Searles plantation captain Glennis Powlett was going to fold now, not with the eyes of the world looking on, and a noisy, expectant Caribbean crowd rocking the Mound Stand. Taking full advantage of the absence of the injured Bob Willis – Mike Brearley chose to bowl Boycott, Larkins and Gooch to make up his overs – King belted 86 from 66 balls, including three sixes and ten fours. His cavalier batsmanship was so intoxicating that local schoolboys waved Union Jacks in appreciation. Richards could only admire the extraordinary looping backlift and contempt for traditional one-day tactics. 'He came and showed me how it's done,' he said afterwards. Inspired, he went on to smack 138 and grab the man of the match award but some in the West Indies dressing room thought King, who had changed the course of the match, was a more worthy recipient.

To outsiders, it seemed that the 28-year-old Bajan, whose position in the West Indies side up to this point had been tenuous, now had enough batting credits to bank a full career in the champion side. They were wrong.

* * *

No one in cricket history had a closer acquaintance with hotel fire escapes. They were King's preferred conduit to the outside world of discos and nightclubs, a way of subverting officious tour managers and captains stationed in musty lift foyers hoping to catch curfew-breakers. 'They saved me many times,' he says. They also revealed to him the slippery standards of tour management. 'Clive Lloyd was a wild BOY!' he hollers.

On Test debut at Old Trafford in 1976, King snuck out to a disco in Nelson, 35 miles from Manchester, where he'd played in the Lancashire League. 'I knew full well it was my first Test match,' King says, revelling in his youthful audacity. 'The great Sir Gary Sobers would drink a bottle of whisky and play the next day.'

He didn't make it back until 1.30am, an hour and a half after curfew, but utilising the tried and trusted fire escape method, climbed to the second floor to catch the lift to his room on the fifth. 'I pressed the lift button on the second floor,' King says. 'When the lift opened, who was there? Clive Lloyd in a suit. He looked at me and I looked at him, and he said, "Kingdom, you ain't seen me and I ain't seen you." I said, "Fair enough, captain, good night." He swung left and I swung right.'

He especially enjoyed putting one over Clyde Walcott, a revered member of the 'three Ws' of West Indies batting folklore, but a stickler for touring etiquette. 'He used to come and check everyone was in bed,' King says. 'I used to lay under the covers in a suit with a sheet up to here.' He points to his neck. 'I used to rub my eyes like a vampire, ruffle my hair.' The trick worked. "Well, well, I never thought I would see Collis King in bed at this time," Walcott would say. I'd say to myself yeah, yeah ... idiot.'

There was clearly no love lost between King and Walcott. 'He play a lot of fucking with people, man,' Murray pipes up.

'Clyde Walcott was the cause of me going to South Africa,' King rages. 'He fucked up my tour,' he adds, referring to the 1980 West Indies campaign in England. 'I could have played 70 Test matches like any of them.'

Coming off the back of a century against New Zealand in Christchurch and his now legendary World Cup heroics, King's tour was blighted by injury and indifferent form; his only Test, the fifth at Headingley would turn out to be a swansong.

Walcott's enduring gripe, King and Murray agree, was the timing of King's signature shot. 'He said Collis square cut too early,' Murray says. 'Batting number four, he said it ain't a batsman's stroke. He had something against it.'

King rises to the top of his drunken toes, heroically musters a modicum of big-man elegance and thwacks an imaginary short ball through the covers. 'If you don't have a square cut in your repertoire, put down the bat,' he thunders, returning to the stability of his rum glass. 'As long as you control it, it doesn't go to gully for you to be caught. If you're on your toes that ball will never go near, but if you're flat on your heel, the ball goes in the air.'

In Murray's and King's opinions, the square cut phobia only served to mask a far deeper Walcott grievance, a grievance that disturbed the older man's pride and sense of belief in the cricket establishment order of things. A grievance that Glennis Powlett inadvertently helped trigger. 'It was you leaving Spartan to YMPC. Because of that. He had animosity,' Murray says.

King cusses. 'He was a nasty piece of material. People don't know. Walcott said, "As long as I have anything to do with cricket, you cannot play."'

If King was at loggerheads with senior management, he was never more popular with team-mates. They admired his direct manner and dedication to the cause, whether on the pitch or in a flash London disco.

Wicketkeeper and vice-captain Deryck Murray remains a great fan. 'I had, and have, a lot of time for him. A tremendous guy. One hundred per cent straightforward; doesn't apologise for the fact he drinks too much. He gives you 100 per cent on the field and 100 per cent off.'

Like a lot of his team-mates, a huge chunk of that off-field commitment was aimed at women. 'We made a sport of it,' King says. 'Women loved me. Everybody eat pussy.'

To conceal extra-curricular activities from team management, he would rent out cheap hotel rooms to entertain female fans in. 'Once a King always a king, once a knight is NEVER ENOUGH!' he whoops.

But being a fun team guy with an unquenchable appetite for the opposite sex was never going to be enough to persuade Lloyd, whose speed obsession rendered the likes of medium-pacers such as King and Bernard Julien surplus to his head-hunting requirements. It didn't matter that his batting, given an extended run, could have filled the number six spot soon to be vacated by Alvin Kallicharran. Nor did it matter that in the 1981/82 Shell Shield season he clobbered 319 runs at 53.17. His lead role in delivering the West Indies World Cup success already felt like ancient history, as if he was forever destined to be king for that one solitary day in 1979, and no more.

Just as at Spartan more than a decade before he wasn't getting the opportunities he wanted, and just as at Spartan he needed Glennis Powlett-like cut-through. That came in the form of an offer to tour the apartheid republic of South Africa with a West Indian XI comprised of many of his Bajan buddies. Realising he would probably never represent the West Indies official side again, King jumped at the chance. 'I said to myself if I was playing badly I could see why they left me out. I'm a professional cricketer looking to make a living for my family and I'm not in the team when I'm supposed to be.'

He was undeterred by the argument that playing cricket in South Africa served to shore up apartheid. 'Let me tell you something. All of the countries of the world were trading with South Africa. You tell me I'm a cricketer and you're trading but I can't play.'

At Grantley Adams Airport, the eight Barbados rebels gathered for their flight to New York. King was filmed walking to customs with what looked like a straw hat covering his face. Was the straight-shooting people's hero ashamed of the journey he was about to undertake? 'A lot of people talk about that and say I was trying to hide my face but that couldn't be further from the truth,' King says. 'I always wear my hat pushed forward. Even when I'm putting on my cricket hat it goes down my face. I had nothing to be ashamed about.'

The first published press photograph of the Barbados contingent arriving in Johannesburg shows a laid-back King clutching a can of Lion Lager and sharing a joke with Alvin Kallicharran, Emmerson Trotman and Richard Austin.

The white South African press and public eagerly embraced the fun-loving Bajan. King, explosive and unpredictable at the crease, fitted their romanticised idea of the quintessential Calypso cricketer. His confident, outgoing demeanour contrasted with their apartheid experience of black people as disgruntled menial workers and angry trade unionists. 'I've never met blacks like these fellows, without any sign of a chip on the shoulder,' a patronising white businessman flapped to the *Sunday Times* correspondent at a Port Elizabeth function.

South African newspaper sub-editors went into overdrive, conjuring new nicknames to describe King's volcanic batting style: 'Calypso Collis', 'Barbadian Bomber', 'King of Clout'. And when they found out he was a reggae fan, 'Cool Breeze' screamed from their mastheads.

He was great copy for reporters too. 'It is my policy that whenever I decide to attack the ball, I attempt to hit it for six,' he said. 'It serves no purpose to hit it at half strength.'

He didn't disappoint. In the second 'Test' at Wanderers, a ballistic 101 off 114 balls, including 15 fours and a six, rescued the rebels from a perilous 39/3, inspiring two white boys to run on to the field brandishing a banner reading 'Coll is King'. In the second innings, he defied extreme leg cramps that were so painful that five of his team-mates had to hold him down in the dressing room, to partner Alvin Greenidge in a match-winning 71-run stand.

His battered and bandaged four-year-old Slazenger V12 bat became an object of fascination – and veneration – in the press. A gift from best mate Sylvester Clarke, King says he banged nails into it to prevent it falling apart. When asked why he didn't trade it in for a shiny new willow from one of his sponsors, his answer was typically to the point: 'It hits so good.' It was hard to argue when he topped the first tour averages with 518 runs at 51.8.

He also proved a canny on-field motivator, provoking Hartley Alleyne into a spell that broke Pollock's arm with the gee-up, 'You bowling slow. I can bowl quicker than you!' and commanding a hungover Clarke, whom he'd spent the previous night boozing with, to observe their 'party hard, play harder' mantra during the burly Bajan's incredible 7-33 at Wanderers.

His off-field relaxation rituals were the focus of intense interest. The *Rand Daily Mail* reported on the massive 'two-way, three-dimensional sound system, powered by nine batteries' that King lugged with him all over the republic.

Such was the extent of the goodwill that he could even sport a bad-taste T-shirt bearing the phrase 'The unforgettable gift – herpes' and get away with it.

He gave batting lessons to eager white pupils at Johannesburg's King Edward VII school, the alma mater of golfing great Gary Player, Ali Bacher and Graeme Smith. But it was his relationship with the fans and their generosity towards him that left a lasting impression.

After a day at the 'Bullring' in Johannesburg, King and Clarke were treated to a complimentary 'braai', roast beef on a spit, by a street vendor who'd seen them ogling the barbecued meat on the way to their hotel. As they tucked in – 'Sylvester ate half the cow', according to King – a young white fan mustered the courage to ask the star all-rounder for a souvenir. King was at a loss – his cricket equipment was too big to be useful – until the boy spotted the chunky gold chain dangling from his neck. 'I had bought it for 250 rand a couple of days ago,' King says. 'But I saw he wanted it and thought what the hell ... and I handed it to him. He was so excited. He went to his daddy and said, "Daddy, Daddy, Mr King gave me his chain. I will treasure it for life."'

About ten minutes later, the boy's father returned, offering the chain from his own neck as a thank you to King for making his son's day. Despite King's protestations, the man insisted he take it. Before the campaign ended, the touring party were bussed to a jeweller's shop to gorge themselves on South African gold. King showed the jeweller his newly acquired chain. He offered him US$10,000. 'It was the most beautiful chain I'd seen in my life. It used to dazzle the eyes when the sun shone on it.'

King had accepted that his West Indies career was over, but in England, as news of his rebel heroics reached the counties, his star was in the ascendant again. He had a contract with Colne in the Lancashire League and Worcestershire snapped him up as a replacement for injured Australian swing bowler Terry Alderman. The rebels, untroubled by West Indies Test commitments, were now being seen as good-value investments by county sides.

Even the reception back in Barbados wasn't as hostile as he'd feared. 'I would say that 90 per cent of the people are behind us,' he told the *Rand Daily Mail* on his early return to South Africa for the second tour, where he acclimatised to local conditions by playing Sunday league cricket with Balfour Guild in Johannesburg.

The standout moment was an uncharacteristic dour effort in the second innings of the third 'Test' at Wanderers while suffering from chicken pox. His room-mate Hartley Alleyne had contracted the disease, and the fast bowler says SACU president

Ali Bacher, a doctor by profession, advised King to change rooms. 'But Collis said, "No, doc, I've got so much alcohol in my body – it will stop it,"' Alleyne recalls.

It didn't. He broke out in sores within hours and was in bed slathered in calamine lotion when desperate team manager Gregory Armstrong phoned his hotel room at teatime on the third day begging him to pad up. The rebels were 99/6 chasing 205 to win but King, running a temperature, courageously answered the SOS to guide the rebels to within five runs of victory in blazing afternoon heat.

Playing with Natal in the Currie Cup after the tours gave King a chance to experience the real South Africa unvarnished by tour niceties. It wasn't always pretty.

In January 1985, police shot at his car, piercing the head rest on the passenger's seat as he drove in the early hours of the morning. According to them he'd been driving recklessly, but would they have fired on him if he were a white man? Understandably spooked, his then girlfriend returned to England, unable to cope with the incessant racial grind.

Another time, he and Clarke, who was contracted to Transvaal, were evicted from a bar in Johannesburg.

King also witnessed black on black violence at the Kwa Mashu township, north of Durban, between Inkatha and ANC supporters, having to flee sporadic gunfire nursing a pipe gun given him by a hotel worker he'd dropped off from the Holiday Inn where he was staying.

But he says racial profiling could be just as bad in England. He remembers a rainy winter's night in London in the 1980s and being confronted by a bobby because he was sheltering under the awning of a jewellery store waiting for a taxi. 'He said I was a thief because I'm a black man,' King says. 'He raised his club, but I got him. His knees turned to fuckin' jelly and he went down and I took off.'

It's the kind of story Glennis Powlett would have liked. 'My father was not scared of anybody,' he says, raising his glass.

Nor was his mate Sylvester Clarke. 'When that man died, he took a part of me,' King says of Clarke's premature death in 1999. 'You ask David.'

'He crying,' Murray replies.

King had seen his great drinking partner and fellow cricket nomad just two days before the fatal heart attack. When he got the news, he'd just finished a morning coaching session with future England seamer Chis Jordan at Queen's Park. 'He was a mate, through and through. Syl call whisky, brandy, big-mouth drinks. If you got whisky there, Syl would go and push it off the table.' He pauses to keep his emotion in check. 'On Sunday morning, I went for him.' He looks at Murray. 'We left David's place and we drink at every rum shop for a radius of two miles. We could not get drunk for shite.'

Emboldened by the memory of a hardcore dad and a hard-boozing friend, his Mike's Bar musings take on a darker hue – for a moment or two he's like Samuel L. Jackson's character in *Pulp Fiction*, but instead of dispensing hitman advice from the Bible, his targets are former team-mates who he feels betrayed him, and the intellectual elite.

Remembering how Michael Holding and Clive Lloyd condemned the rebels in the harshest terms, he says, 'They can talk what they like but I know for sure that they don't know the true facts. Why didn't Holding come and ask me: "Kingdom, was it true you signed something saying you're honorary whites?" And I would have said to him: "Holding, listen, no, that is not the case." Instead of running your blasted mouth off! Lloyd. They never came and talked. I would tell them to fuck off. You understand that? I know I speak the truth.'

He rails against prominent Barbados academic and cricket historian Hilary Beckles, a vocal opponent of the tours. 'He is a joker. It's amazing how some learned people can be so ignorant of the facts. I have no regrets. I know no one can tell me I went to South Africa was wrong. If it happened again I would do it better,' he adds.

David Murray grunts his approval, leans drunkenly on his friend's shoulder and blubbers, 'I love you man, always. You are King. You are free, Llewellyn.'

The conversation is four bottles of rum old. Many years ago, King chortles, Andy Roberts bowled him a series of net bumpers laced with vengeance because he'd slept with the moody quick's girlfriend.

He sends a shout-out to an old flame. 'Fiona from Adelaide. I'm not sure if she's alive. Tell her I send my best wishes. Aussie girl.' There's a vague recollection of a threesome in Murray's hotel room in 1980, which draws howls of laughter.

Despite his rum-fuelled ire, King can afford to laugh. In 2011, the WICB (having by then dropped the 'of Control' from its name) honoured this favourite Bajan son by naming the Super50 one-day award for best all-rounder after him, a sure sign that his rebel sins had been forgiven, if not forgotten. And despite beating an unconventional path to cricket immortality, he has always been able to weather the criticism levelled at him because of the rebel tours, whereas others, such as his friend Murray, have not.

Perhaps it was the uncompromising old-school influence of Glennis Powlett that steeled him better for life's battles. King says if his father were alive today, he'd be a man out of time destined for an early grave. 'In this modern-day world, you see a father hitting a boy and you're looking at death. The youngster shoot you, and stab you, that's how the world's gone – ballistic.'

'Ballistic missiles?' Murray slobbers, having lost track of the midnight narrative.

'Listen, I'm home,' King says. 'I've had a good life if I die tomorrow. The Bible say you get three score and ten years, so if I get to 70, fuck the rest.'

Sylvester Clarke

'Nah, I gonna hit he'

BARBADOS WAS in mourning. Sylvester Clarke was in mourning.

It was Friday, 3 December 1999. Almost a month earlier, Malcolm Marshall, the man who snatched Clarke's place in the West Indies fast bowling battery, died of cancer. A day earlier, another favourite Bajan cricketing son, Sir Conrad Hunte, dropped dead in Sydney after a game of tennis. It was as if the cricket gods were conducting a pre-millennium purge. But it wasn't over yet.

'He [Sylvester] called me at work to tell me Conrad had died,' says Peggy RockClarke, remembering her husband's sadness.

Clarke hadn't been well himself. For a few weeks he'd complained of stomach problems and had been to see the doctor. A heavy drinker throughout most of his adult life, he'd recently cut down on the booze. 'I remember one evening when I reached home from work,' Peggy says. 'He was saying that he felt so badly – he had gas – and he felt he was going to die, but he was seeing the doctor.'

Typically on a Saturday morning, their four-year-old son Shakeem hung tight with his daddy, knowing that if he strayed too far his old man might head off to the local cricket ground without him. Not that Clarke, with his ailing stomach, had played too much for his club side Crusaders of late.

Peggy knew her husband was out of sorts that morning because Shakeem complained that his daddy wasn't helping him draw pictures. She made Clarke a cup of ginger tea to settle his stomach, but when a friend phoned, Clarke asked Peggy to tell them he'd call back in the afternoon.

Later that day, Clarke got Sasha, their 12-year-old daughter, to fetch him a can of Sprite. 'It was strange because he was not one to have fizzy drinks,' Peggy says. But the burly fast bowler, the man Steve Waugh said taught him the meaning of fear, would never get to drink it.

'Sasha was the one telling me he was dead,' Peggy says. 'He collapsed on the floor.' A heart attack caused by acute leukaemia. The cricket gods had recalled another Bajan Test star to the pavilion. 'He used to say as soon as Shakeem reached five, he would walk all over the island with him. But that never happened,' added Peggy. Clarke was just 44 years old.

* * *

There's a momentary silence, filled in by the whirring of a desk fan. It's mid-afternoon at the Eagles Preparatory School in Bridgetown where Peggy teaches. Shakeem, now 23, and a first-class paceman like his father, is sitting across from his mother in an office room. A gold chain bearing miniature stumps and a six-stitcher dangles over the Barbados Pride shirt he's wearing. Tall and lean, he cuts a more athletic figure than his thickset father – but he has his same economy with words.

Was growing up without a dad hard? 'I didn't really know him, so I didn't miss him in that way.'

Do you feel pressure to emulate him? 'Sometimes it can feel that way.'

Do you like to terrorise batsmen like your father did? 'Not really.'

There can be little doubt that Sylvester Theophilus Clarke did. It was joked that the big Bajan's strike rate wasn't measured in balls per wicket, but in how many batsmen he hit. In his autobiography, *Out of My Comfort Zone*, Waugh talks of the fear he felt facing Clarke, who was contracted at Surrey, during his stint with Somerset: 'Pace and bounce of the kind Clarke could muster is something you can't prepare for; it's an assault both physically and mentally, and the moment you weaken and think about what might happen, you're either out or injured.'

It was a common experience in English county cricket during the 1980s. Legend has it that the more lily-livered county batsmen would invent all manner of absurd excuses to avoid a pitch encounter with him. Ian Botham writes about taking part in a fabricated drinking contest with Clarke in order to get the paceman so drunk that he would be too hungover to headhunt Botham's Somerset team-mates on a lively Taunton surface.

But the caricature of Clarke as some kind of laconic behemoth with a thirst for batsmen's blood and over-proof rum is misleading. His was a surgical brand of intimidation, borne out by the extraordinary success he had – 591 wickets at 18.99 – in county cricket for Surrey.

Yet compared to Michael Holding's rhythmic gazelle or Malcolm Marshall's quick-stepping roadrunner, Clarke's shortish run-up was more of an ambling wildebeest; there was little hint of the G-forces he would unleash at the popping crease. Once there, he made the most of his barrel chest, and 6ft 2in frame, meeting the batsman front-on – which only emphasised his hugeness – and ripping his arm over. His natural delivery was an inswinger, or off cutter, which when pitched just short of a length, morphed into a throat ball.

Former England opening batsman Alan Butcher was one of Clarke's best mates at Surrey. He was present at Clarke's wedding to Peggy in the 1990s and gave a eulogy at his funeral. He says the hard-nosed character on the field was replaced by a gentle giant off it; a warm, generous guy whose natural shyness peeled away once he felt comfortable. He also says that when Clarke was directed by his captain to bowl straight or a good length, he would reply, 'Nah, I gonna hit he.'

'It's disingenuous to expect fast bowlers to be nice guys on the field,' Butcher says. 'Their job is to intimidate and get people out and use their pace and bounce – that's what they do.'

In September 1978, Clarke, 23, had already played for the West Indies, but his caps were earned while the regular frontline bowlers – Holding, Garner, Roberts and Croft – were marketing bumpers and burgers for WSC, so he still had to prove to Surrey management that he could fill their import spot.

It would take only two balls. Butcher, then on the cusp of selection for England, was the test dummy chosen by Surrey manager Mickey Stewart to face the untried Bajan and offer his assessment. All on an unprepared Oval pitch. The first ball, delivered off an unimposing 15-yard run, spat up from just short of a length and sailed across his body past the left shoulder towards slip. The second did the same. Butcher knew he'd seen more than enough. Clarke's reign of terror had begun.

Yorkshire and Surrey are hotspots of English cricket, areas that have produced myriad Test players and delivered the most county championships. Their rivalry spans the game's history. During a Gillette Cup semi-final in 1980, it was the backdrop to what Butcher believes was Clarke's most destructive spell. It was also the era of the Brixton riots and the targeting of black sportsmen by racist spectators. During a game in Hull, Clarke had endured monkey calls for an entire afternoon, reducing some of his team-mates to tears. When Yorkshire returned to SE11, Clarke had revenge on his mind.

'The weather hadn't been great so the start of the game had been delayed,' Butcher says. 'It was cloudy, there were flashes of lightning and thunder. It was a really dramatic sort of a day.' The Yorkshire section of the crowd were getting restless. When play finally resumed, so did the abuse. 'I can remember going on the field, with the crowd having had a few beers, and having a go at Clarkey. And the thing was, with Clarkey, there was history with Yorkshire because of what happened in Hull; the bananas and monkey calls. It was the most violent

and charged atmosphere I can ever remember playing cricket,'
Butcher adds.

Critics of Clarke's relaxed approach observed that he barely
got out of second gear when there was nothing to prove, no one
to cut down to size. On this day he would smash top gear. 'He
absolutely steamed in; he split Bill Athey's helmet in two, was
far too quick for Geoff Boycott, and bowled one bouncer that
almost hit the sight screen. He got four for nothing in his early
spell. He was always ready to steam in against Yorkshire because
of Hull. It was a bit unfair because their lads in the team weren't
like that. They were fine.'

Turning it on when he wanted was good enough for Surrey,
and also on the occasions he represented Barbados, but at the
very elite level, in a West Indies side chocka with the finest Test
pacers of a generation, it wouldn't cut it.

Deryck Murray, one of the senior figures during the founding
phases of that all-conquering West Indies side, and a close
confidant of captain Clive Lloyd, wasn't the only one to notice
Clarke's inconsistency. 'If he had a weakness it was because some
days he would be as quick and lethal as any of the others, and
other days he would be innocuous. But everyone knew when
we [Trinidad] played Barbados that he would be a threat and
a danger, bowling with Garner and Marshall and Daniel, they
were going to put you under a little bit of pressure.'

In Michael Holding's autobiography, the outspoken Jamaican
gently chides his fast-bowling amigo Joel Garner for not quite
making the most of his talent, for enjoying a night out a little too
often, despite a stellar Test career that yielded a world-beating 259
Test wickets at 20.97. If this was the kind of thinking occurring
at the top level of West Indian cricket, what hope was there
for someone like Clarke, a guy Butcher jokes must have been
dyslexic, because he always seemed to mistake 'gym' for 'bar'.

Garner says it wasn't Clarke's taste for liquor that restricted
his Test career, but laziness, an inability to work on the fabled
'one per centers'. 'At any time, the West Indies always had four

fast bowlers trying to get wickets,' Garner says. 'You had to get yours because when the ball goes away from you, you don't know if you're going to get it back.'

Complacency was the enemy. Garner adds, 'Clarke was one of the most-deadly fast bowlers. But if you take it for granted, you pay the price. He was unlucky in that they didn't select him on more occasions, but there were nine or ten players competing for four places. I don't think he liked training. That was part of the problem. He was just lazy. He didn't like training like we did. I don't think drink had anything to do with his performances.'

Others did. Even Clarke. Legend has it that, post-retirement, when Clarke was asked by a journalist in Barbados whether it was Clive Lloyd's selection policies or the rebel tours that stalled his career, he pointed instead to a bottle of rum on the table.

Whenever Warwickshire played Surrey, all-rounder Paul Smith and seamer Gladstone Small would hit London's black nightclubs with Monte Lynch, Clarke and Collis King. Smith was impressed by the big man's ability to inhale superhuman quantities of alcohol and perform superhuman deeds afterwards.

He remembers the Singapore Sixes in 1995, the last time he played alongside Clarke. 'In the hotel room he drank three-quarters of a bottle of vodka while ironing three shirts. He just necked it in 15 minutes. We went out after that and made a night of it. Ended up playing cards at 6am before returning to our hotel for breakfast and then on to the ground for the second day's play.'

The capacity to drink till dawn then get up the next morning smelling like a distillery was considered a badge of honour in the 1980s; indeed to some it was a proof of manliness, but there was still a sense that Clarke was overdoing it.

And despite maintaining a relationship with Peggy in Barbados, womanising was also a distraction. Even Mickey Stewart, Clarke's coach at Surrey, could be called on to be the fast bowler's go-between. During an important county match, an agitated Clarke approached him. 'He said, "I've got girl number one and girl number two here and I've left tickets for them both,'" Stewart recalls. 'I said, "What did you do that for?" He told me, "One's in one stand, and one's in the other." I said, "Well, they won't meet then." "But the problem is," he said, "I've got the third one coming as well!" I had to keep them apart.'

Like a lot of sportsmen, Clarke had a support system that enabled him to conceal professional indiscretions. Percy Plunkett, an expat Jamaican garage owner, put Clarke up in his three-bedroom Thornton Heath terrace during the paceman's early days in London. He remembers taking Clarke, who was never comfortable with England's indifferent weather, to Alf Glover's indoor cricket school in Wandsworth in the winter months, and the sound of leather cannoning into the protective canvas behind the stumps as his friend unloaded on legions of Caribbean batting prospects. He also recalls devoted fans helping Clarke out when lack of discipline threatened his Surrey contract.

'He used to have a friend called Vic from Barbados,' Plunkett says. 'Used to chauffeur him around – he just loved the guy. Vic used to get him to cricket matches when he probably should have left together with the team at the Oval. He used to make sure he got to the ground on time.'

Those same fans also appreciated Clarke's generosity of spirit. At the Surrey Tavern, he would buy supporters beers and replay the day's highlights with them. 'People took advantage of his kindness; it was always him paying,' Plunkett says. 'He was extremely kind-hearted.'

'Too kind-hearted,' Peggy adds. 'I remember one time when he returned from England and he came back with so many socks and he gave them all away, and then he had to go out and buy his own pair of socks for himself. He was that kind of person. He would loan money and it would never come back.'

In October 1980, armed with 79 county scalps at 21, and a growing county reputation for making batsmen quail, Clarke marched back into the West Indies Test squad for the tour of Pakistan. It was a series that would both make and break him.

Senior paceman Andy Roberts had been rested because of a back injury and Michael Holding aggravated a shoulder problem in the first one-dayer, which ruled him out of the Tests. That left Croft, Marshall, Garner and Clarke to shoulder the burden on pitches that proudly bore the designation 'fast-bowlers' graveyard'. But such was the fierce competition for places and pressure to perform that the makeshift four-prong attack overcame the unresponsive conditions to dominate the four-match rubber. Garner, whose position in the quartet was probably the most secure, says Clarke won the series for the West Indies. In ordinary circumstances his stats – 14 wickets at 17.29, and a man of the match award in Faisalabad – made for excellent reading. The CANA correspondent described his pace as 'unplayable'.

A frustrated Michael Holding, forced to look on from the dressing room, feared Clarke was edging him out of the West Indies line-up. The Bajan was as close as he would come to cementing a permanent position in the Caribbean pace battery, the most elite club in world cricket. But in the final Test in Multan, Clarke lost his most significant battle with discipline. Pakistan in the 1980s was a difficult proposition for tourists. Hotels were of varying quality, crowds volatile and the poverty in your face.

'A lot of things happened on that tour that never came out,' Garner says. 'Nobody talked about it. They tried to overturn the bus we were in after we finished the game in Karachi. We were lucky the bus driver heard them talking about it and instead of taking the normal route, he drove away from the crowds. When you play away from home you expect pressure, but you don't expect it like that.'

Newspapers reported that Clarke was pelted with oranges, but according to West Indies team-mates, there were also nuts, bolts and stones in the cocktail of projectiles hurtling from the grandstands. Fielding at third man, Clarke resisted the urge to return fire, accepting that as a professional sportsman in a foreign country he would have to endure crowd trouble from time to time. Then he snapped. Picking up a brick used to mark the boundary line, he hurled it into the stands, striking a spectator in the face. Not just any spectator, but a well-known local student leader. The sight of him being stretchered out of the ground, blood streaming from a head wound, triggered 20 minutes of crowd unrest that threatened to spill into a riot.

Only the quick thinking of Alvin Kallicharran, the sole man of subcontinental descent in the side, saved the day. 'I was fielding in the gully, and most of us didn't see it,' Garner says. 'Kallicharran came running up and said to Lloydy, "Skip, skip, we've got a problem." And when we turned around, Sylvester was walking towards us from the boundary.'

The diminutive Guyanese, Kallicharran, moved to position himself in front of the stand where the student leader was injured, and knelt in prayer. The enraged crowd was calmed, but the damage to Clarke's Test career was immeasurable.

On the face of it, Lloyd was sympathetic to his strike bowler's brain explosion: 'I don't know if it's the wrong type of people who are watching sport these days,' he told reporters. 'Clarke might have lost an eye.' But he and manager Jackie Hendricks were forced to spend the next few days apologising for Clarke and visiting the injured student leader in hospital.

Butcher says Clarke admitted it was a silly thing to do when he was back at Surrey. But he also saw the lighter side.

Dennis Lillee remembers sharing a dressing room drink with Clarke during the West Indies' 1981/82 tour of Australia, only weeks after the Australian paceman had himself been embroiled in controversy, having kicked Pakistan captain Javed Miandad following a mid-wicket collision in Perth. 'Sylvester was a man of few words, but he had a dry sense of humour,' Lillee says. 'We were having a rum or something and he suddenly looked up at me and said, "Me bricky, you kicky," because of my thing with Javed, and just pissed himself laughing.'

But now Clarke was a wildcard, an unpredictable force with the potential to jeopardise team harmony. 'This was obviously part of the discipline thing,' Butcher says. 'The incident fed into that idea of Sylvester Clarke as a nasty, brutish guy, but he wasn't that at all.'

At first, there were no official sanctions against Clarke, and he was selected for the opening one-dayer against the touring Englishmen in St Vincent in February 1981, but at a WICBC hearing about the incident, which Garner says took place, somewhat bizarrely, in the middle of Barbados's Shell Shield match in Trinidad, Clarke was outed for three games.

Holding was rushed in as a replacement, the capacity Arnos Vale crowd erupting as he first skittled John Emburey and then Chris Old, closing out a West Indies victory by two runs.

'My place in the team was again settled,' Holding, who is ten months older than Clarke, wrote. 'But I'm not so sure it would have been had Clarke not thrown that brick in Pakistan.'

Clarke wasn't considered for the home England series, but with Andy Roberts's age and fitness again coming under scrutiny, he secured a berth on the West Indies' 1981/82 tour party to Australia, alongside Marshall, Croft, Garner, Holding and Roberts. But he was no longer a first-choice selection. His appearance in the second Test at the Sydney Cricket Ground, in place of Marshall, who was deemed unfit, was a perfunctory affair. There were glimpses of the fire and fury – he struck a hooking Bruce Laird on the shoulder – but YouTube footage from the match has commentators Richie Benaud and Ian Chappell bemoaning Clarke's lack of pace and enthusiasm. It would turn out to be his last official Test. He did better in the one-dayers, nabbing 3-22 and 3-30, but Marshall, three years his junior, more consistent and less inclined to court trouble, was now ahead of him in the fast-bowling pecking order.

As Roberts quietly slipped from view, Marshall, Holding, Garner and Croft shaped as the pace battery's principle drivers. The likes of Clarke and Wayne Daniel – both feared in England – were reduced to bit players on the international scene, while a younger generation of quicks, in the form of Winston Davis,

Courtney Walsh, Ezra Moseley and Patrick Patterson, threatened even more destabilisation.

Being condemned to the fringes didn't sit well with Clarke, who was still only 27. Deryck Murray understood his resentment. 'A lot of us were playing county cricket at the time so they were earning reputations in county cricket and they were being told they were the best fast bowler ever, yet they still couldn't get into the West Indies side. So it would be very frustrating.'

Back at the Oval, Clarke unburdened himself to his pal, Butcher. 'We discussed whether his career with the West Indies was over and one of the things he said was, "I can't get no play." He felt he wasn't going to get a game so he may as well go down another route. There were lots of quick bowlers about and he would have to change people's perceptions of him and whether he was prepared to do that was another thing.'

The other route would lead to South Africa.

* * *

In June 1982, Ali Bacher, in his dual role of SACU board member and managing director of the powerful Transvaal Cricket Council, flew to England to put out feelers for an unsanctioned West Indian tour of the republic. After the visit of a disappointingly mediocre England XI in 1981/82, Bacher was keen to win back the public's trust by signing the best cricketers in the world, the West Indians, to a series of matches. Clarke inadvertently became a vital link in the chain of events that would lead to the tour's formation.

Bacher saw an enthusiastic Colin Croft in Manchester and met Marshall and Clarke in Portsmouth, where Hampshire were playing Surrey. According to Bacher, both were interested in South Africa, but momentum stalled. Back in Johannesburg, he sent a contract to Clarke via a business friend, who, rather optimistically, attempted to hand it to him at Lord's after Surrey's NatWest Trophy Final victory. But Clarke was in celebration mode and in no mood to be bothered by contractual fine print, so he took a business card instead.

At home in Barbados, he passed on the business card and his knowledge of Bacher's plans to retired Bajan paceman Gregory Armstrong. Armstrong, a fledgling entrepreneur, had recently staged a day/night tournament on the island. Armstrong immediately saw the financial potential of a rebel tour and became Bacher's go-between in the signing of new recruits. The wheels were in motion.

* * *

Barry Richards didn't retire because of Sylvester Clarke, but he sure made him aware of his batting mortality. Chosen by Don Bradman to open for his dream team of the 20th century, Richards was limited to only four Tests because of the international ban on sporting contact with South Africa. At 37, the master batsman was ready to chuck it in, the year-in, year-out grind of county and Currie Cup cricket all but killing off his motivation. 'I was just proving myself over and over at the same level,' he says.

But the chance to test himself one last time against a world-class attack led by Croft and Clarke was hard to resist. He trained like a prize fighter, the bowling machine, cranked up to 100mph, his double-end bag. His plan to combat Clarke's signature throat ball and yorker revolved around what he calls 'batting awareness', the ability to anticipate good deliveries and be prepared for them. That meant getting behind the ball and using a short backlift – Clarke always had an attacking field set up so there was no need to increase risk factors – and a 'thought process, where if you got a couple of runs and manage to hit a four off him, you knew the bouncer wasn't far away'.

It worked well in the first 'Test' at Newlands, where Richards stroked a free-flowing 49, but at Wanderers in the second 'Test', Clarke delivered him a 'ripsnorter that went past my nose and kicked my glove', and he was caught by Kallicharran without scoring. In the second innings, he says Lawrence Rowe taunted him on the way to the wicket: 'You ever got a pair, mon?' But he scored a decent 59. 'I was happy. But I knew I wasn't quite in the zone as I had been ten years previously. The enduring memory is the control of the lethal deliveries he [Clarke] had – far better than most people I faced,' Richards says. 'Sylvester was one of those guys who could pull something really quick without seeming to change his action at all. It was on you in a flash. He was one of those guys who in another era and with another selection committee could have got 250–300 Test wickets.'

Clarke's second innings rout of South Africa in that Wanderers 'Test' secured his legacy in the republic. After having lost the first 'Test', the West Indies were desperate for a win to show South Africans and people back home in the Caribbean they were more than a rag-tag bunch of mercenaries. But with Richards and Cook motoring along to 87 without loss, the fourth innings target of 211 looked well within the Springboks' grasp.

The night before South Africa's run chase, West Indies captain Rowe had turned to Clarke and King and warned, 'Don't go out tonight.' Clarke responded, 'OK Yagga.' It was a well-worn ritual none of the participants actually believed in.

It's no exaggeration to say Collis King was Clarke's best mate. They grew up together in the Christ Church parish, shared the same mercurial talent – King had brutalised England's attack in the 1979 World Cup Final – and, significantly, the same love of rum. But whereas Clarke was naturally reserved, King was always on, the supreme entertainer. 'Yagga knew when the ball was thrown to us, we would do the work for him,' King says. 'No matter what we'd been doing.'

That night they stayed out to 2am. 'We were warming up,' King says, 'and Yagga said to me, "Jesus, Kingdom, man. I can smell the rum fumes. There are 20,000 here." He knew.' But this time the magic wasn't working. 'After his third over, Clarkey came over to me and said, "Kingdom, I don't feel so hot." He was depressed.'

What King calls 'alcohol bubbles' – a hangover sweat – was seeping from the big man's pores. 'I said, "Clarkey, you can't pull out now. You have a job to do."' He reminded his pal of the sportsman's drinking code: 'If you play hard by night you play hard by day.'

His mate's booze-shaming spurred Clarke on to one of the greatest spells of his career. Between lunch and tea he blasted out six batsmen, the first, Cook, caught appropriately enough by King at second slip, and also the prize scalp of Pollock, again snared by King, after a diving David Murray had knocked the ball past first slip. His 22.2 overs of two-way swing and seam garnered 7-34 as South Africa crashed to 181 all out, losing by 29 runs. His match figures were 12-100. Rodney Hartman writing in the *Rand Daily Mail* called it 'the finest strike bowling performance ever seen at the Wanderers'.

What followed bordered on a moral panic. White South Africa was already fretting over a new constitution that extended parliamentary representation to 'Indians and Coloureds' – blacks were still excluded. Now the press was building Clarke into another bogeyman. The headlines and captions screamed: 'Terrifying 5 1/2 ounces of leather that talk for Clarke', 'Brooding West Indies meanie', 'Clarke haunts the Boks'. Film stills of the 'chest-on bowling action that has made Sylvester Clarke one of the most feared pace bowlers in the world today' were analysed by experts, and even Eric Rowan, a septuagenarian former Test batsman, who had faced Keith Miller and Ray Lindwall without gloves or a box, was wheeled out to give his considered opinion on how to combat the 'lethal' quick.

Tellingly, there were few quotes from the man himself, other than a report that his favourite bowler was Dennis Lillee.

There were upsides too. Never one to miss a commercial opportunity – and exploit Clarke's notoriety – Bacher organised a competition to find 'Soweto's Clarke', with 1,000 rand donated to the best local black pace bowler by TV2/3 and SA Breweries. He also made sure that Clarke signed a Transvaal contract, much to the chagrin of North Transvaal, who were already peeved by their rival's monopolisation of South Africa's best talent. It meant Clarke would now be employed as a professional cricketer for ten months a year in the county championship and Currie Cup, insulating him from the financial consequences of a lifelong Test and first-class ban in the Caribbean.

Along with best buddy King, whose freakish batting and carefree approach turned him into something of a cult hero, Clarke was the star of the rebel tours. The two of them were regularly featured on newspaper front pages together, once even pictured with a cassette player listening to a ten-minute song recorded by locals in honour of their Wanderers performances.

After the tours ended, King stayed in South Africa with the Natal franchise and their double act continued. 'When he was playing for Transvaal and I was at Natal, he would come down to Natal and he would only bring 100 rand so I would have to look after him. When I would go up to Transvaal, I would carry 100 rand and he would look after me there. That's how it was. If it was 2am and Sylvester said why don't we drink a bottle of rum, then we would. I'm still like that today.'

But living on a day-to-day basis in South Africa wasn't as pleasant without the curated comfort of five-star hotels and managed social activities. The pillars of apartheid had been shaken by economic and sporting sanctions, but racist attitudes and infrastructure still prevailed. Elite sportsmen such as Clarke were exempt from carrying passes that guaranteed black people freedom of movement, but that didn't guarantee freedom from discrimination. What was colloquially known as 'honorary white' status allowed Clarke to live in an affluent white area of Johannesburg with his girlfriend at the time, a South African-born 'coloured' woman of mixed race. But a racist incident in a local bar forced them to reconsider their lifestyle. Clarke and King, in Johannesburg for a Currie Cup clash, had been drinking quietly when they were asked to leave. When the manager found out they were the famous black cricket stars, he intervened and invited them to stay. They declined the offer. 'I'd rather not have people make an exception for me just because of who I am,' Clarke told a newspaper reporter.

From that moment on, he and his partner decided it was better to spend leisure time at home watching videos than suffer the embarrassment of falling foul of segregation laws.

Clarke may have been living in forced seclusion, but his reputation for hostile fast bowling continued to grow across the cricketing world. Ex-Australian captain Kim Hughes encountered Clarke in the Australian baggy green and while batting for Natal late in their careers. Like countryman Steve Waugh, he was intimidated. 'Sylvester was nasty and deceptive. He had a good change of pace. A real handful. A bugger to face. A lot of blokes thought he bent his elbow because of the force he hit the pitch at.'

Former England and Middlesex seamer Mike Selvey wrote that Clarke 'had a glare that could freeze hell'. Warwickshire opener Dennis Amiss called Clarke's bouncer the 'trapdoor ball' because the batsman wouldn't pick it up until inches from his eyeballs. But perhaps the greatest accolade of all came from Viv Richards, who maintained that Clarke was the only bowler who made him feel uncomfortable.

However, past achievements and plaudits stood for little when Surrey decided to terminate his employment early in the 1989 season for 'persistent breaches of the terms and conditions of his contract'. With the passing of time, few remember why he was dismissed, but roguish behaviours that were tolerated when he was younger, at 34 began to appear unprofessional. He was still on top of his game – the 1988 English season produced 63 wickets at 14.49 – and orchestrated one final campaign on the highveld, but the lure of a quieter life with Peggy, who remained his abiding love, and their young child Sasha in Barbados beckoned.

Intermittent sightings only burnished his reputation. His *Wisden* obituary retold the story of a practice session on England's 1993 tour of the West Indies, when Clarke, buoyed on rum, and decked in only shorts and plimsolls, offered his services as a net bowler, tormenting Graham Thorpe off a short run, with pace the equal of anything the tourists faced that series.

* * *

On the concrete backyard of the Eagles Preparatory School, fringed by lunch tables and candy-coloured bins, Shakeem Clarke emerges from the shade. The run-up is smoother than his father's and, because of his leaner build, only the facial features suggest a famous lineage. But the action is classic Sylvester – front-on and a whippy arm rotation. 'They say I look and walk like him,' he says, with barely concealed pride.

In 2016, he participated in an exchange programme organised by former South African seamer Fanie de Villiers, turning out for the Irene Village club in Pretoria and coaching at a private college. In the heart of his father's old stomping ground, Shakeem was met with warmth and goodwill as former team-mates, administrators and fans showered him with stories of his dad's exploits. 'They told me the two things he was passionate about were cricket and rum,' he laughs.

Peggy interrupts him. 'There were times when I thought he was drinking too much,' she says. 'Of course, I told him, but his response was it was never too much for him.'

But in the last few years of his life Clarke mellowed. He even attended services at St Patrick's Anglican church in Christ Church, where he would ultimately be buried. Getting over his death, Peggy says, took a long time. 'Things happen and you think, I will tell him, but you tell yourself you can't tell him because he's not there,' she says.

The whirring of the desk fan seems to amplify the sadness. 'He would have been very proud of Shakeem.'

Derick Parry

'They thought I looked like Pelé'

MARIA PARRY is a garrulous woman. She wears a bright floral dress and enjoys talking about the island of Nevis and the colourful characters she has met in a life spanning more than eight decades. But her voice quivers when she recalls leaving her two-year-old son, to find work and prosperity in England. 'I was very sad, you know. I always have a thing in my heart about leaving him. He was a handsome little lad.'

In the lounge of her Nevis home in the rural village of Cotton Ground, a framed photograph of a dapper young boy wearing a starched white shirt, blue bow tie and long trousers hangs from a wall. It's the son she has never really known.

In the mid-1950s, post-war Britain, suffering from a labour shortage, reached out to its colonies to fill the menial jobs that white Britons wouldn't do. For Mrs Parry, living off subsistence farming in a far-flung speck of the empire, following her husband to Birmingham and his new job as a bus conductor was the sensible thing to do, even if it meant entrusting a toddler son to the care of his grandmother and selling all the family's sheep to pay for the fare.

The intention was for that 'handsome little lad' to eventually join his parents and growing band of siblings in England, but it never happened. By the time his mum returned to the island to live, Derick was already a middle-aged man, a retired West Indies cricketer, and a Nevis favourite son.

'I still can't say mummy or anything like that,' he says of the relationship with his mother, whom he now sees regularly. 'It doesn't feel right.'

In many ways, Derick Parry had no right to an extraordinary sporting career. But Nevis is no ordinary Caribbean island. Despite a population of only 12,000, an economy dependent on tourism and offshore tax haven dollars, and an uneasy bond with its big brother St Kitts two miles across the channel, it has nurtured eight international cricketers, a per capita record better than Barbados, the traditional hotspot of the West Indies.

Its first Test representative, trailblazing left-arm off-spinner Elquemedo Willett, paved the way for the likes of Viv Richards, Andy Roberts and others from the Leeward and Windward islands. Cricket is in Nevis's cultural DNA. It has helped nourish the tiny island's psyche.

That link was never more evident than when, in 1970, the ferry MV *Christena* sunk crossing The Narrows strait en route to Nevis, killing 233 people. The disaster threatened to plunge Nevis into a collective depression for years, but the all-conquering island cricket side, competing for the Hesket-Bell Shield, the symbol of Leeward supremacy, gave the grieving nation comfort and cheer. Locals packed the homely Grove Park, as it was then known, to watch local heroes Livingstone Sergeant, Willett and Parry.

* * *

Cotton Ground is a rustic collection of homes painted in the soft pastels of the old Caribbean, grog shops, timber churches and the occasional colonial-era stone building once occupied by sugar cane overseers, all in the shadow of the mighty Nevis Peak. Packs of hungry goats and sheep, which roam freely on the island, keep gardeners out of work, trimming back the tropical foliage. Monkeys steal mangoes. Cotton Ground is, at least on the surface, a throwback to a gentler age.

On the rocky cricket field, Parry and his schoolmates, weaned on faded *Cricketer* magazines and ancient tomes from the mother country, styled themselves after W. G. Grace, even adopting the great man's surname. 'We had a Grace clique,' Parry says, in his softly spoken manner. 'There were four of us: Kelvin, Earl, Higgs and myself. I was D. Grace and there was E, H and K. He was the man.'

But the secret to his signature aggressive brand of off spin is found nearby on a cracked concrete path that leads to the pitch-width front door of the Georgian-era nurse's quarters. There, Parry and school friend Godwin Warner, unhindered by the need for flight or accuracy, would practise their craft, focused solely on ripping as much spin, and putting as many revolutions on the ball as teenage fingers could muster.

No further than a crisply struck boundary away was the tiny shack where Parry, his cousins and half-brothers slept, four to a room and on the floor, knackered after long afternoons recreating the shots and mannerisms of an ostentatious 19th-century Englishman. His grandmother would rise early to till the fields of the small plot of land she owned outside the village. 'We had cows and land to grow veggies, sava, potatoes, yams, any provision you want,' Parry says. 'In those days, fish were plentiful. You could swim out and dive for conch, bring them back and eat them. Everything was plentiful. Money wasn't an issue.'

And endless cricket, during and after school, and on the weekends watching the working men of Cotton Ground take on village teams from Charlestown, Brown Hill and New Castle fuelled his hopes and dreams.

It didn't seem to bother him that his parents were carving out a new life 4,000 miles away in England, an occasional letter to his grandmother the only form of correspondence. When he accepted a contract to play for Milnrow in the Lancashire League in his mid-20s, his mother and father were there to greet him at Heathrow. But it wasn't an emotional occasion. 'No. I was an old dog by then,' he laughs.

If anything, the only legacy of that separation is Parry's natural reserve, a kind of gentlemanly shyness. Humbleness seeps from every pore of a long, wiry body that still performs wonders in seniors cricket matches.

All over the island, Nevisians respect Parry's achievements and lack of ostentation. To them, he's the guy whose cricket feats helped put their 36-square-mile nation on the map in the 1970s and 1980s, but he's also the guy who runs a successful car hire business, a guy they deal with on a daily basis. Everyone has a Parry story.

But that intra-island admiration would be severely tested during the early 1980s, when St Kitts and Nevis society segmented into pro- and anti-rebel tour camps, as the Lawrence Rowe-led tour inflamed racial politics across the Caribbean.

Elquemedo Willett's successful ascension to the West Indies side in 1973 was a game-changer for young Caribbean cricketers from outside the traditional Test breeding grounds of Barbados, Jamaica, Trinidad and Guyana. The smaller islands had only recently switched from two-day to four-day matches, and now they were being taken seriously. 'It was like, I know Elquo, I have played against him and he's a human,' Parry says. 'You see and hear of these other guys and you think they're superhuman, but he was evidence they were just like us. I could do it too. I could play for West Indies.'

Having started as a medium-pace bowler, aided by the pebbly quirks and vagaries of the Cotton Ground pitch, Parry switched to off spin, observing that the Test incumbent, veteran Lance Gibbs, was nearing retirement. But it was a decision that unwittingly put him in conflict with the emerging zeitgeist. His distinctive double-skip run-up, high action and supple fingers had enabled him to extract spin and bounce where others failed, thrusting him into the Combined Islands Shell Shield side but, in 1976, the Caribbean's attitude towards spin bowling changed forever.

The West Indies, already smarting from a 5-1 defeat at the hands of Australia's snorting, long-haired pacemen, were locked

Rebels Herbert Chang (far left), Lawrence Rowe (third from left), Everton Mattis (dark cap behind wicketkeeper Jeffrey Dujon), Ray Wynter (obscured white hat, fourth from right) and Richard Austin (third from right) leave the Arnos Vale ground in St Vincent during their last Shell Shield match together for Jamaica in April 1982. Courtney Walsh is fourth from left.

Mr Popular: Franklyn Stephenson signs autographs during a one-day international at the Kingsmead ground in Durban, February 1983.

Openers Richard Austin and Alvin Greenidge were at the crease when the bar on sporting contact between South Africa and the West Indies was broken.

Collis King was a major drawcard in South Africa — newspapers dubbed the Barbados all-rounder the 'King of clout'.

*Rebel captain and Test
triple centurion Lawrence
Rowe shakes hands
with Springboks skipper
Peter Kirsten at the
toss in Durban.*

Sylvester Clarke, described as a fast-bowling 'meanie' in the South African press, delivered some of the most hostile spells ever witnessed in the republic.

Legendary South African wicketkeeper Johnny Waite rated David Murray's smooth glovework on the tours among the best he'd seen.

Bernard Julien, veteran of 24 Tests for the official West Indies team, displays his technique to enthusiastic young spectators during a match in Durban.

Franklyn Stephenson, pioneer of the 'slower ball', is momentarily airborne as crouching umpire Dudley Schoof observes play.

Colin Croft came to South Africa with a fearsome reputation but a persistent back injury curbed his output.

At a glance, it was easy to mistake the rebels' cap for official West Indies maroon; a 1983 cartoon in Johannesburg's Rand Daily Mail *summed up the new reality for budding Caribbean cricketers.*

Four-Test batsman Everton Mattis grew up in the ghettos of Kingston, Jamaica; he now calls Poughkeepsie, New York, home.

Alvin Greenidge coaches the Barbados Defence Force cricket team in Bridgetown.

West Indies great Alvin Kallicharran, scorer of 12 Test centuries, resides in Raleigh, North Carolina.

Unsung fast bowler Ray Wynter in front of the Kensington Cricket Club scoreboard in Kingston.

Driven away by anti-rebel sentiment in Jamaica, batting legend Lawrence Rowe sought refuge in Miami in the mid-1980s.

'The best all-rounder the West Indies never had', Franklyn Stephenson, at his academy in St Thomas, Barbados.

Long-time buddies David Murray and Collis King at Mike's Bar across the road from the national stadium in Barbados.

David Murray, drinking at Pirate's Cove in Bridgetown, says he still gets called a traitor.

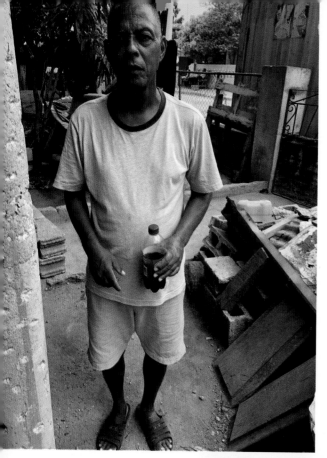

Left-handed batsman Herbert Chang, pictured in Greenwich Town, Kingston, suffered a breakdown after the rebel tours.

Off-spinner Derick Parry was sacked from his coaching job in Nevis because he had played in South Africa.

Now based in Orlando, Faoud Bacchus scored 250 in a Test against India in 1979.

Tour manager and two-Test veteran Albert Padmore relaxes in the foyer of the Hudson Hotel, New York.

Two-Test all-rounder Richard Austin begging on the streets of Crossroads, Kingston, in May, 2003.

The rebels were feted almost everywhere they went in South Africa. These photographs were taken on paceman Ray Wynter's camera at a gathering hosted by SACU president Joe Pamensky in Johannesburg, early 1983.

Franklyn Stephenson, Ray Wynter and Collis King enjoy the hospitality; critics claimed the rebels were 'honorary whites'.

Lawrence Rowe (left) and Richard Austin, who was always the life of the party, with a friend.

A smiling Bernard Julien (second from left), Everton Mattis (second from right) and Joe Pamensky (right).

Barbados speedster Ezra Moseley (front) in pensive mood while Herbert Chang (left) chats with a guest.

It was said he would happily bowl bumpers at his grandmother, but off the field Colin Croft cut a relaxed figure.

Bernard Julien in party mode as Ray Wynter practises his dance steps.

in a home battle with India. In the third Test at Port of Spain, their one-off spin trio of Raphick Jumadeen, Imtiaz Ali and Albert Padmore proved ineffectual against Gavaskar, Viswanath et al, who racked up a record fourth innings total of 406/4 to win the Test match. It was a humiliating loss. Burned once, captain Clive Lloyd vowed never to put his trust in spin again. 'Lloyd just didn't like spinners,' Parry says, looking back at his career.

But Lloyd was occasionally willing to reconsider if they were taking wickets and scoring runs. In the 1977/78 Shell Shield season, Parry snared 19, including two five-wicket hauls. He also belted 96 against the fearsome Barbados pace machine. The 23-year-old's form was irresistible, and with Michael Holding injured, and Australia fielding a WSC-depleted line-up, a virtual second XI, the selectors felt confident enough to blood an off-spinning all-rounder.

Parry debuted alongside Desmond Haynes and Richard Austin at Queen's Park, Port of Spain, his first Test wicket being the impressive scalp of veteran Australian captain Bobby Simpson, who pulled a wide off break on to his off stump.

But if the Aussies were no match for Croft, Garner and Roberts, they were still first-rate sledgers. It was an ear-opener for Parry. 'There was sledging between the islands, but playing against Australia it was something else,' Parry says. 'Steve Rixon behind the stumps would be talking all the time. And Simpson would say things too. But I just got on with it.'

The first Test was also infamous for the skidding Andy Roberts bouncer that felled Peter Toohey in a pool of his own blood. Press photographs of Viv Richards cradling Toohey, in a Jesus-like pose, fanned a sense of horror back in Australia, as the West Indian fast men pummelled their way to victory. Parry was fielding at short leg. 'I remember the blood pouring out of his forehead. It was sickening.'

The fourth Test, also in Port of Spain, was Parry's apogee in a West Indian cap. The bulk of the side from the first two Tests were missing, having resigned in protest at the board's decision to drop three of the WSC-contracted players, and under new captain Alvin Kallicharran, Parry was given greater opportunity to settle as a Test bowler. In the second innings, he castled the last four Australian batsmen to go with the earlier wicket of Graham Yallop, yielding figures of 5-15, as the Frank Worrell Trophy was returned to the Caribbean.

'You look at the pitch, and if it's going to do something, you have to bowl differently, really grip it and bowl quicker,' Parry says of his performance. 'If the pitch is not going to spin, you have to bowl higher and get some bounce and variation. That day it was doing something. Bruce Yardley also bowled well. It was purchasing a bit.'

Parry's output in the series included two half-centuries, which cemented his position for the tour to India later that year, in what was essentially a West Indies second XI. But it was a long and grinding campaign. Contrary to expectations, turning wickets were rare – the fourth Test pitch was a Madras green-top that produced some of the slipperiest bowling seen on the subcontinent – and Parry was unable to make any headway.

When the warring WSC and establishment boards patched together a truce in 1979, Parry was one of only four establishment players included in a squad of 16 for Test series in Australia and New Zealand. With Lloyd back in the big chair, opportunities were limited.

Just 25 at the time and with 11 Tests under his belt, he was relegated to the fringes as the pace quartet of Roberts, Garner, Croft and Holding destroyed a shell-shocked Australia led by Greg Chappell. He played two one-dayers, but in the majority of games, part-timers Viv Richards and Larry Gomes were called on to bowl out the designated overs. To a specialist off-spinner with genuine batting credentials, it was insulting.

Typically, Parry bears no lingering resentment towards Lloyd. 'We had a great team and Lloyd was a great man manager; he brought everyone from the islands together. But as a really deep captain, I found he was good, but he kept on winning because he had four quick bowlers and Viv and Gordon.'

Of the legendary pace quartet, Parry was closest to Andy Roberts, the thinking man's fast bowler. They had played against each other in the Hesket-Bell Shield for Nevis and Antigua respectively, and represented together for Leeward and Combined Islands. He'd also felt the bone-crushing pain of a Roberts bouncer. 'Andy broke my nose in my first game for Nevis,' Parry says. 'He pitched up a couple of cover drives and I was still going on the front foot instead of waiting, and his bouncer struck me going forward. It was a lesson in technique.'

Parry finally got his chance on the New Zealand leg of the tour when Roberts pulled out of the first Test in Dunedin with a leg muscle injury. But the Antiguan's influence was all-pervasive even if he wasn't on the pitch. 'I wouldn't say he was the bowling coach, but I really respected him,' Parry says. In this instance, a little too much.

New Zealand were cruising at 133/3 in response to the West Indies' paltry 140, when Parry struck, removing debutant Peter Webb for 5, and top-scorer Bruce Edgar for 65, both lbw. He had two for next to nothing; the quicks were momentarily forced to take a back seat. Parry's time had arrived. But when he was brought back on to snuff out a nuisance tail-end partnership between Cairns and Hadlee, Lloyd and Roberts encouraged him to give the ball flight. It was a mistake. Brawny Cairns, swinging like a lumberjack, belted Parry to all corners of the small Carisbrook ground, and his figures blew out to 2-63, still respectable but not quite good enough to convince the doubters.

Looking back now with the knowledge that it was the last time he would bowl for the West Indies, Parry regrets that he didn't follow his own instincts. 'When I think about that, I could have changed and bowled flatter, and made him make a mistake, but Andy would say flight it. Lloyd and them kept telling me to flight it. There was no coach like there is now to tell you what you had done wrong. You were on your own. Nobody would come and say hard luck or encourage you. You had to read between the lines.'

New Zealand's second innings was rendered infamous by Michael Holding kicking down the stumps in frustration at the somewhat dubious local umpiring, as Lloyd reverted to type with Garner and Croft the only other bowlers (apart from a solitary King over) in a rare West Indies defeat.

Over the next two years, Parry would occupy the token spinner role on tours to England and Pakistan, as the West Indies, stung by criticism that it was over-reliant on pace and intimidation, sought to keep up appearances by including a slow bowler in their squad. But Trinidad trundler Rangy Nanan was preferred to Parry in Pakistan, and the unheralded Harold Joseph got the nod for the Australian tour of 1981/82, while in Guyana, Clive Lloyd's compatriot Roger Harper, the man whose action, some said, resembled a wounded seagull, was being groomed as the next token finger-spinner.

Parry was only 28, a veteran of 12 Tests, but he sensed that his West Indies career was over. Beyond the Shell Shield, he was plying his trade with Horden in the Durham League but, back home, his natural reticence and the disadvantages inherent in coming from a small island meant there was no media cheerleader to spruik his case for a return to the West Indies squad. 'I remember rebel tour organiser Gregory Armstrong came to Nevis, got a taxi and came right to Cotton Ground,' Parry says. 'It was a straightforward decision. There was no future for me in West Indies cricket.'

* * *

Parry had accepted a US$100,000 contract to play for a rebel West Indies XI in South Africa; however, his journey to the republic would turn out to be the most arduous of all the tourists.

First up, he had to inform his team-mates in the Leeward Islands Shell Shield side. Parry was vice-captain to Viv Richards.

The world's best batsman wore a red, gold and green sweatband to indicate his support for the Pan-African ideal. He was the sport's most recognisable face in the struggle against black oppression, a vocal opponent of apartheid and the rebel tours. Privately, however, he was more sympathetic. At a two-week training camp in preparation for the 1982/83 season, Parry told Richards and coach Danny Livingstone that he would be catching a plane out of Antigua the next day to join his rebel compadres in New York en route to Johannesburg.

'Viv had no objection to me going at all,' Parry says. 'I wasn't as close to him as I was Andy but there was no problem.' Richards's blessing was the least of Parry's problems. At what was then known as Coolidge International Airport, the Antiguan head of immigration, Inspector Jeremiah 'Dods' Joseph, arrested Parry, confiscated his passport, and threw him into detention. In a scene more redolent of a totalitarian regime than a tropical democracy, Parry was given no reason for his arrest. 'It was a scary experience,' Parry says. 'It was in the back of my mind that I wouldn't get to South Africa.'

Aside from Richards's vocal stance, Antigua wasn't renowned for its anti-apartheid rhetoric. In fact, in 1981 the government was scandalised when a weapons company was exposed for funnelling arms through Antigua to South Africa. Was Parry's detention the action of an over-zealous official, or a fearful government trying to impress its Caribbean neighbours with the strength of its principles?

Parry believes the former. 'The chap just looked pompous,' he says. 'That's the way he acted.'

When Parry was released 24 hours later, still without any justification, he was met by his friend Andy Roberts, who put him up until the next available flight.

There was also friction at the highest levels back in Nevis. Joseph Parry was one of the cousins with whom Derick shared that hard and cramped bedroom floor in Cotton Ground. Six years his senior, Joseph had helped form the Nevis Reformation

Party, which, in coalition with the larger People's Action Party in St Kitts, governed the two-state federation. The man who would lead them to independence from Britain just eight months later, Prime Minister Kennedy Simmonds, was virulently against sporting contact with South Africa.

As Secretary for Nevis Affairs, Joseph Parry began to feel the heat. 'There was a lot of political pressure being exercised,' he says. 'People were sounding off. In Nevis there was a black consciousness movement. Intellectuals and pseudo-intellectuals were mainly talking about it. I was in a very awkward position. I regarded Derick as a younger brother, and I understood these men had to make money. No one came to me and said I had to pressure Derick, but things were being said.'

In South Africa, Parry found that Rowe, like Kallicharran in India, was more open than Lloyd to using him as an attacking force. He also found the younger Rowe, renowned for his laid-back approach, easier to work with. 'You could talk with Yagga. Lloydy as a captain, you couldn't really go and talk to him. Yagga was a good captain.'

For his part, Rowe says, 'Parry is the best spinner we had since Lance Gibbs.'

During the first tour, the captain's faith in Parry paid off. At Newlands in the first 'Test', his figures of 5-117 included the wickets of Peter Kirsten and Clive Rice. On a flat wicket, Parry's 'flighted off spin proved to be skipper Lawrence Rowe's main weapon as the faster men struggle to gain lift' wrote Brian Crowley in *Calypso Cavaliers*.

But it was the duels with the great Graeme Pollock, then 38, that tested Parry as a professional and brought out the best in him. Most of the Springboks used their pads to nullify the turn Parry extracted, but Pollock led with his bat and his feet. It reminded Parry of his battles with Viv Richards. 'With players like Viv and Pollock, you cannot settle. They're going to come at you. You have to keep pushing them. Other batsmen, they let you bowl. If you bowl a bad ball, they hit you.'

Parry wasn't ignorant of the suffering of the black South African population, though he didn't interact much with them, other than hotel staff and occasional coaching clinics. He knew that black liberation organisations had implicitly condemned the tours. Still, he says the focus was on cricket and staying out of trouble. 'We heard maybe they didn't approve but we didn't sit down and discuss the consequences. We were just trying to make a living. We were careful not to go to the wrong places, because mad people might attack us or something. We didn't see any protests. A lot of the time we spent in each other's rooms watching videos or having a drink.'

Colin Croft, who was injured for most of the tour, was his room-mate, and because of a pinched nerve in his back, a poor sleeper. Ironically, Parry quiet and even-tempered, was closest to the *enfants terribles* Clarke and King. 'We had a good time congregating in their rooms having a few beers and relaxing,' he remembers.

Back home in Nevis, the debate about the pros and cons of the rebel tours was escalating. High school students were asked to write papers on the subject and the rumblings in authority grew. As in the rest of the Caribbean, fault lines between the educated political class and ordinary citizens widened. There was a general sense among islanders, many of whom knew Parry personally, that as a poorly paid professional cricketer who had brought acclaim to the nation, he had the right to pursue playing opportunities wherever he could.

'People understood the economics of the time,' says Carlise Powell, father of current Nevis Test batsman Kieran Powell, and former manager of the Leeward Islands side. 'People didn't want Derick to fall on hard times. There was a tremendous amount of understanding and respect for Derick Parry and his judgement. What happened to the guys in Jamaica … Derick didn't get that treatment in Nevis. He was loved and is loved.'

The second tour proved less fruitful for Parry. He performed well in the first two National Panasonic 'Tests', outscoring recognised batsmen with a total of 151 runs at 75.50, and claiming the prized wicket of Pollock twice, but pre-match speculation that the Wanderers pitch for the third encounter would provide an even contest between bat and ball was enough to tip the balance in favour of the four-pronged pace attack of Clarke, Moseley, Stephenson and fiery Bajan newcomer Hartley Alleyne. Not for the first time, the amiable Nevisian had been sacrificed on the altar of pace. 'I really wanted to play, but it was back to the old formula. They really wanted four quickies.'

It didn't help that Alleyne delivered a blinder, taking 4-54 and 5-62 with his chesty missiles, as the rebels recorded a series-levelling one-wicket win, ensuring his place for the final showdown.

It was a long ten-week campaign and, towards the end, enthusiasm waned, as the jaded tourists began to focus on how they would spend their booty. Parry thinks some had given up long before that. 'The saying was "come to collect". There were guys you could tell who didn't come to play cricket at all,' Parry says.

There were also squabbles over sponsorship payments, as the initial contracts didn't include provisions for prize money but, overall, Parry felt the tours were a success and the spirit of camaraderie was high, despite the looming life ban from Test and Caribbean cricket.

In the wake of the tours he was offered a spot with Western Province in the Currie Cup but knocked it back for the chance to coach schoolchildren in Nevis. It was, he thought, an opportunity to give back to the island that had given him so much.

But anti-apartheid sentiment was, justifiably, still at high levels, and the rebel tour fresh in the minds of politicians. Pressure to be seen to be doing the right thing in the eyes of the Caribbean was immense. It threatened to tear Parry's family apart.

According to Joseph Parry, the decision to terminate his cousin's coaching contract came about because of a push from CARICOM (Caribbean Community). At least, that's what he was told. Prime Minister Simmonds, steadfast in his opposition to the rebel tours, was happy to oblige them, reigniting old tensions between St Kitts and Nevis. 'Simeon Daniel was leader of the Nevis Reform Party in coalition,' Joseph Parry says. 'He said Simmonds was pressuring him and told me it had to be done. I felt he should have stood up to them in St Kitts.'

The man tasked with wielding the axe was Joseph Parry. 'I was in a helpless position. Derick came to my house. It was a hard conversation to have. I was so frustrated because I could do nothing.'

What made it more frustrating for Parry was that when he approached Western Province the next season, he couldn't even get through to the switchboard. Fortunately, he was still contracted in England with Horden, where attitudes towards the rebels were much more flexible, even if his exotic homeland continued to invite curiosity and ignorance in equal measure. 'They thought I looked like Pelé,' Parry laughs. 'They always asked, "Where in Jamaica or Barbados are you from?" They would say, "Where in Jamaica is Nevis?" They had no idea.'

And unlike some of his rebel brethren, he invested his South African money wisely. League cricket in England brought him only a few thousand pounds for four months of the year, but in Nevis he had no job, so he had to live frugally and put money aside. When he did splash out, it was on a two-storey house overlooking the Caribbean Sea in Spring Hill, where he now lives with his family. He also bought land in Charlestown, the historic Georgian-era capital, and later sold it to fund the car hire business that he runs today.

In 1989, the WICBC rescinded the rebels' life bans from Test cricket, but it came too late for the 35-year-old Parry, out of the first-class arena for too long to compete for a maroon cap. He was free to coach – with a catch. He had to write a letter to the WICBC apologising for his involvement in the rebel tours. Parry felt he had nothing to apologise for, and still doesn't, but if it meant he could draw a line under them once and for all, it was worth doing. 'I thought "whatever they want". I wanted to coach. So I did it and they accepted it.'

After years in the wilderness, it seemed he'd been reintegrated into the mainstream of Caribbean cricket. The Leeward Islands coaching job followed, as did a stint as a West Indies junior selector. He even coached for government schools in Nevis, until petty island politics intervened once more. Parry had played first-class cricket with Vance Amory in the 1970s. The right-hand opening batsman from the Gingerland parish in the south-east of the island compiled many elegant mid-range scores but could never convert them into centuries that would arouse interest from West Indies selectors. The two were friends – or so Parry thought. But Amory had founded the Concerned Citizens Movement in opposition to Joseph Parry's Nevis Reform Party, and when he took over as Nevis premier in 2013, promptly ended Parry's tenure as a government coach.

His links to his cousin had put him in hot water again. 'People said to me I have the wrong name,' Parry laughs. 'Vance wrote me a letter and fired me. And then a couple of days later he said he wanted to help me. He wanted to give me a hug. "Oh, long-lost friend," I said. "Look, you just fired me!"'

* * *

At St James Primary School on the north of the island, a barefoot boy with the kind of fast twitch muscle reactions that coaches salivate over, sizes up the length of the yellow ball, leans back on his right leg and tonks it with a plastic bat in the direction of Nevis Peak. More boys in red shorts and white T-shirts tear after it, and the bowler, all corn rows and floppy red bow, exhorts them to return it to her pronto. It's a colourful scene that momentarily gives the lie to the idea that cricket is in slow decline on the island. Directing it is Parry, who has arranged the coaching session, a West Indies Cricket initiative, with his good friend, ex-Leeward Islands opener Livingston Lawrence. 'When I was growing up it was spontaneous everywhere,' Parry laments. 'Every boy played. Now it's only on Saturday morning.'

And even those games are not always the idyllic palm-fringed encounters of the popular imagination. Lack of economic opportunity, drugs and the aping of American gun culture has seen youth homicide explode in the federation. Cotton Ground hasn't hosted a game for the past two years because of it, and Parry witnessed first-hand the murder that caused the shut-down. 'A chap sitting down next to us was shot in the back of the head by gunmen, while the match was going on,' Parry, who was coaching Cotton Ground, says. 'He was from the Gingerland side, but he didn't get a game because he was late. So he sat there for about an hour and a half. All I heard was da-da-da-da-da, and when I looked, I see the two gunmen running with the gun in their hand, two masked men dressed in black. Then I saw him and there were two holes in his head.'

Understandably, local youths have been afraid to set foot on the ground since. 'This year alone we have had 15 guys shot,' Parry says.

* * *

It's a typically warm and sticky late afternoon in Cotton Ground, and Maria Parry is recalling the disappointment she felt when she, like many of the Windrush generation, arrived in London. 'We thought the streets would be paved with gold,' she says. 'But it was no fairy tale.'

There's a minor lull in her story as Nevis's notorious power grid, unable to cope with the demands of another steamy day in paradise, temporarily clocks off. It's the cue to change the subject and ask Derick, who never ceases to be amazed by his mother's ability to talk for long periods at the kitchen table, how, 35 years on, he feels about taking part in the rebel tours. 'I have no regrets,' he says.

Early that evening, Parry's hire car rumbles past 17th-century St Thomas Church, the oldest Anglican house of worship in the

Caribbean. It backs on to his alma mater, St Thomas Primary School. Near the entrance, there's a sign bearing the motto 'Learn today/Earn tomorrow'. Words of faith for Parry, a man of quiet perseverance and enduring achievement. A man whose close connections to community and respect for the gentle rhythms of island life spared him the hardships that so many of his rebel brothers would endure.

Hartley Alleyne

'He would try to kill you'

IF THERE are only 21 seconds of your sporting career on YouTube, you'd better hope they count. Hartley Alleyne's shaft of internet immortality shows him felling Graeme Pollock with a bouncer that strikes the South African batting great on the right earlobe. It's the only time in his 27-year first-class career that Pollock was hit on the head. It counts.

The pity is that there isn't more footage of Alleyne in the public space. In the early 1980s, county opponents rated him quicker than Roberts, Holding and Marshall, but to the wider cricket-loving public, he's the fastest bowler you've never heard of.

Port Elizabeth is Graeme Pollock's hometown. He always liked to do well there in front of his friends and relatives. The previous ball had rocketed off the St George's Park pitch, hissing feet above his blue helmet. It was laced with the greeting 'Nice to see you, Graeme'. The 39-year-old took guard again with the familiar wide-legged stance that many a pulverised bowler had come to resent over the years.

'He went around the wicket and he was a little bit of a round-armer,' Pollock says of Alleyne's action. 'And it came quite wide and I didn't pick it up.' The ball cannoned into the side piece of his helmet, and Pollock crumpled into the turf clutching his bloodied head.

'I was scared,' Alleyne confesses. 'He was laying on the ground.'

The cut required four stitches, but Pollock was aware that the bigger damage could be psychological. He returned the next day in a vain attempt to help the Springboks save the game. 'Once you get hit on the head you've got to get out there as quick as you can to get it out of your system.' But he told reporters that Alleyne's blow had made him think seriously about retiring. 'You had to very careful with Hartley,' he says now. 'He was very fast.'

Don Bradman rated Pollock alongside Gary Sobers as the two finest left-handers to have played the game. Indeed, Pollock ultimately decided to bat on, plundering 144 against the Australian rebel attack of Alderman, Rackemann and Hogg in 1987, aged 42.

So how did a paceman capable of ruffling the game's most elite feathers not reach its highest level? The complication with Alleyne's 21 seconds of YouTube fame is that it portrays him unfairly as cricket's version of a psychopath, forever slashing open a batsman's head.

'He was fucking mad,' says Alvin Kallicharran. But madness and fast bowlers have always been co-conspirators in the batsman's horror show.

John Vanderpool played youth cricket with Alleyne in Barbados in the early 1970s. They trialled together for the national under-19s side. Commentator Tony Cozier rated opening batsman Vanderpool as West Indies material. In the nets against Alleyne, he was terrified. 'Hartley would actually get a new ball to bowl at me, and every other ball was usually a bumper,' Vanderpool says. 'It was not that he didn't like me – we were very close, but he was a little crazy. He was wild. He had no respect for anyone when it came to bowling at a batsman. He would try to kill you.'

All broad shoulders and straining biceps, Alleyne's athletic sprint to the wicket enabled him to thump the pitch at furious speed. Former Australian captain Kim Hughes was his skipper at Natal in the late 1980s when both men were playing out their careers in the dying days of the apartheid republic. 'He had a beautiful build for a fast bowler,' Hughes says. 'He was a six-footer, not like those really big guys you get now. And he was sharp. In another era he would have been in the top two or three West Indian bowlers. He was just born in the wrong era.'

When Alleyne came to Australia to play Melbourne club cricket with St Kilda in 1981/82, the normally staid *The Age* newspaper splashed its front page with 'World's fastest bowler here'. Loyal readers may have expected to see a picture of Andy Roberts or Michael Holding in their pomp; instead they peered at Hartley Leroy Alleyne following through at a suburban oval – a man most of them knew nothing about. The story went on to claim that the mystery paceman's speed out of the hand 'makes Wayne Daniel look medium pace'. Well, so said his county opponents. It also referred to the six quicks in the West Indies touring squad to Australia that season – Roberts, Holding, Croft, Garner, Marshall and Clarke – and the WICBC's desire to use Alleyne as a replacement if one of them broke down.

Captain Clive Lloyd reinforced their interest: 'The boy will never know how close he was to being picked to tour Australia.'

As it turned out, Sylvester Clarke sustained a bruised heel after pounding down on the hard Aussie surfaces, and Lloyd, Alleyne says, called him to join the squad as a standby. It was the nearest he got to representing in the maroon cap. 'They kept Sylvester on the team, and he got fit. And then I couldn't get in. I wanted them to send him home,' Alleyne laughs.

Lamenting the glut of once-in-a-generation talent that diverted their route to the West Indies dressing room is a familiar refrain from many of the rebels, but there's no doubt Alleyne had extraordinary competition to contend with. And that's not including young Bajan countrymen Ezra Moseley and Franklyn Stephenson, and the hulking Daniel.

Alleyne's first appearance for St Kilda sent a shiver of collective fear though the district competition. Phil O'Meara had played Sheffield Shield cricket for Western Australia. He was Alleyne's captain. 'We were playing at the old Footscray football ground. We had selected Hartley without seeing him bowl. I was in the slips and I've never stood so far back, and I played against guys like Lillee at the WACA. I reckon we were 30 yards back. Our keeper was taking the ball on the up. He only bowled five or six overs in his first spell after we batted first, but he had four wickets by the end of it. And the word went around Melbourne: this guy's seriously sharp.'

Helmets, which were still considered less than manly in the grizzled, macho world of Australian grade cricket, in essence a confession of fear, were soon de rigueur for St Kilda games.

But Alleyne's second spell was never quite as threatening. 'He would drop from 150km per hour to 125km per hour,' O'Meara says, and hitherto frightened batsmen would learn to tough out the opening bumper barrage knowing the second Alleyne coming would be a gentler, less combative affair. His propensity for targeting the throat, like many a newcomer seduced by Australia's bouncy wickets and, in O'Meara's opinion, pitching too short, meant once opponents had mastered the art of ducking and weaving, they could navigate Alleyne's overs unscathed. 'They learned how to handle him, so he didn't get the wickets he should have,' O'Meara says.

But he was still a popular figure at the club and a huge drawcard, especially among young women. 'He was a party boy and he had those big shoulders and slim waistline; all the ammunition was there,' O'Meara laughs. More importantly, his St Kilda stint kept him on the West Indies selection radar as competition for places in the famed pace quartet intensified.

In the previous northern hemisphere summer, Alleyne, then 24, had stormed into contention with 8-43, including a hat-trick, for Worcestershire against Middlesex's international-studded line-up. *The Guardian* headline topping the match report joked: 'The fastest waiter in Worcester', alluding to the absurd irony that if he were an Englishman he would be playing Test cricket, not pouring ales to help make ends meet. The observation spoke volumes about the grim economic reality of life for many of his Caribbean compatriots.

Like a lot of West Indian pacemen, Alleyne was a gun for hire for 12 months a year. His bespoke pace bowling service found custom in England via the Lancashire League and in the county and minor county championships, the Shell Shield in Barbados, district and sub-district cricket in Australia and the Currie Cup in South Africa.

But wherever he went he left a unique mark – and not just in bruises. The New Zealand all-rounder Dipak Patel was his flatmate at Worcestershire. Like O'Meara, he admired the young Bajan's aptitude for partying. 'We used to call him "Hartley Man" because he used to say "man" after everything. He was never a great drinker – he didn't handle it that well, but he loved his dancing and was very successful with the ladies. If you stuck close enough to him at nightclubs, you'd get some of his palm-offs and they weren't the worst.'

Alleyne's quirky habits and his fractured relationship with the English weather was a source of great amusement to Patel and his team-mates. 'He couldn't stand the cold. I remember it had been hot outside for a week. I'd gone out to play golf and I walked in on Hartley with not a stitch of clothing on ... with the gas heater on at full blast with the curtains closed, listening to his music and dancing. He was a great character.'

In January 1983, Alleyne was earning Aussie dollars coaching in Melbourne. His tenure as club pro with St Kilda had been controversially terminated in November because of what team insiders termed a lax attitude. He also lost his position as second overseas professional with Worcestershire, who were seeking scapegoats for a disappointing 14th-place finish in the county championship.

Wickets were money, and while he wasn't taking them his bank balance suffered. But he wasn't stewing; there was the upcoming Shell Shield season to prepare for and the company of Bajan friends Malcolm Marshall and Desmond Haynes to enjoy. There were no Tests scheduled in the Caribbean until late February, so Marshall and Haynes were plying their trades in the sub-district competition with Moorabbin and Dandenong respectively. The three of them lived nearby and their close proximity made it easier for Ali Bacher to factor them into his plans for a West Indian rebel tour of South Africa.

Alleyne says the course of Caribbean cricket would have changed irredeemably if Bacher had been able to arrange a face to face meeting with Haynes and Marshall. All three had received offers over the telephone, but the human touch was needed to get the Test men over the line. They were so close to going, airline tickets from Melbourne to Johannesburg had been arranged for them to collect from a travel agent. 'I reckon if Bacher and Pamensky had flown to Melbourne they would have changed their minds,' Alleyne says.

The three mates had talked extensively about their offers and the ramifications for their careers. But whereas Haynes was ensconced at the top of the West Indies batting order, and Marshall, Alleyne's junior by a year, had 12 Test caps to his name and was looming as Andy Roberts's likely successor, Alleyne had no guarantee of a future at the highest level.

What stopped him succumbing to Bacher's predations was the health of his father back in Barbados. 'He was suffering with his heart,' Alleyne says. 'I didn't want to go to South Africa and hear my father died. I would have taken his death to heart and felt that I'd caused him to die. I also thought I could still make the official team.'

He called Clyde Walcott's brother Keith, the Barbados chairman of selectors, and reassured him he would be ready to go for the first game against Leeward Islands at Kensington Oval.

The 1983 Shell Shield would turn out to be both his season horribilis and mirabilis. Wicketless in the Leeward Islands game, he was then best-on-ground against Jamaica at Sabina Park with match figures of 7-83. But in the second ball of his third over, charging in from the press-box end, he was called for chucking by umpire Wesley Malcolm. Alleyne was devastated. 'Man, I just stood there and cried,' he told *The Age*'s Patrick Smith a few months later. 'A big man like me just cried.'

The chucking contagion has a dark history of infecting umpires, making them see murky shadows where none exist. In the final match of the Shield in Port of Spain, official Mohammed Hosein cautioned Alleyne twice during the second innings as he blasted Barbados to victory with 4-43. The incident still preys on Alleyne's mind. 'The other umpire came over to me and said, "You're not chucking," and he said he did not know why his colleague called me. I played a lot of county cricket in England and never once was called.'

Looking back through the prism of history, he thinks the no-balling was a function of the exceptional lift he got when other bowlers struggled – lift that umpires thought must have been derived through illegal advantage. 'The other players couldn't believe why I could get the extra bounce.'

County team-mate Patel says there's no doubt Alleyne bent his arm on rare occasions but so did Sylvester Clarke and just about every quick bowler that ever laced a boot.

There was little support from Barbados officials, who Alleyne accuses of being distant and more concerned with etiquette than supporting team members in moments of crisis. 'Clyde Walcott and those guys never got close to the players. They were cliquey and would assess you from a distance. At trial games they would come around and see if you had the right table manners and how you ate with a knife and fork.'

It didn't seem to matter anymore that at the conclusion of the season Alleyne sat at the top of the bowling averages, ahead of Marshall, Roberts, Daniel and Winston Davis. Rightly or wrongly, at 26, his career was irreparably tarnished.

There was also the issue of temperament. The previous year with Worcestershire, he was suspended for remonstrating with seasoned umpire Mervyn Kitchen. Clive Lloyd had the finest battalion of quick bowlers in the history of cricket at his disposal. He could afford to be picky; and the superfast party boy with the questionable action might be more work than the ageing captain could bear.

Alleyne knew it. He also knew the hyper-competitive Marshall was the favoured son. 'To be honest with you, I reckon Clive Lloyd liked Marshall. If he didn't like you, you didn't get in the team. That's when I decided to bugger off to South Africa,' he says. If Bacher and co. came brandishing a blank cheque book again, that is.

In England, he was still a sought-after commodity in the leagues. When Worcestershire let him go, Haslingden, a Lancashire League club north of Manchester snapped him up. During Alleyne's four-year tenure at the mill town club, his hard-earned reputation for slippery bowling and carousing was cemented.

Mike Ingham is the leading run-scorer in the Lancashire League's 118-year history. He recalls 'H' with a mixture of affection and amusement. 'He was a great team-mate,' he says. 'He was a nutcase. Complete madman. He was just a crazy individual to be around – the crazy things he said and did. He liked a rum or two. When he was with Oldham's Franklyn Stephenson there was always something going on when they were in the room together. I once called him "bungalow". He said, "Ingham, why you call me bungalow, man?" I said, "Basically because you've fuck-all upstairs." "What do you mean, man?" he asked.'

Over the years, Haslingden has been home to fast bowlers with the calibre of Andy Roberts, Allan Donald and Merv Hughes. Rival league sides sizzled with Imran Khan, Michael Holding, Wayne Daniel and Joel Garner. Ingham faced them all. He's in no doubt who was the quickest. 'Hartley is the fastest thing I've ever seen by a country mile.'

The man who inked the deal to sign Alleyne was Haslingden club chairman Ernie Taylor. He was like a father figure to Alleyne, helping the young Barbadian come to grips with life and cricket in England. 'H was brilliant for us,' Taylor says. 'He gave 100 per cent all the time. I once said, "Franklyn Stephenson bowls a slower ball, Hartley, why don't you?" He said, "I don't bowl slower balls. I tell you what I do, Ernie, I bowl a quicker one." He was something else.'

Taylor rescued Alleyne from many off-field scrapes, especially of the romantic variety and was a trusted confidant in times of crisis.

* * *

In November 1983, Alleyne returned to Melbourne to take up a deal with Brighton in the sub-district league. It could have been interpreted as a retrograde step in light of his messy departure from St Kilda the previous season, but his new contract coincided with the West Indies' participation in the triangular one-day series that was the hallmark of Australian summers in the 1980s. He told *The Age*'s reporter, 'I just need a break to get selected ... if anyone in Australia breaks down this summer I hope they consider me as a replacement.' It was a forlorn hope.

His stay at Brighton lasted only two games. It was distinguished by a swashbuckling 55 that ended with a bouncer crashing into his face, the suspicion that he was more interested in his female companion than what was going on pitch-side during the next game, and Pakistan Test star Younis Ahmed smashing him to all corners at Malvern.

But if Alleyne seemed a little distracted, it was with good reason – Bacher had telephoned him from Johannesburg again. The SACU bigwig wanted another fast bowler to replace Jamaican slinger Ray Wynter for the second West Indies rebel tour. Having squared it with his parents back in Barbados, Alleyne was leaning towards accepting the US$100,000 offer.

His new employers were aghast. Brighton wanted to hold on to their marquee signing for as long as possible. They also felt that Alleyne still had a chance of representing the West Indies. 'My captain Rod Sayers said, "Hartley, don't go to South

Africa. You will play for West Indies." I said, "I don't think I will."'

Alleyne says that to convince Sayers that his West Indies dream was dead in the water, he asked him to phone selector J. K. Holt, the former Test batsman, in Jamaica. 'Holt told him I'm off the record,' Alleyne says. 'How could I be off the record when I hadn't even gone to South Africa? Rod said, "It seems like they have got it in for you." I reckon from the chucking business they had it in for me.'

It was all he needed to know to confirm he was making the right decision – even if a life ban from Test cricket was the outcome.

Back in England, Ernie Taylor was glad his charge had decided to chance his bowling arm with the rebels. 'He used to say to me that Lloyd promised him he would play Tests, but nothing happened,' Taylor says. 'It annoyed him. For a kid from Barbados, and he'd left Barbados in his early 20s, to try to make a life with a cricket ball, I thought if things with apartheid are going to get better, why not go. What an achievement. That's how I looked at it and how I spoke to H about it. It was the money that swung it for him.'

In an article in *The Age* signalling his departure, Alleyne was obviously conflicted by the decision. But he also hit out at his treatment by the West Indies hierarchy. He said Clive Lloyd telephoned when he was close to joining the first tour back in January, insisting he was still in the champion side's plans. 'They never said don't go, they just told me I should not ruin my chance of playing for the West Indies. They said I would get my chance soon.'

The big kick in the guts was when teenage Antiguan fast bowler George Ferris was put on standby for the Test tour of India later in the year. 'Man, if I had a bad heart I would have collapsed there and then. I couldn't believe it,' Alleyne said at the time. 'I had the performances on the board. It hurt me, man, it really hurt me.'

He also offered the familiar 'cricket-is-my-trade' justification for taking the apartheid nation's money. 'I'm not qualified for anything else and I only have a short time as a cricketer. I want to sit down at the end of my career and say I haven't wasted my days.'

Alleyne's arrival in Johannesburg gave Lawrence Rowe the final piece in his four-prong pace jigsaw. Sporting a tight T-shirt that revealed bulging biceps, the new recruit was pictured relaxing in a park in affluent Sandton alongside tour manager Gregory Armstrong, David Murray and Collis King. 'His lean, muscular build reminds you of an Olympic athlete', the accompanying report in the *Rand Daily Mail* suggested.

'It was a good vibe,' Alleyne says. 'We all knew each other from the West Indies, so it was like seeing your buddies again. All the boys were great.'

After a match against provincial opposition in the conservative Afrikaner heartland of Bloemfontein, the tourists were filmed in a bar mixing with white fans and businessmen. The camera zooms in on paceman Sylvester Clarke, who is wearing the prototype cricketer's attire of polo shirt and jeans, as are most of his team-mates. Except Alleyne. Gold chains dangle over a trendy grandpa collar T-shirt as he launches into another fast-paced story for eager fans. He's clearly enjoying himself.

There's also footage of him in sunglasses drinking gratis champagne served by a pretty air hostess on the squad's flight from Johannesburg to Durban. 'I was humming,' Alleyne says of his time in South Africa.

His form was humming, too. A blistering 4-26 against Eastern Province in Port Elizabeth put him in contention for the first 'Test' in Durban.

North Transvaal batsmen rated him the slipperiest of all the rebel quicks. Then he contracted chicken pox. With Colin Croft unable to regain the form that had made him one of the most feared bowlers in the world, Rowe's plans for a pace battery foursome were in tatters. 'Dr Ali Bacher came to see me and I said how could I catch it – I was 27!' Alleyne says. It kept him out of the selection mix until the third 'Test' at Wanderers.

For Alleyne, the third 'Test' was the highlight of his career so far. 'It felt like a real Test debut. I've still got my cap and blazer back in Barbados. All the guys were playing for the West Indies. We didn't want to go to South Africa and get demoralised. That would have given the people in the Caribbean a lot to say.'

He didn't disappoint. In cahoots with fellow Bajan quicks Ezra Moseley, Sylvester Clarke and Franklyn Stephenson, he registered figures of 4-54 in the first innings and 5-62 in the second as the West Indies XI levelled the rubber at one-all. Alleyne was man of the match.

It was in the second innings of the deciding fourth 'Test' that he poleaxed Pollock with that fabled bouncer, triggering an outbreak of panic in the Springbok dressing room. If their best batsman could be hit, what chance did the rest of the side have? From 65/2 they collapsed to be all out for 127. The rebels won in a canter. Although Sylvester Clarke deservedly won all the plaudits with match figures of 10-68 it was Alleyne who'd changed the course of the match.

Captain Rowe credited his presence with turning the series. 'Ever since we started using all four of our quickies, it's made all the difference to our performance,' he told the *Rand Daily Mail*.

Off the pitch, Alleyne's main companions were King, Clarke and Nederburg Stein wine from the Western Cape, although his consumption of rum wasn't in the same league as the booze brothers.

He says the tourists were well received wherever they went. One night at Derby's Corner bar in Durban with King, they were the recipient of largesse from an unlikely source. 'These beers kept on coming to us,' Alleyne says. 'And I asked the barman where they were coming from.' He pointed to a tall, thick-set white guy in the corner of the establishment. 'He played rugby for Natal,' Alleyne says. 'He was about 6ft 7in, an Afrikaner – a massive, massive man. I went to shake his hand, and he said,

"No problem. I thank you for coming to this country. If you have any problems, let me know and I will take care of you. You fellas have a lot of pressure on you and I'm so happy you came because I don't believe in what's going on in this country.'"

Most of the tour passed off without incident, although vice-captain Alvin Kallicharran recalls, with a smile, a shaken Alleyne getting stuck in the Holiday Inn lift at Sandton: 'He was white when he came out, sweating profusely.'

The only thing that bothered Alleyne was a nagging suspicion that the cricket establishment wasn't as hostile to the tours or South Africa as they publicly made out. He smelt hypocrisy. 'Ali Bacher said to me, "When you get back to Barbados, please give my regards to Clyde Walcott." I said, "Pardon?" I couldn't believe what I was hearing. These men are buddies? And yet we were being banned. It was like they were in on it.'

What he encountered when he returned to Barbados only strengthened his belief that the West Indies authorities were, privately at least, keen supporters of the rebels' fortunes on the pitch. 'One of them said to me, "Oh, Hartley, you boys did so well in South Africa," and I said, "But I thought you weren't interested." He said, "No, we followed you guys and how you progressed." I said, "Thank you very much indeed." And these were the guys that had banned us for life!'

Back at Haslingden, Alleyne settled into the gentle routines of an English cricket summer. Only now he had a huge sum of money burning a hole in his pocket. The temptation was to spend it on the flashy baubles of excess as many of his team-mates did. Fortunately, chairman Ernie Taylor could be relied upon to help curb what he describes as Alleyne's 'Big-time Charlie' instincts. When his impulsive fast bowler asked him along to a showroom in London's Hanger Lane to buy a 'souped-up Ford', Taylor put his foot down. 'I said, "What do you want to buy a car for?" He said he wanted to take it back to Barbados. He probably wanted to show off in front of the birds in Bridgetown. Something young men do. I've done it myself, so I talked him out of it. "You're only in Barbados two weeks a year, who will look after it?" He said his brother would. So I asked him, "What's the most important thing you want in life?" He said, "I need to build a house." I replied, "There you go then. Why buy a car when you can build a house?"'

Alleyne's father, a contractor, was also insistent that his son channel his new fortune into bricks and mortar. 'I got collared by him,' Alleyne says. 'He said, "Now listen. Either build a house or you can leave my house." So I did – in St James, near where Desmond Haynes comes from.'

At the end of the year he returned to South Africa to play for Natal in the Currie Cup, where, he says, he was still treated like a king. He was regularly invited to barbecues and hung out in shebeens, the once illegal township bars that were forbidden during apartheid. Locals, he maintains, were interested in how a man of the same skin colour had prospered in a world stacked against black people. 'They would ask me where I was from because I was walking so confidently. They could tell from the way I moved I wasn't from there.'

The only grief he encountered was when a Belgian national stole his seat at a bar and attempted to have him evicted. 'I said, "Hang on, you're dealing with a different black man here. I'm not from South Africa." I pushed him out of the way.'

In the autumn years of his fast-bowling life, Alleyne alternated between Natal, the Lancashire League and Kent where he now lives. He's married, has two sons and coaches at St Edmund's school in Canterbury. The 'crazy' man has mellowed. His treatment by selectors and cricket officials still rankles, but even he and Clive Lloyd, the man who had the power to make or break so many careers, get along fine. 'I saw him at Garfield Sobers's 80th birthday in Barbados in 2016, and he said, "It's nice to see you." He never brings up South Africa,' Alleyne says. 'I remember when Clive was the manager of the West Indies in the late 1990s and I'd been to watch them practise and I was walking across the ground and he said to me, "Hartley, when I saw you, and knowing you couldn't get in the team back then, that made me sad. Look at what I have to work with now. These guys are no good."'

On the subject of the 1983/84 rebel tour, Alleyne is certain its effects were overwhelmingly positive. 'History will look at us more kindly. I know one day they will say these boys who went to South Africa had a lot of influence, did a lot of good.'

He's just as upbeat about his bowling career, even if a short YouTube video is all the wider world knows about it. 'I'm very happy. When people heard about Hartley Alleyne, they were looking for someone who was 6ft 5in. They didn't understand I had leverage and I was a very aggressive individual. I used my wrists – and that wrist snap, and the way I brought my wrist down. Like Jofra Archer does. It wasn't copybook. But you've got to let people go with what the Lord has given them. I had some great times. I enjoyed the battles: Allan Border, Viv Richards, Geoffrey Boycott, Kapil Dev. They would smash you if you didn't put it in the right area. I did as good as I could.'

Bernard Julien

'A very, very handsome guy'

THE MIDDLE-AGED resident points to an apartment at the top of block D. 'I think it was the one with the satellite dish,' she says. 'I know his was the biggest.' Powder Magazine Phase 2 is a Trinidad Housing Development Corporation project off the Diego Martin Highway, four miles north of Port of Spain, the capital. Its dull cream, green and amber-painted blocks tower over patches of yellowing grass and the occasional park bench. Bernard Julien lived here once.

'He's the cricketer, right? I haven't seen him for a few years here now.' And even when he was there, no one saw him often. Julien has led a nomadic, intermittently reclusive existence for some time now, beholden to government and private handouts.

Friends all have different ideas on where he lives. Some say the affluent northern Port of Spain suburb of Maraval, others say he's further south in a Couva apartment whose stairs he has trouble climbing. His 'cousin' Terry Joseph swore he was somewhere in the vast grimness of the Powder Magazine Phase 2 complex. There's even speculation he's still in Carenage, the fishing village where he grew up.

In the past ten years Julien has battled throat cancer and depression as recognition of his own mortality hit home hard. The anxiety has pushed him closer to God but further from old friends. Yet there are days of unexpected vigour, as if his captain has asked him to muster all his energy for one final spell. Days when his supernatural hand-eye coordination is in evidence on the golf course or in coaching sessions. But they are fewer and farther between. Unpredictable is his new normal.

'We often invite him to gatherings of Trinidad players,' says Deryck Murray, the man who kept to Julien in all his 24 Test matches. 'He comes to some but not others. When you see him now, he is sometimes very reserved, which is very unusual for him, and other times he's almost normal. It's a lottery.'

His reluctance to socialise is understandable given the terrible toll the disease has wrought on his mind and body. A help provider says he has lost his teeth. The handsome face female fans all around the world adored is gaunt and frail.

Stephen Gomez played with Julien in the Trinidad under-19 side in the late 1960s. The son of former West Indies all-rounder and administrator Gerry Gomez, he's bewildered and saddened by his old friend's decline. 'Really and truly, he has just dropped out. Nobody knows where he is. I ask a few friends and they phone around and it's negative, negative, negative.'

My first contact with Julien is a long-distance call from Sydney. His voice is dry and brittle, his tone mildly irritated. He tells me he's writing an autobiography so he can't reveal too much about what happened in South Africa. But the more he talks the less it seems to be a real possibility. 'I feel a bit down sometimes,' he sighs. 'It fluctuates a little bit.' He reveals that he didn't know what apartheid was; he was just a sportsman looking after his family – a familiar rebel refrain. 'I was overlooked, I was unemployed,' he adds, before asking me to 'give us a shout' when I'm in Trinidad.

Planning a meeting with Bernard Julien is an exacting science. The phone call response rate is about 25 per cent, and even when he does answer, he leaves open the possibility that he may pull out of any engagement.

Deryck Murray, a former diplomat to the UN and ex-chairman of the Trinidad and Tobago Transparency Institute, is a man you can rely on. The diminutive keeper with the trademark goatee beard was a mainstay of the all-conquering West Indian sides of the late 1970s and has remained a friend to Julien throughout his troubles. Warm and hospitable, he tees up a lunch for the three of us at the Queen's Park Club, the home of Trinidad cricket, but warns that he has been trying to organise a game of golf with Julien for the 'longest while' and that still hasn't eventuated.

The first signs are ominous. Phone calls go unanswered, and the message 'BJ is not available, please leave a message' becomes a regular source of frustration. A week out, he finally picks up and, although he sounds faint, conveys a somewhat unconvincing desire to keep our lunch date.

Scenic Queen's Park Oval, flanked as it is by the rugged hills of the Northern Range, was the backdrop to some of Julien's finest moments. It may be an exaggeration to say Geoffrey Boycott was Bernard Julien's bunny – he took the obdurate Englishman's wicket four times in 15 innings – but there's no doubt those dismissals stung Boycott more than most. In the fifth Test against England in March 1974 at Queen's Park, Boycott had laboured in typical fashion over six long hours for 99, when Julien tempted him on the on side with an inswinger that must have screamed 'century'. But as the ball moved off the wicket, it gathered in pace, and despite catching the full face of Boycott's glancing bat, the speed of the ball propelled it within Murray's arc, allowing the keeper to pull off a spectacular diving catch. It's the all-rounder's most memorable wicket.

It was almost a rerun of Boycott's 97 at The Oval the previous year, which had terminated in another leg-side catch to Murray off Julien. The Trinidadian's wide-angled run-up – it almost seemed as if he was tearing in from mid-on or mid-off – on characteristic stiff legs, enabled him to maximise slant at the moment of delivery. 'Boycott never seemed comfortable against left-arm medium-pacers,' Murray says. 'You didn't have to be quick. Just swinging the ball in. So we always knew Bernard and

Sobers would have a chance with him. In that match Boycott made 99 in the first innings and a century in the second so he was denied two hundreds. Whenever he sees me and Bernard, that's how he greets us, remembering that.'

The Queen's Park bar waitress has brought two orders of Cajun chicken to the table, a fruit juice for Murray and a Carib beer for me. Julien hasn't arrived. I send him a WhatsApp message. 'Sorry couldn't ... sick' is the reply.

'I think Bernard's problem is psychological,' Murray says. 'Nervousness about meeting someone new. Bernard's always been a little irresponsible in terms of timing, regularity and responsibility. That's nothing new. That's from his school days. We tried to make him a coach at Queen's Park but it didn't work out. He didn't realise that you put up with a certain amount when you're a player producing, but you can't have 20 kids waiting for you to turn up and you don't turn up or you are half an hour late.'

* * *

The first half of Julien's career reads like a cricket fairy tale. Uber-talented all-rounder from sleepy seaside village wins scholarship to elite St Mary's College ... debuts for Trinidad at 18 ... gets fast-tracked into a Kent county contract by Colin Cowdrey ... belts a 90-minute century against England in his third Test. At ease bowling left-arm seam, swing, off spin and Chinaman, exhilarating in the field and dynamic with the bat, he's feted as the new Gary Sobers, even while playing alongside the old Gary Sobers.

He's also charismatic and good-looking. With his fashionable Afro and angular sideburns, he has the dashing air of martial arts movie star Jim Kelly or funk-soul icon Sly Stone. He's a magnet for women and a hero to men. He's the personification of calypso cricket. But there are hazards and distractions that come with being the pretty face. 'I think it's putting it mildly to say that sometimes you wondered whether women weren't his real priority,' Murray says. It was a common perception.

When Wes Hall was West Indies team manager in the 1980s, middle-order batsman Gus Logie remembers the legendary paceman observing that Julien would have been the world's greatest all-rounder ... if only he'd been born ugly. And it's said that West Indies captain Clive Lloyd often moved Julien around the field to interrupt his flirtations with women in the crowd and keep him focused on the game at hand.

Barbadian all-rounder Franklyn Stephenson, Julien's room-mate on the first rebel tour to South Africa, remembers the difficulty of having to sidestep his team-mate's female conquests in the morning. 'Bernard Julien is a legend,' he says. 'A very, very handsome guy as well. He had a lot of attention but sharing a room with him you would have a lot of girls in your way.'

During the 1975/76 West Indies campaign in Australia, the tourists began to embrace the commercialisation of the game, appearing in a cheesy calypso jingle for Brut 33 shampoo. Of course, Julien, a natural in front of the camera, was chosen for lead vocal: 'New ball bowler's swinging late/though his hair is looking great/use Brut 33 Shampoo, batsman lbw.'

In studio rehearsal footage, Julien catches the eye in a flamboyant brown and white patterned, wide-collar shirt. Lean and smooth-faced, he's the star attraction in a team full of stars. And if he appeared to crave the limelight a little too much at this point, it didn't seem to matter. He could still back it up on the pitch.

Already he had an imposing highlights reel: an explosive Test century at Lord's, 5-57 against England in Barbados, a dominant role in West Indies' 1975 World Cup success. He also had recognition from his countrymen in the form of the nation's second highest honour, a gold Chaconia medal for 'meritorious service'.

But the 1975/76 series Down Under would prove a turning point. Billed as an unofficial world championship, the West Indies, unable to cope with the menacing pace of Lillee and Thomson, were duly hammered 5-1. Julien's contribution wasn't insubstantial: 11 wickets at 27.55 and 124 runs at 31 in three Tests. He would have played more but for a broken finger sustained fending off a Thomson lifter in the fourth Test. Images of him courageously clubbing one-handed boundaries offered rare consolation for disappointed fans back in the Caribbean.

But the issues facing West Indian cricket were bigger than Julien's crushed digit or bravery under fire. Lloyd understood that pace underpinned Australia's smashing triumph. Max Walker and Gary Gilmour had ably supported the Lillee and Thomson bouncer barrage. The constant onslaught, littered with broken bones, had shattered the Windies' confidence.

It was a formula Lloyd would seek to replicate. He had Andy Roberts, the inscutable Antiguan with the lethal bouncer, and young Jamaican Michael Holding had been all promise and tears in Australia, but he was still short of the kind of pace quartet that could threaten the world. Julien had to perform, or face being subsumed by a snarling four-headed monster. Calypso cricket was about to be eclipsed by something harder and much less photogenic. There would be little room in the new regime for an ambidextrous playboy all-rounder.

In his first eight Tests, Julien's record was stellar: 392 runs at 43.55; 23 wickets at 28, but in his last 16, the stats told a different story: 474 runs at 24.94 and 27 wickets at 45.33. Clearly, he hadn't maintained a standard that would allow him time to remould his game in the image of a fast-bowling hitman.

Yet, initially, Julien had seemed to thrive on the unreal expectation that he would inherit Gary Sobers's mantle. But when results didn't go his way it forced an uncomfortable level of introspection.

Murray witnessed his team-mate's turmoil: 'There will never be another Gary Sobers, in the same way there will never be another Don Bradman,' he says. 'I suppose if you're a target of that, you start believing it, and when it wasn't happening it made him question himself. I noticed the inconsistency of his performance, not only from one day to the other, but from one spell to the next. People with less natural talent performed better than him, but it was not that they had improved, it was that Bernard was not performing to his maximum. When selecting teams, you go with the performers, not with the potential that is not being fulfilled.'

Julien would play his last Test just days after turning 27.

* * *

After lunch, I send Julien a WhatsApp text – by now his phone pick-up rate is below 20 per cent – wish him better health and propose a catch-up. His response: 'Try my best to.'

Conversations with Queen's Park Club members suggest he could be staying in Valsayn, an upscale residential area four miles east of the centre of Port of Spain. I offer to meet him there. He hangs up on my phone call.

* * *

In Caribbean folklore, Trinidad is the party island. Every year, carnival draws thousands of revellers from around the region. It's said that if Trinidadians are not celebrating carnival, they are probably getting ready for it. The festival's drug of choice is 'rum', the local word for all types of alcohol. A 2015 Pan-American/World Health Organisation report found that Trinidad and Tobago had the highest rate of booze consumption in the Americas.

Like his fellow citizens, Julien loved to drink. But some observers believed he indulged too much and too often. There was a history of alcohol abuse in his family, and when he played in England, he was known by some as 'Ale Man'. But he was hardly Robinson Crusoe. Alcohol is the currency of celebration across the cricketing world, and the West Indians were renowned for their liberal intake. Yet with his position in the side under increasing scrutiny, tolerance for a hungover full-toss or long-hop was low.

Julien's final appearance in an official West Indies cap was in an ODI against Pakistan in March 1977. He was still capable of pulling off the spectacular – his catch to dismiss Zaheer Abbas certainly impressed the CANA reporter: 'The athletic Julien leapt high in goalkeeper fashion to bring off a magnificent catch at short backward square.' But the man who delivered the ball from a bloody great height was ODI debutant Joel Garner. Ultra-tall and menacing, Garner had a natural flair for bruising batsmen's ribcages. The other debutant was the burly Guyanese Colin Croft. He had a similar knack for rattling ribs. Lloyd's four-prong vision was slowly taking shape.

Even so, Julien was still an integral part of the West Indies set-up. Sure, his Test output was inconsistent – he played in only one of the five-Test series against Pakistan that year – but his all-round skills could certainly be utilised in the burgeoning one-day arena.

When the West Indies signed en masse to WSC later that year, Julien was part of the defection. He had reservations; administrator Gerry Gomez and WICBC president Jeffrey Stollmeyer, virtual godfathers of Trinidad cricket, were huge supporters of his, but the colonial-era cricket establishment across the Caribbean wouldn't be able to prevent the inevitable rush to professionalism.

Checking the West Indies Supertest averages for the two seasons of WSC makes for sobering reading. Julien failed to appear in any of the 11 matches against the Australia XI and World XI. With Wayne Daniel vying with Garner and Croft to partner Holding and Roberts there was little room for Julien's stuttering heroics. On the few occasions that selectors turned to a jack of all trades, big-hitting Bajan medium-pacer Collis King was preferred. Julien had some success wearing the magenta flannels of the Windies' International Cup side, earning a place in the historic first day-night one-dayer at the SCG on 28 November 1978, but he also spent time slogging around rural Australia in the Country Cup, an exhibition series for squad leftovers.

Julien's reputation hadn't been enhanced by WSC. Confirmation of his reduced standing came when the 1979 World Cup squad was named. King snaffled the all-rounder's spot and Malcolm Marshall, a young paceman with a lightning run-up and skidding bouncer, padded out the fearsome pace troupe of Garner, Roberts, Holding and Croft. There would be no place for the 1975 World Cup winner.

Julien was also bereft of a county contract as Kent had decided to part ways with their Caribbean import. In a telling statement, they maintained it had nothing to do with Julien's allegiance to WSC.

The next three years were tough on Julien. Despite banking a windfall from WSC – Carenage residents still remember the shiny new Toyota Corolla he brought back from Australia – his first-class outings were limited to, at best, four matches in the Shell Shield per year. In 1980, he was 29 and supposedly at the peak of his powers as a professional cricketer, but his days of gracing the international stage were already over.

Gus Logie hails from the small village of Sobo in the south-west of Trinidad. The tiny right-hand batsman and brilliant cover fieldsman carved a niche for himself as a mostly reliable but unspectacular run-gatherer in the Viv Richards-led Windies sides of the late 1980s. Ten years Julien's junior, he'd grown up admiring the all-rounder's on-field and off-field achievements. 'For us young guys, he was one of the guys you wanted to emulate in some way. He had that star quality. The way he walked, the way he talked, the way he did things with grace and panache. One of the guys you would pay any amount of money to come see him perform.'

He and Julien first played together in the 1980 Shell Shield, but it was a dismal campaign for the senior man. The CANA reporter previewing Trinidad's Easter weekend game against Jamaica wrote: 'The once ebullient Julien appears to have lost his sparkle and looked woefully out of touch against Barbados', calling his bowling 'unpenetrative'. He wouldn't appear at all in the 1980/81 season.

'To him, it was disappointing,' Logie says. 'There was a little spell where he was off the game. Here was this guy who had all this ability and talent. When you think you are in your prime and you expect something in return and it's just not happening. It was a transitional period from being at the top of his game and then not being able to showcase his talent to the wider world. It was a difficult time for him.'

But Logie was still a believer. As were his team-mates. Before the 1981/82 season, he says they attempted to lure Julien back into first-class cricket, visiting him where he was living in Diego Martin in the north-east of the island and encouraging him to return. The ploy worked. But to some it only revealed the character flaws at the centre of Julien's personality.

Internationally renowned Trinidad-based cricket commentator Fazeer Mohammed sees Julien's demise as an indictment of the Caribbean macho stereotype. 'Julien preferred people to come to him rather than him going to you. He was frustrated with the game, but you have to beg him to come back. It would fuel his ego because they begged him to come back. He always wanted to give the impression that he was too cool to care. You have to understand the environment he came from, and that still exists across parts of the Caribbean. The whole Caribbean macho man thing. It's typical about the Caribbean male because they only want to hear the positives. They don't want introspection. They don't want knowledge of their own faults.'

For a while Julien's comeback bore fruit. The sparkle had returned. Against Jamaica at Queen's Park in March 1982 he took a career-high 9-97, the second-best return in Shell Shield history, making full use of overcast conditions that, according to the CANA reporter, were 'made to order for his swing bowling'. His game figures of 10-109, his sole ten-wicket haul in first-class cricket, earned him the man of the match award. But in the following match against the Windward Islands in Grenada, he was forced to retire hurt after ducking into a Winston Davis bouncer. His season haul of 21 wickets at 20.09 was bettered by only one established Test player, Andy Roberts, but the West Indian selectors had long ago closed the door on a recall to the Test side.

Just 32, and without a professional contract, he would be an easy target for Bacher and Pamensky's big-money plays later that year. 'It was the only option I had,' Julien told me during our stilted phone conversation. 'I didn't think there would be consequences. I had no idea there would be a life ban. Family and friends supported me.'

Although there was sympathy from the general public for his decision to join the South African rebel tour, the official government response was damning. Foreign Minister Basil Ince told a press conference: 'They are mercenaries fighting the cause of apartheid on the backs and blood of black people of South Africa.' He even floated the idea of the rebels having to apply for a special visa to re-enter the country. Julien was stripped of his Chaconia medal, as was rebel captain Lawrence Rowe, who had been awarded it in an honorary capacity. Julien's government coaching jobs were gone, too.

In South Africa, Julien would confront the same selection problems he'd faced in the Caribbean. To counter Springbok batting colossi Pollock and Richards, captain Rowe settled on his own four-prong pace attack of Barbadians Sylvester Clarke, Ezra Moseley, Hartley Alleyne and Franklyn Stephenson. Julien felt that he was harshly treated because he was the only Trini in the squad, but in reality he was a casualty of the ubiquitous fashion for fast bowling batteries.

Room-mate Stephenson was sympathetic. 'From his point of view he definitely didn't get picked enough. He wasn't at his peak. I had set myself a goal in the first leg of the tour to be that third seamer. I saw it as Sylvester Clark, Moseley and myself. I saw myself bowling holding spells to let them come back. Bernard was probably a little past his best.'

Yet he could still swing the ball prodigiously. 'I remember facing him in the nets and he was amazing,' Stephenson says. 'He bowled me four big outswingers over the wicket, and the ball was getting closer and closer to the edge. I wanted to hit him over extra cover. Halfway through the shot I had to get my bat out of the way. He's bowled me a massive inswinger and it came back and bowled me.'

Perhaps as a result of not being on the selectors' radar, some team-mates said Julien seemed uninterested and had 'come to collect', the phrase used to describe squad members who appeared more interested in their fat pay cheques than beating the South Africans.

Off the field, as usual, Julien was a huge drawcard. Apart from the bevy of women Stephenson remembers the all-rounder entertaining, Julien, a smooth-talking and worldly Test veteran, was often the centre of social events. Ray Wynter's snaps of a party at Joe Pamensky's house in Johannesburg show him dressed casually in a dark red shirt and blue jeans, holding court to a gaggle of adoring young white men and women. In *Windies Whirlwind*, the documentary of the second tour, there's footage of the rebels on a flight to Cape Town. Typically, the camera zooms in on Julien and paceman Hartley Alleyne, another flamboyant character, as they lap up the hospitality.

Although his only 'Test' outing was average – he had match figures of 1-82 and 51 runs for once out – younger players such as Surrey batsman Monte Lynch appreciated the time he spent with them passing on the benefits of his vast experience. It pointed to a future role as a coach. The problem was finding an opportunity when he finally came home.

Trinidad authorities had been vociferous in their condemnation of the BCA for allowing Bajan rebels to play club cricket; they were hardly going to permit their own rebel to coach. Nor could Julien count on the support of the union movement, which had vehemently backed the rights of players to improve their livelihoods with WSC; now they were at the forefront of the anti-apartheid struggle. And unlike in England or Australia, retiring to the cushioned comfort of the commentary box wasn't an option for West Indian cricketers, where big-money TV rights deals were still decades off.

'It was a difficult time,' Julien told me. There were rumours that the money he'd earned was squandered helping family members and servicing his twin demons of women and booze. There was also his natural tendency to withdraw during difficult times, an expectation that because of his status as an ex-Test cricketer, he deserved patronage.

'He carried himself in a way that suggests he felt everyone owed him something,' Fazeer Mohammad says. 'A sense of entitlement. This created a lot of ill-feeling in his own mind, because he felt ignored by the Trinidad public. The story of Bernard Julien and his decline isn't so much about him going to South Africa and playing with the rebels, it was more about his personality. Not reaching out to the public to earn their sympathy.'

In Carenage there's no such cynicism. At the western end of the village, the Alcoa bauxite transfer plant spills into the Gulf of Paria. To the east, the Western Main Road snakes alongside the coast past the new Fishing Centre, a couple of Chinese restaurants and plaques advertising a fisherman's fete till it reaches the health centre on the corner of Constabulary Street. On the opposite corner is a car park where the Julien family home used to be.

I have chartered a taxi here in a last-ditch effort to locate Julien, who is no longer answering my calls. I don't want to hound a cancer survivor, but I do want to understand his journey.

Further up the street is St Peters Catholic Church, a low-slung, late 1960s construction, which replaced the original church that Julien worshipped in, which was toppled in an earthquake. Its white metal gates are open and, as if on cue, a tall middle-aged man wearing a camouflage Adidas T-shirt emerges from across the street. He also wears a permanently disturbed expression, and claims to be Julien's cousin. His name is Terry Joseph, and he offers to help – for a price.

Terry says he saw Julien two weeks ago at 'a golf club' and he was 'good but hoarse when he speaks'. He points to the hall next to the church and recalls Julien batting on its smooth concrete floor where, according to Terry, the ball would come on faster, providing more of a challenge for the ambitious young teenager.

'He used to put 25c on the wicket and I would bowl to him,' he boasts.

He remembers Julien's football skills: 'He had the distinction of being the only guy to score direct from a corner – a left-footer' and says we should visit the Bernard Julien Ground, a local sporting field named in his honour.

Before we leave, Gizelle, a church worker, adds her own Julien observation: 'He was a lovely boy,' she beams with local-lad-made-good pride.

The ground, a five-minute walk away, is arid and sandy with a small tin-roofed grandstand and light-blue painted clubhouse. A boy in a replica Arsenal shirt is kicking a soccer ball with his mates, but there's no signage suggesting this is indeed the Bernard Julien Ground. Terry assures me that's what the locals call it, even though a quick Google search reveals it's named the Carenage Recreation Grounds. What's more important, he says, is the recently erected wall of fame on the far side of the ground, a badge of honour for this small village of no more than a few thousand.

The slogan 'success is a process' greets viewers from the top of the wall and underneath are attached brass-colour plates with the names of Carenage's top sportspeople. In the cricket section, Julien's name takes equal billing with a former Trinidad wicketkeeper and an up-and-coming female batter. There's no indication that Julien is the only person from Carenage to play Test cricket for the West Indies. Either side of the plaques, 'role models' is painted in blue. Julien, the man whose name is on the honours board at Lord's, is one of them – the man whose fridge, some friends say, is captive to hard alcohol and little else.

Terry says I should visit Julien's youth cricket captain, who lives in the lush, palm-streaked hills overlooking the ground. Getting there is a steep climb up stairs with no rails past random sheets of corrugated iron, crowing roosters and blackened concrete homes in various states of Saturday morning activity. Halfway up, Terry turns seaward and points to a couple of clumps of green he says are called Five Islands. Apparently, Julien used to swim seven miles there and back to strengthen his shoulders.

Despite being in his 60s, Lennox Ryan still has echoes of a sportsman's physique. Shirtless and barefoot, his naked torso reveals the kind of broad chest and upper body that Julien must have exercised so hard to achieve. 'We trained a lot together before he made the West Indies team,' Ryan says. 'We used to run and swim and row together. He was always a special individual in the sense he could do things most players couldn't do. He could throw with both hands. He was a natural ball player. Any ball game. When I was captain of Carenage United, he made a century in the morning between nine and one o'clock, then he left and went to QRC [Queen's Royal College in Port of Spain] to play for St Marys and made a century in the afternoon.'

Why did his career tank so quickly? 'I think he lost interest. When players get on top of their game, they don't train as hard, and younger players coming up train harder to get into the team.'

What role did alcohol play? 'When he was called to Kerry Packer, I remember he was in no shape then. He wasn't even playing cricket. He was drinking too much. He went through this up and down, up and down, then he had wife problems. Definitely depression. That caused the slide.'

Terry, face twisted in concentration, says he recalls Julien opening a bar called St Peters down near the water after he returned from South Africa, but Ryan doesn't remember it existing. He does remember the controversy that Julien's decision to throw his lot in with the rebels caused in the village. 'It was 50-50 here ... he was in financial trouble at the time.'

He also remembers Julien's visceral appeal to women. 'He was a real handsome human being, so the girls are going to run into his corner. I think he got too distracted. When you start to run girls and things like that, something will have to give.'

Terry accepts TT$40 for the ad-hoc guided tour through Julien's Carenage past, money he will spend on breakfast, but before we part ways on the Haig Street side of the recreation ground, he gives me a tip-off: his famous cousin is staying at Magazine Phase 2 in Cocorite. It will prove to be yet another red herring.

* * *

When Julien went public with his battle with throat cancer in the early 2000s he'd already been accepted back into the cricket establishment. Because he hadn't ditched his homeland like many of the rebels throughout the Caribbean, there was a degree of sympathy for him and his desire to give back through coaching.

He became a Trinidad selector but his tenure as coach continued to be dogged by periods of absenteeism, and his financial situation dipped further. At one point, he resorted to begging old cricket friends for money.

Stephen Gomez was one of them. 'I remember in the old pavilion at Queen's Park, prior to 2007, I ran into Bernard and he needed money to go somewhere, and he was reduced to asking people, and that's when I realised he was in a state of decline. The amount of money he asked for, which I did give him, was a substantial sum in terms of transport. It was more than just transport. When someone is reduced to that level you don't want to start inquiring and prying.'

Although he'd beaten the cancer, morbid thoughts were still gnawing away at him. In late 2010, according to a report in the *Trinidad Guardian*, he began experiencing severe migraine headaches and sleepless nights, but doctors and specialists in both Port of Spain and Miami were unable to find anything wrong with him. 'The whole problem was going from here to there and taking all these tests and everything was coming up negative and I was still sick,' Julien said.

He lost 11kg (24lb) in six months. 'The biggest challenge was I found myself at home with all these negative thoughts of dying crossing my mind. During that time I got closer to the Lord, prayed a lot and my wife was very supportive.'

But when long-time friend, former West Indies batsman Ricardo Powell, himself often referred to as a 'wasted talent', approached the Trinidad health ministry on Julien's behalf, the ailing all-rounder was awarded $79,595 to cover his health bills. His happy knack for being bailed out of sticky situations prevailed again.

Since then there have been sporadic bursts of vigorous activity. There are press pictures of him at a Digicel coaching clinic in St Vincent, arm wrapped around the man whose shadow haunted his cricket career, Gary Sobers, as they dispense wisdom alongside Ramnaresh Sarwan. When he's feeling well, he plays golf and seniors cricket with the same panache of yesteryear. In 2011 he was inducted into the First Citizens Sports Foundation Hall of Fame alongside Brian Lara and footballer Dwight Yorke.

There have also been dark moments. Reports that he needs someone to caretake his government-subsidised apartment because he can't clean it himself. Reports that a bottle of Johnny Walker is his best mate. That his peripatetic lifestyle is a result of a failure to keep up with rental payments. Among his friends, the fear is that the one-time glamour boy of West Indian cricket may be shuffling towards an inglorious end.

It's a familiar trope in the sporting world: the wayward young genius who gorged himself on the sweet flesh of fame and then spent the rest of his life suffering for it.

It's hard not to feel sympathy. Logie does: 'When you look back and think about other players who didn't have an ounce of the ability he had, and they're making millions of dollars, sometimes it's not difficult to sit there and wonder what could have been. It's human nature for him to feel that way.'

Fazeer Mohammad doesn't: 'He was a tremendous talent who squandered that talent, because he more or less felt he was God's gift to cricket and didn't need to do much, and he more or less allowed himself to become dependent on everyone else after his playing days. And South Africa didn't help. The difficulty you have in getting a proper dialogue with him tells a real story.'

On the cab ride to Piarco International Airport, we pass more dusty cricket fields like the one in Carenage, recreation grounds that cricket writer C. L. R. James wrote once dotted every community in Trinidad. It's still fair to say that cricket looms large in the imagination of the people.

It's no surprise then that the taxi driver, a man in his 60s, has his own Bernard Julien story. He says he faced him last year in a seniors game at Lange Park, a residential area south of Port of Spain, and the former champion took a freakish one-handed catch off his own bowling to dismiss him. He says Julien wasn't that quick anymore but he would 'outsmart you'.

He certainly outsmarted me. In one of my last WhatsApp texts I sent him a photo attachment of his old rebel team-mates Collis King and David Murray drinking rum in Bridgetown a few days before, hoping the nostalgic good times vibe might persuade him to see me. 'Let u know' was his response. He never did.

Albert Padmore

'There are still people who shy away from me'

ON A Calcutta hotel bed at 3am, second-string wicketkeeper David Murray sat, legs crossed and began to cry. His sobbing woke room-mate Albert Padmore. 'Paddy, you will never be the West Indies off-spinner,' Murray wept, 'and I will never be the number one keeper.'

It sounded like a daft, witching hour premonition, but Padmore knew not to take his sensitive friend's comments lightly. 'I said, "D, you gotta be kidding me."'

It was Padmore's first overseas tour with the West Indies side, the prelude to a long Test career. Or so he hoped.

'Let me tell you something,' Murray explained to him. 'They want to play four fast bowlers before they play a spinner.' He was accurately predicting the advent of a four-prong pace battery two years before it became accepted West Indies policy. And he wasn't finished. 'You have a very good arm ball,' he said to Padmore, 'and many people cannot pick it. Our keeper is not picking it up either – and he is not going to be exposed, because on a good day you could cause a problem.' That gloveman, the highly respected vice-captain Deryck Murray, was a cornerstone of the West Indies revival under bespectacled captain Clive Lloyd. An immovable force.

Murray and Padmore's conversation took place on the 1974/75 tour of India. True to Murray's forecast, Padmore didn't play a

Test. Now 74, the memory of his team-mate's early morning lament joins the dots on a two-Test career strained by limited opportunity and the quirks of history.

If Padmore was unfashionable on the pitch, cultivating a craft few in the upper echelons of West Indies cricket would have time for anymore, he was most definitely fashionable off it. English fans recall the oxblood colour leather trench coat and suede baker boy cap he sported during his stint at Marske-by-the-Sea Cricket Club in the early 1980s and its striking impact on conservative locals. In an official team photograph of the first West Indian rebel side snapped in early 1983, Padmore's full-blown Afro and flared white slacks stand out among the more restrained haircuts and attire of his team-mates.

He was also renowned for his taste in music and the huge ghetto blaster regularly perched on his shoulder during international tours. Former Australian captain Ian Chappell doesn't remember too much about Padmore's bowling, but he has excellent recall of the Bajan's monster sound system. 'It was bloody big,' Chappell says. 'One of the West Indies guys told me he paid more for his sound system at home than he did for his house! He had the ghetto blaster he used to carry with him around Australia blaring out at an airport and I'll never forget Ashley Mallett walked over to him and with typical Mallett dry humour, tapped him on the shoulder opposite to the ghetto blaster, and said, "Excuse me Albert, do you like music?"'

Seated in the alfresco area of the boutique Hudson Hotel's Library Bar in midtown Manhattan, Albert Leroy Padmore is laughing at Chappell's anecdote. Prince of Wales check trousers, chunky Invicta diver's watch and fawn sweater indicate a man still possessed of sartorial smarts and, unlike his old friend Murray, his fine-featured face isn't ravaged by hard living. This isn't the ruined rebel tourist of popular myth.

'David Murray was a dresser,' Padmore says. He clearly still feels a lot of respect and affection for the 19-Test veteran. 'He was so smooth. When I was first selected, I roomed with David.

We would save our money on tour and just go buy Italian sports coats and threads. Only Italian gear.'

Padmore says the area he grew up in – St James, on the leeward side of Barbados – was always creating its own trends, in part because of its proximity to up-scale hotels and the mix of well-heeled international tourists and rich white locals.

Music was central to their lives. 'David Murray and myself … we were into it in a big way. We liked soul, the O'Jays, the Dells. We carried music all the time with us.'

It wasn't until 1976 that the full ramifications of Murray's prophecy were realised. And as with WSC and the rebel tours of South Africa later, Padmore would find himself front and centre at one of the great turning points in West Indies cricket. Without the lanky Barbadian, the Caribbean pace platoons that brutalised Test nations for a decade and a half wouldn't exist. No Roberts, Holding, Garner, Croft. No Marshall, Walsh, Patterson, Ambrose.

There's little doubt that the sobering events at Queen's Park Oval, Port of Spain, on 12 April 1976 turned the philosophical tide against spin bowling for generations. The third Test was Albert Padmore's West Indies debut, at the ripe old age of 29. With world-record-holding wicket-taker Lance Gibbs pensioned off against his will, Padmore, whose action was likened to the Guyanese great, got his chance. The previous Test, also held at Queen's Park, had given enough assistance to India's legendary triumvirate of Bedi, Chandrasekhar and Venkataraghavan to convince the West Indies selectors that spin, the flavour of the moment, could fashion a victory. Imtiaz Ali, a promising 21-year-old leggie from the northern suburbs of Port of Spain was duly awarded his first West Indies blazer, and another local, left-arm orthodox spinner Raphick Jumadeen, retained his position from the second Test. They had a mere five caps between them.

In hindsight it seems ludicrous that the West Indies selectors believed that their three Test tyros could compete with the celebrated subcontinental masters in a stadium heaving with a sizeable chunk of Trinidad spectators of East Indian descent. But when Clive Lloyd set a world-record target of 406 on a pitch where India's spinners had taken all 16 West Indies wickets to fall, he felt justifiably confident in his side's ability to stage a crushing victory.

In the first innings, Padmore had bowled impressively, luring Indian danger man Mohinder Amarnath into a stumping trap with his arm ball, and prompting Tony Cozier to write that the debutant 'turned the ball appreciably and varied his line cleverly'.

But Amarnath wouldn't be fooled again. As the pitch slowed, the Indians found their batting feet and ground out the most unlikely of wins with six wickets to spare, surpassing the heroic feats of Don Bradman's 1948 Australians along the way. Lloyd was so exasperated by his spinning trio's lack of penetration that he even bowled himself for six overs. Their collective inexperience had been exposed at the highest level.

Padmore concedes that his fear of stuffing up in his first Test discouraged him from giving the ball air and attacking the batsmen enough. His figures of 47 overs, ten maidens, 0-98 betrayed his stinginess, but the cost was a lack of wickets. 'In Trinidad you have to change the way you bowl because the wicket is slower,' he says. 'You couldn't push the ball, you had to loop it. In the early stages you're feeling your way around. You don't have that knowledge. You're giving it your best shot, but you can't really let your hair down because you want to be in that range.'

He was unaware of Lloyd's building rage. 'Clive was supportive. There were a couple of chances at backward point – the pocket – that could have changed the game. A wicket early boosts your confidence and you can start to do your thing, but when you're not getting wickets you start to be a little conservative.'

In the losing dressing room, a disappointed Lloyd addressed his weary spinners in a tone of biting sarcasm. 'Gentlemen, I gave you 400 runs to bowl at and you failed to bowl out the opposition,' he said. 'How many runs must I give you in the future to make sure that you get the wickets?' It wasn't a question any of the bowlers could answer.

The West Indies captain would never risk a spin attack again. In the next Test, at Sabina Park, 'retired hurt' and 'absent hurt' were the most frequent modes of dismissal, as fast men Michael Holding and Wayne Daniel wrought bloody carnage on a terrified Indian batting line-up. The pace age was born.

If Lloyd was done with spin attacks in 1976, he wasn't done with solitary finger-spinners. Over the next decade, a succession of hopeful tweakers would fill that invidious position in the all-conquering West Indies side, more often as a stopgap, so his high-energy pacemen could recharge their batteries for a few overs before the onslaught began again.

Following the home India series that year, the West Indies embarked on a 30-game tour of England. The five-match Test series was given extra zest when England captain Tony Greig told the BBC's *Sportsnight* programme that he intended to make the tourists 'grovel', an insult with obvious slavery connotations that only served to ratchet up the visitors' hunger for victory. It also ramped up their speed bloodlust. Holding, Roberts, Daniel and Holder – the first West Indies four-prong incarnation – bowled 647.1 Test overs between them, Jumadeen and Padmore just 31. Padmore was picked for the third Test at Old Trafford in place of Jumadeen after taking 6-101 against Derbyshire, but bowled only three overs as Holding, Roberts and Daniel mangled England. Such was their dominance that just before the first of Padmore's 18 deliveries, a fan streamed on to the field to present English opener John Edrich with a cartoonish wide bat so that he might have a chance against the quick men.

Although his Test output was limited, Padmore topped the tour bowling averages. If he was frustrated by the lack of opportunity, he's not keen to apportion blame to others. 'What I would say to my friends was that every time I played was a Test – a test of my ability to perform at this level, even if I wasn't on the Test team.'

Nor does he bear any grudge towards Clive Lloyd. He says, as is the case with any touring side, a player's relationship with the squad's most powerful figure was heavily scrutinised by team-mates to see whether anyone was sneaking an advantage. It was also a source of gentle banter. 'We used to say be careful with him. We used to talk among ourselves all the time. Some of the guys used to say, "I see you with Cappy [captain]. You're very tight with the Cappy." I thought he was cool.'

It was the tour manager, Clyde Walcott, a Test batting legend, who did his head in. 'I had taken the most wickets but, at the end of the tour, Walcott said to me if my hand hadn't dropped in my action I would have taken more wickets. Normally it was on top of my delivery.'

It was a fair though curious call. 'Why would he wait till the end of the tour to tell me that?'

It wouldn't be the last time the notoriously picky Walcott planted seeds of doubt in aspiring cricketers. Walcott was a product of the BCA and the Spartan Cricket Club, which was formed as an elite club for middle-class black players in 1894. Padmore says that a lot of the unnecessary hurdles he faced in his early career can be traced back to the strict social divisions within Barbados society, which played out in the way cricket was organised in the former British colony.

Along with Spartan, Empire, a club for working-class black men, and the two white clubs, Wanderers and Pickwick, formed the backbone of the BCA. To many underprivileged black men, especially from poor rural areas, it was a closed shop.

The formation of the BCL by journalist Mitchie Hewitt in 1937 was a watershed for the sport in Barbados. It enabled those same men the opportunity to play organised cricket, and the game flourished across the island. Soon there were more than 100 teams in the league, and it would count West Indian greats Garfield Sobers, Everton Weekes, Conrad Hunte, Seymour Nurse, Sylvester Clarke and Collis King among its alumni. Its motto, *Non nobis sed patriae* (Not for self, but country), spoke to its breadth of vision.

But the BCA still ran the game. By the mid-1960s, as independence from Britain loomed, the racial element had mostly disappeared from its clubs, but the rigid class structure that filtered members was still in place and, despite its success, there was a tendency to sneer at the BCL as village cricketers rather than a breeding ground for the nation's best.

As a youth in the early 1960s, Padmore had enjoyed the intense local rivalry of BCL cricket, but he says the transition to the elite BCA competition was a 'nightmare'. In his first match against Spartan – the club of David Murray, Wes Hall and, of course, Walcott – he was sledged relentlessly. A wag in the crowd joked after his first delivery: 'He's hopping like Gibbs, but when he leaves here he'll be like Mrs Tibbs,' a reference to a nanny goat from the Royal Reader English textbooks popular in Barbados schools at the time.

Not that it bothered him. Padmore captured three wickets and tied down an end. It was the walk from Queen's Park Oval into Bridgetown to catch a bus home that proved more troublesome. He was followed by an abusive spectator who, Padmore says, was paying out on him because he was a BCL product. 'I couldn't really reply because he would just say it was what you'd expect from a BCL player.'

When Padmore reached Wharf Road, he was so disillusioned that he felt like chucking his kit bag into the Caribbean Sea. He realised that no matter what he did on the pitch, to many in Barbados he was a second-class cricket citizen.

He remembers a net session in Guyana when only the intervention of West Indies medium-pacer Vanburn Holder secured him a bowl and a Barbados game in Dominica, where an experienced team-mate told him he suffered from a complex. 'He tried to give the impression I shouldn't have been there,' Padmore says.

And despite Tony Cozier's praise of his Test debut, Padmore never felt that the famous Barbados commentator, a Wanderers veteran himself, believed in his ability or had his back. Not having a local cheer squad that could be heard above the din of inter-island rivalry was a significant drawback in the quest for West Indies selection. 'I'd be walking down the street and people would say negative things like, "If Cozier says he's not good, he's not good." Tony said this and Tony said that.'

But unlike his friend David Murray, who took criticism to heart, Padmore was resilient enough to withstand the put-downs. He attributes some of that mental toughness to his experience as an Anglican choirboy in his teen years and the discipline and capacity that singing gave him to shut out the world. The rest was sheer grit.

'David was a soft character in a sense,' Padmore says. 'My thing was: I was focused on doing something and I'll find the best way to do it. I never worried about criticism.'

In 1977, the technicolour temptations of WSC lured Padmore and the cream of the West Indies to Australia for their first taste of non-stop professional international cricket. That Padmore was invited showed that, regardless of the Caribbean's new-found reverence for pace, he was still the go-to spinner if and when required. And when required he performed: 4-102 against the World XI in Sydney, and during the WSC Caribbean leg in early 1979 exacting revenge on the ground that had stalled his career three years before by taking 6-81 at Queen's Park in Port of Spain.

'Paddy' or 'P' was also a popular dressing room figure – even if he was 12th man more often than not. A natural-born groomer, he'd practised cutting hair as a hobby in Barbados and, in the pavilion, Viv Richards et al would queue for a trim.

Yet in spite of his good Supertest form – and tonsorial talents – his name was nowhere to be seen when the official Test squad for the 1979/80 tour of Australia was announced later that year. He'd learned of the snub from Andy Roberts. 'He said, "You haven't done anything wrong, but they have a replacement for you,"' Padmore says.

That replacement turned out to be Roberts's Combined Islands team-mate Derick Parry, the man who'd filled the spinner's breach in the official West Indies side while Padmore played WSC. 'At that level it's having the right people like you as a player,' Padmore says.

There were political factors in motion as well. The squad was already chocka with WSC stars; selectors had to find ways to balance the ledger with players who'd stayed loyal to the establishment. Parry, a quality batsman, would now fill the frustrating token spinner role for the next couple of years. He was also eight years Padmore's junior.

At 32, the late starter looked like being an early finisher. But Padmore's attention to detail and astute cricket brain was still held in high esteem in Barbados, and in the 1979/80 Shell Shield season he succeeded veteran spinner David Holford as captain. It helped that he had the meanest fast-bowling attack on the planet at his disposal – Joel Garner, Malcolm Marshall, Wayne Daniel and Sylvester Clarke – and the best openers in Haynes and Greenidge, but a team of champions is no guarantee of success. It was Padmore who nurtured them into a champion team, winning two Shell Shields in three years.

Typically modest, he's underawed by the achievement. 'We had the cream of the crop,' he says. 'It was just another thing. In my neighbourhood I always ended up being the one up front when it came to organising the boys and youngsters in my area, so it wasn't something new.'

In the northern hemisphere summer, Padmore's spinning arsenal and distinctive fashion sense were on display as the club professional with Marske in the North Yorkshire and Southern Durham League. Cricket commitments had long since forced him to abandon his job in hospitality at the Sandy Lane Hotel near his home in St James, and it was while playing in Scotland with Stenhousemuir in 1982 that he first got word of a mooted rebel tour of South Africa. He wasn't interested; retirement and the quiet life coaching in Barbados were beckoning.

But tour promoter Gregory Armstrong, the former Bajan paceman, had been a team-mate at the Empire club and he sought to convince Padmore there was a role for him ... as a manager. He was, according to newspaper reports, in good company. Sir Garfield Sobers had also been sounded out but politely refused, having been the centre of controversy in 1970 when he accepted an offer to coach in white-ruled Rhodesia.

But Padmore says it was only when a group of Barbados players – Test all-rounder Collis King, batsman Alvin Greenidge and young pace bowler Ezra Moseley – paid him a visit that he changed his mind. They had each been approached and, according to Padmore, were keen to sign on, but didn't entirely trust Armstrong's intentions. Padmore's acceptance would help push them over the line. 'I was captain of Barbados, so we were tight. They said they would go if I went,' Padmore says.

He knew opportunities were limited for Barbados cricketers to make money out of the game – government coaching jobs were rare – and the selection logjam at the top of the powerful West Indies side was stalling careers. 'Most of the guys were not going to play for the West Indies anyway,' Padmore says. 'Most of them came through the BCL and didn't work outside of cricket, and we weren't paid to play for Barbados, so this was an opportunity to establish themselves.'

* * *

Persuading Padmore to speak was a difficult assignment. He likes to keep a low profile and his Facebook page is sprinkled with memes referencing black liberation icons such as Malcolm X, the Harlem Hellfighters, Marcus Garvey and Black Lives Matter. (Not an encouraging sign when you're a white author chasing content for a book centred on apartheid.) He is politically aware, and not impressed by Donald Trump. 'He represents the true side of America; what people had in their minds, but they never had the guts to say before.'

So how did he square his sympathy for universal black advancement with touring racist South Africa and pocketing a huge sum of money from a discredited regime? 'We saw it as an avenue to shine a light on what black people could do,' he says. 'There's no colour when it comes to talent.'

But the Azanian People's Organisation and the black-led SACB had expressly censured the rebel spectacle, insisting that any contact with South Africa was a slap in the face for the millions of black and coloured people still denied the vote and freedom of movement.

As manager, Padmore was keen to position his West Indies charges on what he saw as the right side of history. That meant walking a moral tightrope in condemning apartheid, while simultaneously enjoying its profits.

In a letter he sent to the BCA, which circulated around the world, he justified the tour's progress on the basis of the players' lack of financial opportunity within the game, which made it 'impracticable for any of us, from the standpoint of not only ourselves but of our families' to refuse the SACU's offer, and proffered a stern rebuke of the republic's discriminatory political system: 'We, and each of us, loathe apartheid as vehemently as, if not more than, the loudest and strongest opponents of that inhuman practice. We don't subscribe to the view that by playing in South Africa we will make the situation any worse for coloureds and blacks there.'

His main role was as an ambassador, representing the team at post-match functions and giving talks about Caribbean cricket culture and life back home. It was an opportunity for him to tamp down tensions.

At a reception in Port Elizabeth, staged by the town's Afrikaner mayor, Padmore cheekily pointed out that West Indies cricketers had long wanted to play against South Africa's top players. 'Some of our chaps who have played against them at county level rate them as being as talented as we are,' he was reported as saying.

He maintains that black students, who made a point of confronting and condemning the tourists early on, had their viewpoints changed when the rebels beat Transvaal, the top-ranking provincial side. He also dismisses claims made by critics that the tourists were granted honorary white status in order to visit areas normally off limits to black people. 'We never had any police protection walking around with us. We went any place all hours of the night. How could we be honorary whites and not have police protection 24/7?'

But he concedes that the rebels' freedom of movement was in stark contrast to the indigenous population's lack of it. 'I remember in a bar in Johannesburg, this group of black girls came in and said to us, "You know if you all weren't here, we could never be in here."'

In between tours, Padmore returned to Barbados, where, he says, the average man on the street was sympathetic to the rebels' cause. It was the upper echelons of society that were enraged, but not so much out of moral indignation as a sense of inverted class envy.

How dare these common sportsmen bypass their superiors. 'They saw it as we were thumbing our noses at the establishment. A bunch of cricketers who got themselves together as a unit, people who just play cricket, without any of the elite. That offended them.'

The BCA had originally banned the rebels from rejoining their clubs, but Padmore says the fear of what would happen if the popular Collis King wasn't allowed to play for YMPC triggered a back-flip. 'There would have been a riot,' he says. Padmore, who to this day jokingly maintains he never retired from cricket, turned out for Empire.

It was a smart move because on the second tour he was required to roll his arm over. Illness and Monte Lynch's contractual wavering put the squad under increased pressure, and vice-captain Alvin Kallicharran was keen for Padmore to step up. His best figures from three first-class matches were 3-103 against Northern Transvaal, but he suffered at the masterful hands of Graeme Pollock in Port Elizabeth, in what proved to be his last outing at the top level.

Back in St James with his wife and three children, Padmore sought to maximise his South African earnings but found business support was scarce. A car fanatic, he had an idea of starting a parts service but couldn't get anyone interested. He suspects it was because of his rebel connections. 'Up to this day there are still people who shy away from me … people I had a lot of confidence and respect for.'

The goodwill he'd built up over a lifetime on the island soured into suspicion. He'd entered a team of youngsters in the BCL, but on a game day was confronted by police who accused him of stealing grass clippings for rolling the wicket. He had, as he'd done on umpteen occasions, collected them from Sandy Lane Golf course where he worked all those years ago, but now he was trespassing.

And after one of his regular five-mile runs he returned to find his house surrounded by police searching for drugs. 'I barely even drank alcohol,' Padmore says. 'Something strange was going on. A lot of doors closed.'

A relative in Miami gave him an out. He owned a garage and was sourcing parts for the off-spinner's Volvo, but couldn't send them to Barbados, so Padmore flew over to collect them. There they discussed his troubles and agreed it was only a matter of time before the police pinned something on him. That same relative was expanding his business and suggested Padmore stay to help out. A new life in America was born. That was in 1986.

* * *

Beneath a crystal chandelier, which illuminates the few grey hairs on Padmore's remarkably youthful head of close-knit hair, and with a flashy Diesel-brand bracelet clasping his left wrist, the former Test off-spinner demonstrates his technique in front of the Hudson Hotel's terminally uninterested lobby staff. His bowling hand is high and perpendicular to the shiny floor – Clyde Walcott would be happy – but not even two glasses of Stella Artois lager can lift his leading left leg to the heights of yore.

The previous day I had travelled to the quaint suburban town of South Orange in New Jersey in what turned out to be an unsuccessful bid to meet him. The entrance to his two-storey timber house was festooned with violet and gold coloured balloons and other inflated paraphernalia celebrating teenage daughter Kiarra's graduation.

A dark stone Episcopalian church anchors one end of the street in faith and virtue, and tall trees shade the sidewalk. It's a respectable and diverse enclave.

Padmore works as a caddy at the nearby Shackamaxon Country Club. He chats with fellow rebel Collis King on WhatsApp every week and still keeps in contact with ailing all-rounder Bernard Julien, who phones him during our night in Manhattan.

Later that evening, we retreat to Masseria Dei Vini, a trendy Italian restaurant on 9th Avenue, for dinner. Padmore, the super-casual granddad, does not look out of place among the edgy, gourmet-savvy clientele. He orders the orecchiette noodles.

He's content with his lot, even if the politics of his adopted country continue to infuriate him. On the other hand, if he'd declined South Africa's advances nearly four decades ago, he may still be living on the island of his birth. Does that momentous decision ever cause him anguish? 'I'm not the kind of guy to go back and say I regret this or that,' he says in his softly spoken Bajan lilt. 'If I make a decision, I procrastinate a lot about it. I like to think things over in my mind so whenever I decide to do something I'm satisfied within myself this is the right way.'

I ask him about Julien, who eluded my determined efforts to interview him in Trinidad. Padmore says he can tell by his raspy voice that he's not the 'BJ' of old.

It troubles him that Richard Austin, Herbert Chang, Everton Mattis and David Murray had their lives shattered, at least in part, by their South African experiences. 'There's something you have to have inside you that protects you from doing certain things,' he says, trying to explain what separates those who fall through the cracks from those who don't. 'Some of us, we tend to fold under certain pressures. I guess when it seems like the whole world is against you, at some point everything starts to break down.'

Of Murray, the man who accurately forecast Padmore's career trajectory but could never quite regulate his own life trajectory, he says, 'David was a grandmother's boy like a lot of us. She was doing everything for him. He never really had to stand on his own legs.'

Nevertheless, he's still upbeat about the rebels' legacy and what he feels they achieved in terms of making cricket accessible to the black population in the republic. 'They started to see it as a game we can play, not just whites.'

He buys me a Baileys Irish Cream on the rocks and shares rebel anecdotes that the cricketing wasteland of New York has no right to hear. And for a little while, Padmore's spinning fingers are in control of the levers of history.

Monte Lynch

'He could drive you barmy'

IN 2010, former Surrey batsman Monte Lynch was interviewed by *The Times* newspaper for their 'best and worst' segment. Asked to nominate his career nadir, he selected his England debut, a second-ball run-out that preserved the wicket of his lumbering captain Mike Gatting. He also mentioned participation in South Africa with the rebel team. 'I didn't enjoy the tour one bit,' he says. 'A lot of us did not realise the severity of apartheid.' Almost a decade later, he's not so sure. 'I think it opened South African eyes and people in the government especially and said to them black people can compete with white people.'

But Lynch has more reason than most to resent the tour's impact. A promising, if rash, stroke-maker with a kamikaze-like approach to batting, the best years of his county career were spent serving out a rebel-induced four-year ban from international cricket that prevented him representing England. The cruel irony was that the lessons he'd learned in the art of high batsmanship from the likes of Lawrence Rowe and Alvin Kallicharran in South Africa were the very reasons for his success. Returning to The Oval armed with technical tips from the great masters on how to build an innings, he plundered 18 centuries over the next five county seasons. 'They spoke to me in a way I'd never been spoken to about cricket before,' Lynch, who was 25 at the time, says of Rowe and Kallicharran. 'You sit down and talk to Kalli about batting and you think you could bat with your eyes closed.'

But there are regrets. 'Because obviously when I came back I got hundreds ... people in England were saying to me, "Look, if you hadn't gone to SA you'd be playing for England now," but it was six of one, half a dozen of the other. I learned so much from what they said about the game.'

When he was finally given the opportunity to wear the Three Lions after the ban expired, he maintains that his best years were behind him. 'I was too old to play for England. I'd passed my use by date. They should have taken me off the shelf.'

The strange misfortune of Lynch's cricket career isn't so much that he represented his adopted country at a time when his batting prowess was on the wane, but that he found himself stranded in the middle of an international political struggle revolving around race. Because from an early age, in his homeland of Guyana, Lynch had been tilting at racial barriers.

Riven by tensions between the Afro-Caribbean and East Indian communities, the only English-speaking country on the South American continent had descended into full-blown race riots in 1964. By the time Lynch was 12 in 1970, voluntary segregation was the norm. His village of Anna Catherina, then part of the vast Leonora sugar estate just 15 miles from the capital Georgetown, was predominantly Afro-Caribbean in ethnic make-up but with East Indian enclaves. Living on a main road where businesses intersected, he was exposed to Chinese, Indian and Portuguese shopkeepers and their passing trade. His best friends were Asian. As a boy of Afro-Caribbean descent, it was a bold statement.

Professor Walter Persaud, a cultural studies academic based in Thailand, is a former schoolmate. He remembers a 'jolly, chubby' Lynch visiting his home in an exclusively Indian street to play backyard underarm cricket with a rubber ball. 'This was almost an invasion in the context of Guyana at the time,' he says. 'For Monte to have entered into our yard or street, he would have passed the test of being non-racial.' The Persauds' backyard was surrounded by sugar cane and the fence on the off side was so close to the pitch that only shots through midwicket past the storage room at square leg garnered rewards. That hitting arc, an arc of temptation for any right-hander, would be the source of much pleasure and pain for Lynch in later years.

Lynch says he had a terrible childhood. His mother, who he has a difficult relationship with, left for England in the mid-1960s, and his father followed a few years later. He spent his boyhood living with a local seamstress and visiting his grandparents in the bauxite mining town of Lyndel McKenzie in school holidays.

The day of 21 November 1971 is a pivotal day in Lynch's life. He can still remember the fog and gloom of Heathrow – and the unrelenting cold. 'I was standing there in a shirt, short trousers and high socks, freezing my nuts off,' he says. But it wasn't the only shock the 13-year-old would experience in the early hours of that morning. His mother had organised the papers for him to migrate to England and she and his father were at the airport to greet him. He was taken to his father's house at 22 Wimbledon Road, south London – his mother had told him she would see him in a couple of weeks – and put to bed. When he woke up, his life was turned on its head. 'I was introduced to two sisters and a bloody brother I never knew I had! It was a lot to digest,' he says. 'My father was living with a family and he had impregnated one of the women.'

After three awkward weeks with his new siblings, he was moved to rural Walton-on-Thames, 15 miles from central London to live with his father's sister. A market town far from the exuberant West Indian communities of the big cities, Lynch once again found himself pushing racial boundaries. 'I was the only black kid at school,' he says. 'It was a white area in the countryside. My mum didn't want me to be a nobody in London.'

If there were any tensions, they were smoothed over by his ability to pulverise a six-stitcher.

When he signed professional terms with Surrey, he and Sylvester Clarke, the genial giant with the killer throat ball, were the sole black players. They formed a close big brother, little brother bond – Clarke the heavy-drinking West Indies Test paceman four years his elder, and Lynch, the impressionable youngster with a fondness for big hitting and socialising.

Their coach Mickey Stewart observed the effect that Clarke had on Lynch when the beefy Bajan arrived at the club in 1979. 'He not only spent a lot of time with Sylvester, he started speaking like him. Before, he was speaking like a south London boy, now he was speaking like a Barbadian. I thought: what is all this? I can't understand what you're bloody saying.'

Lynch and Clarke called themselves the 'Chocs', playing up their colour and invoking the Spitfire pilot's cry 'chocks away' as they exited the Surrey car park en route to bars and nightclubs. But although he liked a drink, team-mates say his eye was more on the fawning young women than getting plastered.

Former England Test opener Alan Butcher played with Lynch at Surrey for a decade. He recalls that Lynch was never short of female company and cultivated a stylish image to match. 'He would spend quite a lot of time in the mirror before he went out on to the pitch. He would have a lot of Guyanese gold around his neck and be arranging it ... the shirt sleeves ... a couple of turns of the cuff, levelled at both sides and folded immaculately, and he would use an envelope to pat down his Afro to make sure it was level all over. It was quite a performance.'

When he took guard, his immaculately contrived appearance gave way to a gambler's countenance, his Slazenger V12 a loaded revolver in a game of batting roulette. On good days, he would win big, on bad days it looked like he'd pulled the trigger on his own demise. 'He was a loveable person, but he could drive you barmy at times,' laughs Stewart.

Lynch says Stewart was a father figure to him. The future England coach saw great potential in the young Guyanese and took a keen interest in his development as a batsman and a man.

'He was, shall we say, of the West Indian way, just casually floating around,' Stewart says. 'I spent a lot of time with him to get him going and make the most of his ability.'

But no matter how hard Stewart pushed his young charge, Lynch found it difficult to master the mental discipline necessary to grind out consistent scores. 'If he knocked an off-spinner over the top for six and they put a man out there on the boundary, he would look at it as a challenge to hit it over him, and in the same over he would hole out at long-on,' Stewart says.

During a match against Kent at the St Lawrence Ground in Canterbury, Alan Butcher watched from the balcony in a state of nervous anticipation, as Lynch rolled the dice against off-spinner Graham Johnson. 'He would block and suddenly run down the wicket and launch one,' Butcher says. 'This happened three or four times. And every time on the balcony, I remember I was about to go, "Monte, you c***!" and I was just about to drop the C-bomb and it sailed into the marquee. So it became "Monte, great shot!" The margins of success and failure – that summed up Monte.'

If Lynch was a source of frustration – and cardiac arrhythmia – to his coach and team-mates, his cavalier approach was still proving more successful than not. *The Guardian* newspaper's preview of the 1982 county season deemed him Surrey's name to watch: 'Monte Lynch, 23, batsman from Guyana via Walton-on-Thames, who cracks a cricket ball like Viv Richards and seems to be acquiring the ability to stay in too.'

One of those watching was West Indies captain Clive Lloyd. With the departure of stalwart Alvin Kallicharran to South Africa's Currie Cup competition, the West Indies middle order was beginning to look vulnerable and Lloyd saw Lynch as a potential replacement. Although he was qualified to play for England, Lynch still harboured a desire to represent his birth country. 'In 1983, Clive made me an offer to come back and play the Shell Shield season,' he says. 'He took myself and the St Vincent pair, Wilfred Slack and Neil Williams, who were with Middlesex, with the aim of us playing for the West Indies.' Ironically, all three would end up playing for England.

The highlight of his one-off stint with Guyana was a bludgeoning 129 against the fast-bowling might of Barbados in the Geddes Grant/Harrison Line 50-overs competition. 'It was like a battleground and very verbal,' Lynch recalled of the encounter in 2010. 'When Roger Harper came to the wicket, he said he looked at me and could have said anything, but nothing would have registered because I was so fired up.' He had to be, as Malcolm Marshall was at his skidding, torso-tattooing best. Batting at number three, Lynch saw opener Tyrone Etwaroo, second-drop Faoud Bacchus and Lloyd himself cop body blows from Marshall, who gouged 5-38 on a glistening Kensington surface. It's still one of Lynch's favourite career innings.

Afterwards, he says the great Everton Weekes congratulated him on the 189-minute knock and assured him that he had a 'bright future' ahead in a maroon cap. Lynch began to dream. He muscled 47 and 75 against the Bajans in the four-day game at Kensington Oval, but although Guyana won the Shield, with 40-year-old Roy Fredericks scoring 217 in his final first-class game, the rest of Lynch's contributions were minimal. Yet he still had reason to believe.

His 1983 county season was a watershed: 1,558 runs at a selector-friendly average of 53.72, including three centuries. Although he hadn't entirely ruled out the possibility of representing England, at this point his mind was set on joining his Guyanese captain Lloyd on the West Indies tour of India in October. His excellent county form and proficiency against spin – Lynch had served his Surrey apprenticeship mastering the turning deliveries of Intikhab Alam and Pat Pocock – would surely stand him in good stead on dusty subcontinental wickets. His impetuosity at the crease always threatened to backfire, but at 25 he was beginning to show signs of maturity.

When the selectors plumped for Trinidadian Gus Logie and young Antiguan right-hander Richie Richardson, he was devastated. 'Viv [Richards] was practically congratulating me that I was going,' he says. 'Basil Butcher, who is Guyanese, had the casting vote and he chose Gus Logie – that's the story I got told. To go to the subcontinent, I thought I'd done enough. It was a massive disappointment.'

What had made Lloyd's original call to arms all the more urgent was the news that a rebel West Indian side containing several famous names, including Lynch's good mate Sylvester Clarke, had accepted huge amounts of money to tour blacklisted South Africa.

Lynch says he was first targeted as a potential rebel for the second tour when he was in Guyana, through his connection with Clarke, who was a prime mover, initially, in the setting up of the venture. 'They were trying to get Clarkey to contact me, but at that time they didn't have a lot of telephone lines in Guyana. Halfway through the Shell season a lady came to me, who had a shop down the road, and she must have had one of the five bloody telephones in the whole village. I was at the market and she said, "Come, come, come, there is a man who wants to speak with you. He's called 11 times. Some man called Strong Arm."' It was Gregory Armstrong, the rebel tour manager.

The following May, *The Sun* reported that Lynch, Lloyd, Marshall, Richards and Joel Garner had been offered AU$216,000 each to join the second rebel tour of South Africa slated for November. By September, with his West Indies dream temporarily in tatters, and Surrey team-mate Clarke able to reassure him that his South African suitors were the real deal, Lynch was weighing up his options. 'I went to South Africa because I was disappointed not to get into the West Indies side to go to India,' he says.

Saying yes was the easy part, even though he knew it would end his Caribbean Test ambitions for good. Negotiating the maze of moral and contractual ramifications proved more demanding. Surrey cricket club was his bread and butter. They paid his wages for six months of the year. To enter South Africa as a West Indian rebel would change his status in England to an overseas player, which would mean fighting for one of two spots reserved for foreigners in the Surrey squad, currently occupied by Clarke and New Zealand captain Geoff Howarth. But if he went as an England-qualified player, he would incur a three-year ban from representing his adopted country, the upside being that his spot in the Surrey side wouldn't be in jeopardy, assuming the Test and County Cricket Board (TCCB) saw it that way.

Surrey coach and mentor Mickey Stewart was aghast at what he saw as the self-detonation of a future England Test career. 'Having known the lad since he was 16 and seen him progress, I could envisage him being considered for Test matches,' he told reporters. 'That's why I'm sad. I know he's given it a lot of thought. He doesn't want to upset his career with Surrey.'

His family were also disappointed. An uncle, who'd lived through racial turmoil in London's East End, begged him not to go. 'I was very close to him. He was married to my aunty Stephanie,' Lynch says. 'They were in Walthamstow. He was very ill with cancer. He called me over to his house and sat down and held my hand and said, "I'm begging you not to go." He told me about the racism and how I was letting people down. He wanted me to promise I wouldn't go. That was in my head.' It still troubles him.

His then girlfriend, pregnant with their first child, was similarly unsupportive, even though Lynch saw the looming pay cheque as a chance to set up his family. 'With the money I could buy a house and get my life started,' he says now.

When he arrived in South Africa, his mind was in a spin. The TCCB still hadn't made a ruling on his eligibility, and the news reaching him from England was grim. 'From being one of the boys from London, all the people who used to come and see us and say well played were now hammering me,' he says. 'The black activists were waiting to slaughter me when I got back.'

Surrey issued a statement urging him to return home 'in the best interests of his career' but, privately, players and management were more sympathetic. Mickey Stewart was calling Lynch regularly to make sure he was coping with the stress. The club's lawyers were ready to fight a negative ruling. Such was the young batsman's angst that he pulled out of the opening match of the tour against Northern Transvaal to reconsider his decision.

A newspaper report observed him strolling around Pretoria's Berea Park with Collis King's portable sound system, listening to reggae music and chatting to locals – anything to keep his mind off his troubles. When he eventually decided to stay with the rebels, it was because he didn't feel that England selection was a realistic prospect, especially with the number of foreign-born players already in the national team. 'I felt they can't keep picking them, and there would be no room for me,' he says. He also had legal advice that the TCCB would at some point have to recognise him as an England-qualified player.

Ultimately, the governing board barred him from Test cricket for four years but allowed him to continue with Surrey.

In the republic, affable Lynch soon found himself the centre of social interactions with locals. His soft south-London accent was easier than the various Caribbean twangs to understand, and he felt a little more worldly than some of his new team-mates. Plus, he had an imposing kit bag. 'As a county player, I went down there with a coffin of five or six bats, batting gloves, protectors. They had hardly anything. There was an air of jealousy.'

It didn't last for long. Lynch quickly bonded with his rebel brothers. 'We were like a family,' he says. He enjoyed the more relaxed atmosphere compared to the political and media histrionics that had accompanied the first tour. 'I think I came in at the easy part,' he says. 'I shudder to think what the first tour was like.'

The local press announced him to the South African public as 'stocky', with an 'unsubtle' style of batsmanship, recalling a six he clubbed against Glamorgan in Swansea as one of the 'biggest hits possible anywhere in first-class cricket', shattering the window of the secretary's office 'like an exploding shell'. He would add ballast to a fragile top order that was found wanting nine months earlier.

At first he didn't disappoint. A first-up century against Garth Le Roux's Western Province and 241 runs at 40.17 in the other warm-up matches ensured that he got the selectors' nod for the opening 'Test' in Durban. A quickfire 26 on a pancake pitch was cut short by what commentators called an 'irresponsible' heave to Denys Hobson at mid-on, but there was enough in his short stay to suggest a fruitful series ahead.

It wasn't to be. 'Suicidal' was another descriptor applied to his cavalier batting, as form and luck tapered off to the point where he was dropped for the fourth and deciding 'Test'.

Yet off the pitch he was still enjoying himself. Some even observed that he was scoring more with the ladies than he was with the bat.

Lynch says he was ignorant about the true nature of apartheid. 'I wasn't into black history, and growing up in Guyana you don't have that history.' But like all the rebels, he developed a finely tuned radar for what he saw as the double standards of politicians. 'The same black politicians who were saying things were looking for us in the evening to have a drink.'

He was more interested in the plight of the man on the street and in the townships. After 35 years, some memories of the tour are dulled by the wear and tear of time, but Lynch can still recall with fondness the almost rapturous reception he and a posse of his team-mates received at a village in the 'middle of nowhere'. As is often the case with rebel adventures, the story hinges on roisterer-in-chief Collis King. According to Lynch, King met two local women who had invited him back to their village. He persuaded best buddy Sylvester Clarke, off-spinner Derick Parry and Lynch to join him on an unauthorised jeep ride that would deposit them two and a half hours from their hotel. A few miles from their destination, a massive storm of dust, and singing, erupted.

Lynch was scared. 'I was shitting myself. I was thinking if anything happens to us here we've got nothing.' He needn't have worried. The locals, thousands of them, were dancing and chanting in their honour. 'We were like gods,' Lynch says. 'All these kids came running to touch us and rub our hands. The old ladies were clapping us slowly and watching us, then you'd look at one and they'd put their hand on their heart.'

They were treated to a feast that Lynch suspects cost many weeks' wages to prepare. 'It got me to the heart of Africa.'

The heart of white South Africa, he says, was penetrated by Clarke and young all-rounder Franklyn Stephenson. Clarke, the bowling bulldozer, was so devastating at the wicket that he transcended national allegiances to become a people's hero, even appearing in advertisements, while the popular Stephenson's affinity with young spectators enabled white fans to move beyond the colour bars they had grown up with. Lynch feels that they should have been honoured for their role in breaking down barriers.

On-tour camaraderie was central to maintaining discipline over a long 19-match campaign, but it was sporadically fractured because of off-field disputes over sponsorship and the realisation in some instances that careers were crashing to a premature end. Ancient inter-island rivalries buried during good times emerged. 'To be honest, by the end of it, I just wanted to get back to England,' Lynch says. 'I remember something was said, and I said, "Mate, you have to listen to Kalli," and someone said, "All you fucking Guyanese stick together." Far from it, I was making a cricket point. I was respecting his knowledge of the game. There were one or two in our squad that if they said jump, fucking hell, you'd have a fucking good look before you leapt.'

Although his perception of the rebel tour is now clouded by the four-year ban that prevented him representing England at his peak, Lynch insists he was proud to wear a West Indies cap, official or otherwise. 'We were playing against a national side with a lot of great players. I was in awe of all of them.'

And then there were Lawrence Rowe and Alvin Kallicharran, the two Caribbean greats whose sharp batting brains Lynch liberally picked in dressing rooms and hotels across South Africa, ironing out the technical deficiencies that had held his game back. Rowe's popping crease culture had a lasting influence. Encouraged to stand further back against pacemen, Lynch found he now had more time to play. The effect was substantial: 18 bittersweet centuries coursed from his bat over the next five seasons, centuries that under normal circumstances would have propelled him into an England side forever creaking with middle-order frailty.

When he did crack the Three Lions in 1988, after his ban expired, it was for a series of one-day games, ironically enough against the West Indies and some very familiar faces. Gus Logie, the man who edged him out of a tour spot to India in 1983, was batting at number five, and Malcolm Marshall scuttled in from Edgbaston's Pavilion End.

If the 30-year-old Lynch thought his selection had arrived a little too late, Surrey team-mate Allan Butcher wasn't convinced. He thought it well-deserved but surprising. 'I didn't think they would go for him, even though he was good enough to play,' he says. 'He came back from South Africa a more mature person and player, but I was slightly surprised as to who they would think might be an England cricketer. England always thinks about coming from the right family, that kind of thing.'

One family Lynch was now a lifelong member of was the growing band of black cricketers representing their adopted country. His face, along with trailblazers Phillip DeFreitas, Norman Cowans, Devon Malcolm, Gladstone Small and Roland Butcher was helping to normalise colour at the very top of English cricket.

The press generally welcomed the dual national's ascension to the Texaco Trophy side but, writing in *The Guardian*, former England seamer Mike Selvey reported that there was a theory doing the rounds that portly captain Mike Gatting had actually requested lunch not Lynch.

The calling mix-up between the two at Edgbaston certainly warranted mirth but, even without his captain's slowness between the wickets to consider, Lynch could only muster 2 and 6 in the two remaining matches. England swept the series 3-0 but Lynch's official international career was over almost before it began.

During the following county season he broke his ankle playing a charity football game and, as Surrey rejuvenated, he shuffled off to Gloucestershire for a more leisurely swansong. By the end of his career he'd banked 18,325 first-class runs at 35.17, including 39 centuries, plus that treasured England cap – a fair return for a man whose precarious beginnings and temperament threatened otherwise.

But there's still a nagging feeling, team-mates say, that he never quite reached his potential. His notorious lack of discipline at the crease and easy-going nature were obvious factors, but there's little question that South Africa hijacked his ambitions.

The batting success he had immediately after the rebel tour only amplified what he'd missed out on, yet Lynch for the most part is comfortable with his record. What frustrates him more is the never-ending debate about the pros and cons of the rebel tours. 'I don't have any remorse. We helped unite people. Those who still carry on about it have to get a life. It's in history now.'

Yet he does carry some remorse. The memory of his uncle's pleas still haunts. 'He said, "You don't know anything about black history." He didn't speak to me after that. His daughter had a chat with me recently. She said, "Do you remember when Dad told you not to go to South Africa?" She said he was devastated.'

In 2013, CNN broadcast a documentary on the rebels, interviewing some of the main protagonists. Lynch wasn't included. 'It's strange that nobody has ever come and asked us, the players, what our feelings are,' he says. What particularly irked him about the programme, he says, was the attitude of his South African suitors, the men who had lured him to the outlier republic and with whom he thought he had a relationship of mutual respect. 'Joe Pamensky disappointed me the way he bragged afterwards that all he had to do was dangle them some money and they'd come running. He shouldn't have spoken about it like that.'

After Lynch's playing days ended, Mickey Stewart, worried that his former charge would drift in and out of employment, helped him secure work as a coach at Royal Grammar School in Guildford, a job he held for more than a decade. There, Lynch displayed a steely dedication that won the hearts and minds of students and teachers. 'I used to say to him, "If you'd applied yourself with the same mental application you have in order to do what you're doing here at the school, you could have achieved anything,"' Stewart says.

Lynch also coached in his native Guyana and in Africa but often ran up against bureaucratic brick walls and political interference. Working with the Southern Rocks franchise in Zimbabwe and witnessing the country dissolving into economic and social chaos under Robert Mugabe only bolstered his belief that Commonwealth leaders who condemned the West Indian rebels were hypocrites. 'Those who criticise the tours in government, they treated the black man worse than the white man ever did,' he says. It's an argument that can be difficult to sustain considering the ongoing negative effects of colonialism, but it helps Lynch reconcile his past.

Now 62, he runs cricket camps in Surrey and coaches at sporting charity London Schools Cricket Association, whose alumni include Alastair Cook, Denis Compton and football World Cup-winning captain Bobby Moore.

He says he has only been shirt-fronted once in recent times about his involvement in the rebel tours – by former international umpire and Guyanese cricket board member Eddie Nicholls. 'He started picking at me,' Lynch says. 'I said, "I don't want to argue with you. Try looking at my record first … more than 18,000 first-class runs." And he said, "Yeah, but you went to South Africa and sold out we black people." And I said to him, "If you're still thinking like that I can't help you. There are other things in life."'

He has much more time for the likes of Viv Richards, who was a vociferous opponent of apartheid but bears no grudges against former team-mates who played in South Africa. 'People had different views about the tours. I saw Viv at an IPL [Indian Premier League] game and he came running over to me and said, "What about these bats they're using now? If we had bats like them we'd have been charged with murder."'

Lynch would rather people moved on. 'Forgive and forget. To me it's gone.'

Ray Wynter

'The most solid lick I've seen'

SOME FAST bowlers judge their success by the number of wickets they take, but Ray Wynter judges it by the number of batsmen he maimed. 'Driving fear into batsmen is what I liked to do,' he boasts. There are few in the Caribbean who would disagree with that claim.

In the mid-1970s, Neville Walker opened the batting for Jamaica Defence Force (JDF) in the Senior Cup. Reputedly a clean-living Christian, team-mates dubbed him 'Oily Rice' for reasons best left unaddressed, but he was good enough to be invited to trial for his country, and those same team-mates respected his sure-footed approach.

They also thought he was dead. The ball cannoned back way past Ray Wynter's follow-through towards mid-off. Most of those in attendance at the Up-Park Camp ground reckoned Walker must have got some bat on it. But then they saw the white mark on his forehead as he crumpled into the pitch.

'It was the most solid lick I've ever seen,' says Jeff Dujon, a man who witnessed his fair share of carnage keeping to the West Indies' fiercest.

This time he was fielding in the covers for Kingston Cricket Club. 'It hit him flush. Most people get hit and the ball drops nearby. This didn't.' In fact, the ball had lifted so quickly that it struck Walker while still in his stance.

As the JDF opener lay unconscious on the pitch, spectators feared the worst. 'I'm here to tell you I thought that man was gone,' says Kingston CC board member Denis Robotham, who was in the crowd that day. 'When Ray saw it, he said, "Take him off the pitch, don't make him dead on the wicket," [laughs]. As quick as he was, as brutal as he was, he couldn't take the sight of blood. Luckily the man lived.'

It's the kind of tale Raymond Ricardo Wynter revels in. Having never represented the West Indies at official Test level, it enables him to carve out a niche in local cricket folklore as the bone-crunching enforcer; the man who couldn't quite crack the big time, but who could nonetheless crack a skull or two.

Kensington Oval is flanked by the Long Mountain range. Despite its city location in the south-east of Kingston, it has a sleepy, rural feel, with a clump of trees at boundary's end shading an old white-on-black manual scoreboard. Inside the clubhouse, goat's head soup is advertised for J$150.

The clear view through to the mountains ensures that it's one of the best pitches in Jamaica to pick up the ball on. It's not too difficult to imagine Kensington batting heroes Basil 'Shotgun' Williams, Richard Austin, Herbert Chang and the grand master Lawrence Rowe taking supreme advantage of the clean sight lines.

RW Home and Commercial Construction are carrying out a refurbishment on the pink and mint green-coloured clubhouse. The 'RW' stands for Ray Wynter. A one-time Kensington nemesis returned to repair a rival's home. A man who evidently bears no grudges.

It's easy to see where Wynter extracted such fiery pace from. Not even a fluorescent safety vest can conceal the barrel chest and broad shoulders. Assets that compensate for a lack of traditional fast bowling height; assets that allowed him to once sling a cricket ball – some say like Lasith Malinga, others say like Fidel Edwards – at speeds in excess of 90mph.

There's no question that he was quick. Leonard Chambers, recently inducted into the USA Cricket Hall of Fame, is a revered mentor of Jamaica cricketers. Appropriately nicknamed 'Skipper', he represented Jamaica in the early 1970s, sat on the JCA board and acted as a national selector and coach. 'Ray comes from the rural parts of Jamaica, so he has the right stuff inside of him,' Chambers says of Wynter, who grew up in Trelawny on the north side of the island. 'Yam, green bananas and sweet potatoes! Very well-built. Very fast. Always in the 90s [mph]. All he needed was Michael Holding or someone to teach him better control.'

'Fast but erratic' is a phrase that often crops up in conversation about Wynter. Even his good friend Terrence Corke, a Kingston Cricket Club youth coach and former Shell Shield team-mate, concedes that Wynter's bowling could be a lottery. 'One time we were playing against Kensington, and Richard Austin, Rowe, Chang and Williams. We had a plan to bowl short balls to Richard Austin, a really good short ball, then out of the blue he bowled him a yorker and he got him out. And we say, "What happened?" And he said he changed mid-stride. Sometimes he didn't know what was going to come out, but he was very quick. The funny thing is I remember the guys he hit more than the wickets he took!'

Dujon recalls spending all of his time in the nets with Wynter ducking and weaving from bouncers. 'He would try and find a new ball and try to kill me,' he says. 'He got on to you quick, but if he bowled an outswinger it was an accident, and if he bowled an inswinger it was an accident.'

Inside the Kensington clubhouse, surrounded by a bevy of his workers and tradesmen, Wynter is in full control. There is, of course, none of the bone-crunching bravado that characterised his bowling. Instead, a broad smile and hearty laugh are his modes of communication.

He's a successful man. RW Home and Commercial Construction has government contracts and a division in New York. He's an antidote to those critics who maintain that the rebel tours were jinxed. Even so, he's nonplussed that the consensus is that his bowling lacked accuracy, that some people labelled him 'Spray'. 'It happened because I was trying to gain extra pace,' he says. 'You think you can get a batsman out with extra pace, so you tend to go off-line from time to time.'

Oderi Palmer is the project supervisor for the Kensington clubhouse refurb. As Wynter excuses himself to answer a client, the amiable 36-year-old, too young to have seen his boss in his pomp, recalls that budding fast bowlers from his cricket-playing youth were dubbed 'Ray' in honour of the head-hunting paceman, such was his legend.

Wynter's former captains Lawrence Rowe and Maurice Foster maintain that he was better with the old ball, when the lacquer had worn through and movement off the seam or through the air wasn't an issue. 'I'm not so sure about that,' Wynter says. 'I was there with everybody's pace. But we had so many fast bowlers in the Caribbean. Unless somebody was getting sick. And nobody was getting sick ...'

The likes of Andy Roberts, Michael Holding, Joel Garner, Malcolm Marshall, Colin Croft, Sylvester Clarke and Wayne Daniel were a 1,000-plus Test wicket barrier to any aspiring paceman, no matter how many quivering batters he'd knocked unconscious. No one was going to roll over for Ray Wynter.

The *Jamaica Gleaner* sub-editor left little to the imagination: 'Wynter, 5-48, blasts out defending champions' read the 27 January 1976 headline. Just 20 and playing only his second first-class match, Wynter's 15 overs of round-arm slingshots propelled Jamaica to a seven-run first innings victory over Guyana at Jarrett Park in Montego Bay. The 'Antillean sports goods salesman', as he was described, had made selectors J. K. Holt and Alf Valentine 'proud'. His cricket future looked bright.

But in the following seven years Wynter was unable to lock down a regular spot in the national side, appearing alongside Junior Williams and Uton Dowe as a pace spearhead – mainly when Michael Holding toured with the West Indies.

However, his batsmen-busting infamy continued to grow at club level. Elleston Panton certainly rued the day that he informed team-mates and anyone else who would listen of his intention to clobber Wynter. The Police club opener was served a bouncer spitting with indignation that kept climbing on him as he shaped to hook. It launched into the centre of his face, breaking his nose and cutting his tongue so severely that three stitches were required once he'd been rushed to Kingston Public Hospital, retired hurt for 8.

'It made a total mess of him,' Dujon recalls. 'Panton used to bat with three keys on his cap, so we called him "Three Keys". It hit him straight in the mouth and, trust me, cleaned a hole. Ray never liked him. He was an arrogant kind of guy.'

Vengeance had been delivered. 'Stirring up Ray is the worst thing you can do to him,' former team-mate Robotham says.

That was 22 August 1978. Wynter would persist in terrorising batsmen, famously reducing Desmond Haynes to his knees in a limited-over game in Barbados with a ball that smashed the side piece off his helmet. But the bruising blows didn't always add up to wickets. His most solid campaign in a dark blue Jamaica cap turned out be his last, 1981/82, when he appeared in all five Shell Shield matches, snaring 12 scalps.

Yet in the final match against Windward Islands in St Vincent, the last occasion in which Messrs Rowe, Chang, Mattis, Austin and Wynter represented Jamaica together, a frustrated Jeffrey Dujon threw his gloves on to the ground in protest at Wynter's wayward radar. Fast but erratic was still his hallmark.

The next season, despite bowling well in a trial match against Bermuda, Wynter was omitted from the Jamaica squad for the first Shell Shield encounter against Trinidad in Kingston. He was 27. His stop-start career total of 18 first-class matches had yielded 31 wickets at 37.54.

* * *

Colin Croft was crucial to Ali Bacher's plans to recruit a West Indian XI to tour South Africa. So crucial that he signed the burly quick knowing he was carrying a back injury. The snarling fast bowler was a key member of Clive Lloyd's pace battery, a man who pushed on-field aggression to the limit, a man with the kind of Test pedigree Bacher knew would attract other players to his cause. Yet despite receiving specialist treatment in the republic, Croft and his troublesome back were unable to reproduce trademark speed or hostility in the nets or on the pitch. A week into the tour, Lawrence Rowe's rogue side was, in essence, a man down.

Back in the Caribbean, news of the rebel tour of apartheid South Africa was sweeping the islands. The howls of protest and recriminations were loudest in Jamaica, where politicians, clergymen and the media united to condemn the tourists for accepting huge sums of money to play cricket in a country where people of their own colour were treated as second-class citizens.

The effect on the national cricket team was immediate. Rebel recruits Lawrence Rowe, Everton Mattis and Richard Austin were banned from Senior Cup, Shell Shield and Test cricket for life. The pay-off was a contract containing an astronomical sum of money. But would it be enough to compensate for a lifetime of resentment?

The operation to lure Wynter to the pariah republic as a replacement for Croft was a two-pronged affair, with first Wynter's Jamaica captain Lawrence Rowe and then SACU president Joe Pamensky calling to cement his interest. The offer was US$100,000 over two tours – at least five times more than the West Indies' players got for signing with Kerry Packer's WSC five years before.

Cricket-wise, Wynter still harboured dreams of representing the Caribbean at Test level but, realistically, he was in the bottom half of the pecking order. He played the occasional off-season in the Lancashire League and with Cambridgeshire, but he wasn't a full-time professional cricketer. Even though he was still young for a fast bowler, he had less to lose than some of his more high-profile team-mates. 'I was still hoping that it would happen, that I would play for the West Indies,' Wynter says, 'but we had an influx of fast bowlers.'

Domestically, it was a different story. Wynter had a steady job working in accounts at GraceKennedy, the Jamaican food and finance conglomerate. He also had a wife, son and daughter to support. With anti-rebel sentiment strongest in the upper echelons of Jamaican society, would he still have a job when he returned from South Africa?

Kingston team-mate Denis Robotham was his manager at GraceKennedy. When Wynter broke the news to him that he was thinking of going to South Africa, Robotham was impressed by his honesty and openness.

It contrasted with what he perceived as the 'secrecy' and 'hypocrisy' of Rowe et al, who in his mind had deceived the public with their anti-tour pledges. 'The chairman of the company, Carlton Alexander, was very anti-apartheid,' Robotham says. 'We had gotten a shipment of pineapple slices from South Africa and Alexander sent them back. When Ray came to see me, I said, "Big man, you're my friend. I wouldn't go but let me know what's going on. I'm trained, I'm in management, I'm earning reasonable money. You're a clerk. I won't kill you, big man, I respect your opinion." But I said, "You should talk to the chairman before you go."'

Alexander is a towering figure in the history of Jamaican business; the man who turned GraceKennedy into a multinational giant. Wynter wasn't deterred. 'Alexander said if the government doesn't say anything to him, my job would be there when I got back. It was a long, hard decision to make because of the apartheid system, but I discussed it with my wife and family, and I thought we could show blacks they were good enough to play against a white team.'

Just over a week after the last of Rowe's squad had set foot in South Africa, Ray Wynter arrived at Jan Smuts Airport, to be greeted by officials from the Transvaal Cricket Council. Sporting a tight-fitting white T-shirt tucked into belt-topped jeans, he looked fit and keen, happily posing for a photograph with an official's sons.

Five days later he would be playing the biggest game of his life.

* * *

The badge on the rebels' cap features a Caribbean palm tree under an azure blue sky encased in a heraldic shield. The rest of the fabric is a deep maroon colour. At a glance it could be easily mistaken for the real West Indies cap, which is, of course, exactly the effect Bacher and Pamensky were after. What gives it away is 'South Africa Tour '83' and 'West Indies XI' printed in gold above and below the badge. It's one of Wynter's prized possessions.

In the living room of his home in Smokey Vale overlooking Kingston, a large painting of Wynter delivering a thunderbolt at the Wanderers ground in Johannesburg takes pride of place. His call-up for the rebel second 'Test' against South Africa was clearly a great honour. 'I felt proud because most of my colleagues in the team had played for the West Indies before,' Wynter says. They had banked an impressive 159 Test caps between them. 'Although it would have been nice if it had been in the Caribbean so my family would have seen it.'

Had they seen it they wouldn't have been disappointed. But over-enthusiasm and a dodgy boot would almost prove his undoing.

Captain Rowe was a harsh critic of the first 'Test' pitch in Cape Town, suggesting that the Newlands curator had prepared a 'dust strip' to blunt the Windies pace attack. But the Wanderers track met with his approval. 'Green, very hard, ultra-fast – right up the Windies alley,' he told *Rand Daily Mail* correspondent Rodney Hartman.

The first day proved him right as the West Indies were blasted out for 267, just before stumps, with Wynter, a hit-and-miss tailender, contributing in a crucial 34-run last-wicket partnership with Alvin Greenidge, allowing Rowe's pacers two overs at openers Jimmy Cook and Barry Richards. One of those overs was assigned to Wynter. It was a huge show of faith from Rowe. In front of a capacity crowd of 29,000, the Trelawny tearaway would get his first taste of international combat. In the fading Johannesburg light, he steamed in, all nervous energy and years of unfulfilled ambition, but as he propped to launch, delivery arm stretched towards long-on for maximum catapult effect, his right foot gave way, sending him sliding across the pitch backside-down. Fortunately, the result was only comical. Fielding at mid-on, Emmerson Trotman doubled over in laughter.

'It was a stud that was a problem,' Wynter says. 'The same thing happened with my first ball for Jamaica. I was like: why does this happen to me? Is this my destiny?'

Ironically, the fall and outbreak of mirth across the stadium seemed to have the effect of calming Wynter's nerves, of piercing the façade of serious nation-on-nation battle. It was only a game after all. A game that can make a mug of us all.

The next day, after a wobbly start, the South Africans appeared to be cruising at 199/5 when Wynter struck with a three-over spell that changed the course of the match. His first wicket was off his signature delivery, a short ball that reared on Kevin McKenzie, forcing him into a protective stab that nicked the edge to Lawrence Rowe in the slips, terminating a 48-run partnership with Clive Rice. Rice fell in the next over to off-spinner Derick Parry, and although Wynter's blockhole yorker to Garth Le Roux appeared to some to nudge willow, crouching umpire Dudley Schoof had no hesitation in giving him out lbw first ball. In nine deliveries, the Springboks had lost three for five, collapsing to 204/8. Wynter had taken two for two, generating what the *Rand Daily Mail*'s Rodney Hartman called 'awesome' pace.

Wynter exited the field shortly after with bruised toes – those recalcitrant boots were still causing trouble – but he'd left his mark on the game.

In the second innings, suffering from chest tightness because of the high altitude, he bowled only nine overs as Sylvester Clarke bulldozed seven South African wickets for 34 runs in one of the most devastating performances in modern cricket history.

Bryan Crowley, writing in *Calypso Cavaliers*, a review of the series, said Wynter could look back on his international debut, which culminated in a 29-run victory for the rebels, with 'some satisfaction'.

The curiosity is that he didn't play more games on tour. Wynter is sanguine. 'The selectors were trying to give everyone a game.' As it turned out, a tour return of 20 overs, three maidens, two wickets for 59 runs, represented earnings of US$833 per ball. Excellent business by anyone's standards.

But Wynter says he was concerned with more than just the huge windfall coming his way. His first impressions of South African society weren't quite as apocalyptic as the Caribbean media and political class had made out. He told reporters: 'I decided to come and see first-hand what was happening in South Africa. As we will be doing a lot of travelling, I hope to get a general picture ... relations between black people and white seem good. It's different to how I imagined.'

Of course, within the tourist cocoon, where players were shielded from the worst excesses of apartheid, and lavish welcoming parties and five-star hotels were the norm, 'relations' between the races could appear cordial.

There's no doubt – as the extraordinary press coverage and sold-out stadiums attest – that ordinary whites were fascinated and charmed by their exotic tourists. Even in the liberal *Rand Daily Mail*, which expressed mild reservations about the tour, full-colour four-page wraparounds saluting the 'Calypso Kings', and specials on 'How to deal with bouncers' were devoured by enthusiastic readers. But they sat alongside headlines such as 'Coloureds can go back to District Six', 'Racial threats at Windhoek pool' and 'Their cross-colour love lives in black and white'.

Wynter's position was that the tourists, by excelling on the field and behaving with dignity off it, were demonstrating to the ruling culture what the black man was capable of. From his perspective, hearts and minds were being changed. 'I remember one day in Johannesburg Richard Austin and I got a taxi and went to a major department store to do some shopping. I noticed when we got in the store people stood off a little. Normally you go into a store and the assistant comes to serve you. Eventually a white lady came up to us and asked to help. We said yes, and apparently she picked up from the accent that we were not from there. She looked at me and said, "Are you the cricketers?" We said yes, and she shouted to her colleagues and ran to the back of the store to inform the manager. Everyone came running to see us and we signed autographs. The manager even gave us some things we were going to buy. He was making phone calls to people saying the West Indian cricketers are in the store now. They were so excited we were there, and he even paid for a taxi for us to go back to our hotel.'

But what of the football-mad black population, who didn't attend rebel games in the same huge numbers as whites? Beyond the PR-friendly coaching seminars at black and white schools, Wynter made sure he visited the townships. 'Me and Mattis went into Johannesburg to watch football and those black people, they welcomed us,' he says by way of justification. 'They used to say, "We are not making any money, but you guys are black like us and they're paying you good money so take it. We are not against you guys."'

At one of the rebels' matches, Wynter also met Gift Biko, the sister of Steve Biko, the heroic anti-apartheid activist who was beaten to death by prison officers in 1977. Wynter claims she 'accepted' the tourists' presence in South Africa. 'We chatted a lot and she explained the situation and spoke about the death of her brother. We were good friends.'

It troubled him that blacks were systematically denied the right to earn the kind of money he was taking back home to Jamaica. 'I felt a little guilty knowing as a fact they were underpaid. I tried my best to contribute – even to the ANC. When we were there and after I came back I gave them money.'

The sole incident of racism he witnessed played out at a hotel bar in Cape Town. According to Wynter, opening batsman Emmerson Trotman became embroiled in a nasty argument with a white man on a team night out. 'The guy was a racist,' Wynter says. 'Trotty wasn't pleased with what he said. They exchanged some serious words, but it was quickly put down by management. The guy got up and left, and a bunch of white guys came over and said they were sorry and apologised.'

Of course the tour wasn't all international politics and intrigue. Thanks to chief carousers Sylvester Clarke and Collis King, Wynter's room-mate, the day's on-field controversies were regularly replayed over beers at the hotel bar. Sometimes the five-strong Jamaican contingent would set up camp in one of their rooms for a rum-soaked discussion about their futures. Lifetime bans seemed to strengthen the off-field camaraderie of all the tourists. They would never represent their region or nation again, but they sure would enjoy their final moments in the international spotlight.

For most of the rebels, it was the last of many overseas campaigns. For Wynter it was something of a novelty. He was the only one to bring a camera. His snaps show the well-dressed tourists – some still sporting Afros and flared trousers – eating, drinking and dancing, female company never far from view.

Looking back on his short time in the republic, Wynter is certain that the rebels' tour was an important step in South Africa's march towards dismantling apartheid. 'Contrary to what they'd been told before, that the blacks weren't good enough to play against a white team, they could see now that black people could do it, that it was the opposite. I think we played a role in ending apartheid.'

In the Caribbean, a firestorm of establishment anger and hostility was being directed at the rebels. Guyanese sports minister Roy Fredericks, an ex-West Indian opener, and former team-mate of many of the rebels, called on the tourists to resettle in South Africa because they wouldn't be welcome back in the Caribbean. There was even talk of them being banned from re-entering their home countries. Although public sentiment in Jamaica was firmly in favour of the tourists – some 68 per cent expressed their support in a poll commissioned by *The Gleaner* – the movers and shakers in Jamaican society were not.

Wynter's wife, Zeta, worked in the accounts department at Caribbean communications giant Cable and Wireless. Some colleagues had called her husband a 'sell-out' and worse. It heightened fears that the backlash might get out of hand. The Wynters' two young children could also be targeted.

Brooklyn, New York, where Wynter's mother-in-law lived, would provide a refuge in between the tours. Except there wouldn't be a second tour. Bacher had lined up lightning-quick Hartley Alleyne, the former Worcestershire paceman from Barbados, to replace Wynter. It was like for like; in many ways a development that was hard to fathom. Along with Austin and Chang, Wynter would be asked to sit out the second tour. Lawrence Rowe fought the move, but when it became clear that Bacher wouldn't change his mind, the captain insisted his countrymen be paid out in full.

'My concern was the guys who originally took the risk should not be discarded for anybody,' Rowe says. 'I said to Bacher you can add anyone you want to the squad as long as you don't get rid of any originals. They assured me everyone would come back. Then they told me they had to get rid of a few. I said I was not going to stand for them dumping anyone. We were going back and forth and back and forth. In the end, I said the only compromise I will make is you have to pay them in full.'

Wynter wasn't overly disappointed. 'My wife said, "If they are paying you, Ray, you might as well not go." I didn't have a problem with that. I would love to have gone back, but the fact I was getting paid the same money without playing, I just accepted it and moved on.'

A phone call to Carlton Alexander revealed that his old job was still available – the government hadn't pressured GraceKennedy to sack Wynter – but the newly banned fast bowler was busy applying for a green card after nabbing a stock market job at Chemical Bank on Wall Street.

With some of the loot from South Africa he put himself through a course in construction management at New York City Tech, setting up his first building company.

At one point, before the left-hander's slide into mental illness, he even hosted fellow rebel Herbert Chang, who was planning his next move after the rebel tour.

Wynter was still splitting skulls in in the New York Metropolitan Cricket League for Long Island club Westbury – the lifetime ban didn't extend beyond the Caribbean – and in 1990 he became a dual international, representing the US in the ICC Trophy in the Netherlands.

Against minnow cricket nations Wynter was at his intimidating best. 'It was fun,' he laughs. 'There was a guy from Papua New Guinea who hit the ball very hard and I hit the top of his off stump and the bail flew all the way to the sight screen. If the ball had hit him he would have died. Then when I was coming in they all started backing away.'

Former St Vincent and Grenadines youth batsman Mark Audain is the curator of the hugely popular Mark Cricket ProviAuda Facebook page. Fanatical in his devotion to spreading the cricket gospel throughout the US, he remembers Wynter's battering impact on the Metropolitan League in the late 1990s: 'He knocked down so many people. Ray was fearful to face. It was devastating fast bowling. He could hit anyone if he wanted. He was like Jeff Thomson.'

* * *

Winnaz Circle is a small bar-cum-betting house in a plaza off Red Hills Road near the hills area in Kingston's more affluent northern suburbs. On the main street, a bass-heavy dancehall track keeps the beat to a conga-line of cars, some turning into PriceSmart, a multipurpose department store, others heading home for the weekend. There's a hint of ganja in the air.

It's Friday evening, and Ray Wynter is winding down with a few Heinekens, a few mates and his older brother Morris. Garrulous and popular with the bar staff, his booming laugh can be heard above the chatter of eager punters queuing to drop their hard-earned on one of Cash Pot's six daily draws. Wynter cracks a well-received joke about not being allowed to bowl at Morris when they were children for fear of injuring him. The former West Indies XI strike bowler is in his element. At 64, he has hit life's sweet spot.

As well as RW Home and Commercial Construction, Wynter owns a cattle and sugar cane farm in Trelawny. He's a board member of Kingston Cricket Club and an associate board member of the JCA. His son is a fighter pilot in the US Air Force, his daughter a forensic scientist in Orlando. His marriage to Zeta has withstood the pressures of South Africa, relocation to the US and return to Jamaica. It's still a source of strength.

Where did it all go right? Perhaps because he wasn't so well-known, Wynter never experienced the same level of opprobrium heaped on countrymen Rowe, Austin, Chang and Mattis. He wasn't a national legend like Rowe nor a ghetto community hero like Mattis, Austin and Chang. He was the country boy with a taste for making batsmen squirm.

Yet the occasional bumper of criticism never fazed him. The stability of his rural upbringing in Trelawny, where his father was a firefighter and his mother a postmistress, seemed to steel him for life's ups and downs.

Leonard Chambers says that Wynter was always adept at mixing with people of all stripes but knew where to draw the partying line. 'He was the type of person who showed a lot of respect to administrators. And he got along with the players because he was a jovial type of individual. He could make jokes, but he would listen too.'

Wynter credits a lot of his success to Zeta, who has been his rock in times of trouble and a constant stream of sage advice. 'I made good from what I earned in South Africa, but my wife has been a major part of what I have done. We are still happily married after 38 years.'

As for his ailing former team-mates, he says, 'Whoever gave them advice didn't do a good job. And they had domestic problems, too.'

Not that Wynter forsook them. When he returned to Jamaica in 2008 to pursue business opportunities, the rebel tours were a distant memory. He was readily accepted back into the cricket fold, working as a liaison officer for Jamaica and the West Indies during that year's World Cup. He was saddened by the decline of Richard Austin, who was by then living on the streets of Crossroads in middle Kingston, his mind addled by years of cocaine abuse. 'I tried to help him. To give him a lot of things,' he says. 'I felt very sorry for him. People were always trying to help him, but there was nothing you could do for him. I bought the suit he was buried in. I was so sorry that happened to a man of his potential.'

Also present at Austin's funeral was Lawrence Rowe, who'd flown in from Miami. The captain and the enforcer reunited. They spent the evening with other mourners at a bar near the Holy Trinity Catholic Cathedral where Austin's thanksgiving service had taken place, sharing 'Danny Germs' anecdotes – Austin and Wynter had made their Jamaica debuts in the same 1975/76 season – and reliving past glories.

Wynter has also reconnected with Herbert Chang, who suffers from schizophrenia, and offered to help with the renovation of Chang's Greenwich Town home. And he recently helped finance the installation of cricket nets at the Calabar Infant Primary and Junior High School, the alma mater of George Headley, the so-called 'black Bradman'.

* * *

It's 9pm and the Winnaz Circle is at full capacity. The bartender is serving jerk chicken. The Heineken and Red Stripe beers are cold and Wynter is coming off his long run-up.

So did he ever feel a tinge of sympathy towards the batsmen he injured? 'My goal was to get rid of you at all costs, so that my team can win,' he says. 'But I remember with Panton, when it first happened I was like, okay, fine, you are out. But in the long run I was saddened. I think he had real problems after that.'

What does he feel about critics who still condemn the rebels? 'People say things about the tours, but they weren't there. I think we helped the people in the long run. Look at the black players coming through now.'

It's only two miles to Wynter's home in Smokey Vale. In the warm embrace of a mild Heineken high, he will soon leave the Winnaz Circle. But he never leaves the winner's circle.

Everton Mattis

'Every man deserves a second chance'

THE VOICE from the car radio is damning: 'When we sin as Christians, who is accountable and responsible? We are!' Temptation is everywhere, the Jersey Shore Calvary Chapel pastor warns, and only through faith in God may we have the grace to bear it. This is the aural wallpaper of Everton Mattis's daily existence as a medical patient driver in the small Hudson Valley city of Poughkeepsie. It's also a vital cog in his life support system.

Mattis's temptations are drugs and alcohol. 'Sometimes when things don't come right, the devil comes into my mind, saying do this, do that – what's God doing for you?' Mattis says in a quiet Jamaican burr. 'But when you know what God's done for you and where you were before, and now where you are at, you have to be thankful.'

Where Mattis was before wasn't a good place. He walks with a limp thanks to a steel plate inserted where his left femur used to be after it was shattered by a gangster's bullets. His leg periodically makes a sharp snapping sound as the implant catches up with his natural movement – the movement of an elite athlete.

There's six-year-old YouTube footage of Mattis batting in a Southern Connecticut Cricket Association match, lanky frame hunched over an SS bat, lairy yellow-clad fieldsmen unaware that the middle-aged guy tapping his bat at the crease once outscored

Viv Richards. He whips the ball off his toes. This is no suburban hacker. It's not his signature shot, the on-drive, which because of his great height, always appears elegant and effortless, but there's no mistaking the artistry. Only his jerky running style detracts from the scene.

Everton Hugh Mattis looks much younger than his 62 years. A gold chain bearing the image of an Aries ram rests on his chest and he often wears a red baseball cap and shorts. He recently scored 60 in a New Jersey League match for Montego Bay Cricket Club.

The well-defined rituals of cricket, like those of the Church, offer Mattis an escape. Since 2009, he has been facing the prospect of deportation to Jamaica, his country of birth. In an era of increasing paranoia about foreign nationals, a catalogue of drug-related offences over nearly three decades finally exceeded the patience of US immigration officials.

Mattis lives in in a rented two-storey house with his wife Tasha and 17-year-old daughter Treasure. He has already done time in Immigration Detention – for two years he was shuttled between Monmouth County Jail, Berks facility in Pennsylvania and Varick St centre in Manhattan. To telephone home, Tasha had to deposit money in his account – detainees are not allowed to hold cash. Visits were difficult because of the frequent changes of address. It was almost a tipping point in their relationship. 'It was rough,' she says, perched on their living room couch.

'Tasha stood by me,' Mattis says, sipping from a can of Red Bull. 'She worked, took care of the house and our daughter. I love that woman – I respect the ground she walks on.'

It was during one of those many dark moments in detention that he made a life-changing pact with his God. 'I said, Lord, if there's one thing I want you to do for me, don't let them send me back to Jamaica because I am going to die. And if you help me I will serve you for the rest of my life.' And so far he has.

When Mattis utters the words 'South Africa' he chuckles to himself, as if he can't quite believe the impact that country – so far removed from his upbringing in the Caribbean – has had on his life. In his eyes, there's no question that a 36-year-old decision to join the rebel tours is the root of all his problems.

The background to that decision begins in the ghettos of Kingston, Jamaica. Mattis was born in 1957, one of four children. His father worked as a 'higgler', buying and selling used goods at Coronation Market, the huge cast-iron framed hall in downtown Kingston. It was a bare-bones existence. 'At least our parents would provide us with something to eat,' his younger brother Michael recalls. 'We were never hungry two nights in a row. There was always a sandwich.'

They lived close to Wilton Gardens, or Rema, as it's commonly called, one of several government housing projects built in the 1960s and 1970s to replace heavily polluted slums and shore up political power bases. These projects in the Trench Town and Jones Town areas of west Kingston quickly became a lightning rod for violent crime, as local gunmen, known as dons, sought to purge them of political enemies and turn them into voting garrisons.

The Mattis family house was on Asquith Street off Seventh Street, on the frontline of the ghetto wars – a solid Jamaican Labour Party enclave, constantly under siege from surrounding People's National Party gangs.

The Mattis home was down the street from the Ambassador Theatre, a once-elegant 1950s outdoor cinema, effectively in no-man's land. Today it's rarely used. The surrounding area is scattered with rubble and the cracking cement foundations of buildings that were razed during the worst of the violence. In its heyday it played the gun-toting westerns popular with young Jamaican males. An unfortunate consequence was that many youths adopted the brutal eye for an eye justice they saw on the big screen.

The community was perpetually on the edge of conflict. 'We would be watching a movie and people would be flinging bottles and other stuff over the walls at us,' Michael says. 'You would hear this boom-crash-boom. People would get hit. It was chaos.'

By the mid-1970s the 'Bass' was being used to stockpile firearms and as a base to launch attacks on Rema, as downtown Kingston degenerated into a war zone. 'It was rough growing up,' Mattis says. Official figures show that the murder rate increased threefold during his adolescence. 'You would lose friends who got killed.'

Sport, in the time-honoured fashion, was a way out. Mattis attended All Saints Primary School alongside fellow rebel Richard Austin and played cricket and soccer with the Boys' Town club made famous by Collie Smith and Frank Worrell. Warfare ended his involvement. 'After a while we had to stay on our side of the divide; it wasn't safe anymore.' Mattis laughs at the madness of it all.

The Hi-Lo supermarket in Barbican, just north of New Kingston, has a massive car park, a perfect batting outfield for young boys and their cricket dreams. When he was 14, Mattis's parents moved the family out of Jones Town to escape the carnage. Every Sunday, local youths would play on the car park asphalt, and it was soon apparent that the tall teenager nicknamed 'Peashead' was a class above. 'They couldn't get me out,' Mattis says.

Although Barbican was something of a safe haven compared to downtown Kingston, it wasn't immune to poverty or developments downtown. In the early 1970s, Rastafarianism, Jamaica's home-grown religion, began to impact on mainstream society, and many young men were attracted to its message of black empowerment. A counterbalance to the plague of gun violence and extortion sweeping the city's poorer areas, it gave peaceful voice to an underclass of men struggling with their nation's history of slavery and oppression. Its musical cousin, reggae, became the sound of the bullet-blistered streets, as ghetto songwriters such as Bob Marley and Peter Tosh spread the gospel.

'Yes, I was a Rasta man,' Mattis says. 'That was the in-thing at the time. I used to grow my dreads. Most of the older guys we looked up to were Rastas. They were good guys, and they encouraged me to go as far as I could in cricket. And for a while I thought Rasta was the way.'

Central to the Rastafarian creed is marijuana, which is used for meditation purposes and to heighten a sense of community. Mattis liked the single-mindedness it gave him – even on the cricket field. 'I used to smoke weed before a game when I was leaving my house. That's how you had to do it without letting the authorities know. It made me real focused. All during my career I did it.' It was a habit he would find hard to kick.

His dreads would also become problematic as his career progressed, putting him in conflict with the conservative Jamaican cricket establishment.

It was while carving up another supermarket car park century that Mattis was spotted by ex-West Indian all-rounder Reggie Scarlett and slotted into the Sports Development Community competition with Ashanti. He scored heavily, earning a spot in a Sports Development Community representative tour to Antigua. At the pre-tour camp, J. K. Holt, a West Indian batting legend and Test selector, gave him an ultimatum: cut his dreads or cut his ties with Jamaican cricket. Mattis chose the former.

It's a quirk of Kingston cricket that two of the city's most prominent clubs, Kensington and Lucas, are located opposite each other in the working-class eastern suburb of Rollington Town. Mattis's natural inclination was to play for Kensington alongside his friend Richard Austin, but the knowledge that he would have to bat way down the order at number seven or eight, behind the likes of Lawrence Rowe, Basil Williams, Herbert Chang and Austin, forced him across the road.

Named after Slade Lucas, a Middlesex batsman who donated equipment to kick-start the club in the late 1890s, Lucas was the first Jamaican club to represent the country's working-class black population. Cricket historian J. Coleman Beecher labelled it 'the most important event in the history of the island game'. It was a good fit for Mattis. Under the guidance of former West Indian players such as Easton 'Bull' McMorris, Mattis quickly graduated into the Jamaican national side. He was only 19.

Quiet and unassuming off the field, his straitened circumstances were noticed by more class-conscious team-mates. They saw him overeat at lunch – even if he was batting and not out – then go out and bat again. The conclusion they drew was that he didn't get fed enough at home.

Right-hand batsman and current Melbourne Cricket Club president Mark Neita was one of Mattis's closest friends in the Jamaican side. 'Matto was a super talent but because he came from a humble background, he did not have all the social graces,' he says. 'And when we played, persons used to hold that against him, to put him down. A lot of guys in that side had aspirations. People scoffed at people who were less fortunate than themselves. If you came from a rural area you were considered a "country man", and if you came from the inner city, you were considered from the ghetto. I was considered "uptown" because my father was an attorney. I really took exception to the way the established guys treated the country and ghetto guys. They would mock the way Matto held a knife and fork – that kind of thing.'

In Barbican, there were no such reservations. The first man from that area to represent Jamaica, he was becoming something of a local hero. After scoring 95 in Barbados in February 1978 (where he was referred to as the 'tall Lawrence Rowe'), Mattis was met at Norman Manley Airport by locals in an open-backed Bedford truck and paraded through streets of appreciative fans in Barbican. To them, and his Rasta friends in particular, he was a symbol of what could be achieved in spite of your roots.

In 1980/81 he finished second in the Shell Shield averages to Clive Lloyd, plundering 332 runs at 55.33. With a hole opening up in the West Indies top order because of a finger injury to Alvin Kallicharran, Mattis was ushered into the Test side against the touring English at Queen's Park Oval in Port of Spain. Batting at number four behind Viv Richards, he fell to John Emburey's gentle off spin for a duck, caught by Geoff

Miller. 'The ball just stuck in his hand,' Mattis says, as he was trying to work the ball through the on side. But as the series wore on, Mattis and his chunky SS Jumbo grew in confidence, and in the fourth Test in Antigua, he made 71. Writing in *The Guardian*, Frank Keating said of Mattis: 'You sense he is very nervous out there, but in every innings that he has played since the duck in the first Test he has stood taller and revealed additional classy bits of business.'

The high point in a plum-red West Indies cap came at a one-dayer in St Vincent. Batting at number three, he was last man dismissed for 62 in a total of 127, run out by Geoffrey Boycott's flat throw that, according to *The Guardian*'s match report had Mattis 'diving into the crease, a jumble of arms and legs and a cloud of dust – an undignified end to a graceful innings.'

And then there was nothing. To this day, Mattis can't quite figure out why he was never given another opportunity. Later that year, he was siphoned off into a Young West Indies tour of Zimbabwe along with Test hopefuls Desmond Haynes, Faoud Bacchus and Gus Logie. In Harare, he smashed the first West Indian century against Zimbabwe, but when the 1981/82 squad to tour Australia was announced, the selectors preferred the uncapped Trinidadian Logie. 'They should have taken me or both of us,' Mattis says. 'They took a spinner named Harold Joseph and he should not have gone on that tour.'

What made Mattis's sense of frustration more acute was that captain Clive Lloyd seemed to be a supporter of his – at least publicly. He told the *Jamaica Gleaner* after the England campaign that Mattis's transition to Test cricket hadn't been without its problems, but 'he is a good player, pretty straight and he will certainly develop vastly in the years ahead.'

Conrad Hunte also commented on his 'sound technique, temperament and variety of attractive strokes'.

The problem that fringe men like Mattis faced was that Lloyd and the selectors had a bevy of batting talent to choose from. They could afford to be picky.

Although he can't be certain, Mattis feels that, of all things, his hair, which had grown into a mini Afro, and his goatee, the only outward sign of Rastafarianism, affected his Test career. 'I remember at Sabina Park, they told me to get a haircut, and I was like: I like my Afro, because at that time a lot of us wore our hair that way, so I didn't get my hair cut. Apparently, they didn't like that I didn't get it cut, and sometimes I feel that's the reason I didn't get back into the side.'

'I know that I was capable,' Mattis says. 'Look at that team I top-scored for, with Greenidge, Haynes and Lloyd. So I had the ability, but I didn't get a good run like Logie or Richardson.'

Certainly, Mattis's form during the 1981/82 Shell Shield warranted further consideration from the selectors. Still only 24, he topped the averages with 441 runs at 49.

And then the South African bombshell hit. It was Lawrence Rowe, Mattis's Jamaican captain and national sporting hero, who telephoned him about the SACU's attempt to organise a Caribbean tour of the pariah republic. Mattis idolised the batting stylist. 'From the moment I first saw him play I always wanted to bat like him.'

He was immediately interested. 'As long as I kept scoring runs I thought I might get back into the West Indies side but I didn't think it was going to happen because I really believe Lloyd didn't want me. They killed my spirit not picking me for that Australian tour. I told Lawrence I would think about it.'

Mattis was working part-time for sporting gear shop, Andrew HB Aguilar Ltd, earning a modest wage selling SS bats and coaching with the Institute of Sport. The offer of US$80,000 to play 12 weeks of cricket over two tours was an incredible financial opportunity. It was 60 times more than the average annual wage of US$1,330 and 240 times what a Jamaican worker could expect to earn in the same time period.

He also had a wife and five children to provide for. The national unemployment rate was 27.6 per cent. It was a no-brainer. 'People like Everton really only had cricket,' says Neita.

'Shell Shield was just five games. There might be a game against a touring side and a few one-dayers. We earned a pittance. It was an economic decision for him. Would I have gone? Maybe not, but I had a job in the financial services industry to go to.'

Mattis knew there would be repercussions. He discussed the offer with his family and sensed their unease about apartheid and the potential for a backlash. He was aware he would be banned from playing cricket in the West Indies, but he didn't think it would be for the term of his life. 'A couple of teams went before us and they got short bans. We thought, okay, we are going to get a little two- or three-year ban. We can work with that. But oh boy ...'

Mattis's Rasta friends in Barbican advised him not to go. Now he wishes he'd listened to them. 'Apartheid and the suffering of blacks put me in two minds, but we thought we could make a difference by going there and letting them see what they could do.'

The vibe in the media and among the political class was hostile. Former Prime Minister and leader of the opposition Michael Manley weighed in, calling the rebels 'mercenaries who had humiliated their race for a mess of pottage'.

Mattis was only 25. In hindsight, it's easy to conclude that he acted prematurely in ending a promising Test career, given Lloyd's stated public belief that his best years were still to come, but the payoff – a ticket out of grinding poverty – was too tempting for a man from the ghetto.

Looking back, he recognises it as the biggest mistake of his life. A mistake he feels he's still paying for. 'I don't care what nobody's going to say. Those tours caused a lot of anger, stress and regret. If I could do it all over again I wouldn't go. I am still suffering from South Africa.'

On 12 January 1983, Mattis left with Richard Austin for London, where they boarded a South African Airways flight to Johannesburg. Photographed wearing a shiny black jacket and smoking a cigarette, Austin by his side, he told reporters, 'I have no second thoughts about coming. This is something I want to do.' On the aeroplane, it was a different story. 'We were nervous, but we also thought we had to make the most of it.'

They were the first of the rebels to arrive at Jan Smuts Airport – flights had been staggered to put the world's press off their scent.

At their hotel, the cumulative effects of weeks of insecurity, pressure and paranoia kicked in. Even the contents of the minibar couldn't calm their nerves. 'We wondered if the other guys would chicken out at the last moment,' Mattis says. 'We'd be stuck there with nothing. It was tense.' That tension was relieved the next day when the bulk of the squad – the eight-man Barbados contingent – landed.

At a meeting with Ali Bacher and Joe Pamensky, the tourists were made aware of their responsibilities and how best to avoid butting up against apartheid. Certain bars were off limits, and beaches and public transport were still segregated. The South African constitution excluded blacks from voting.

Mattis knew he was in an abnormal country. 'All you would see were signs for whites and blacks. You couldn't fool yourself. We just avoided it.'

His scores on the tour were mediocre, his highest being 21. He offers no excuses for his indifferent form, but the horror stories he was hearing from the press and family back home must have affected his ability to concentrate out in the middle. Banned for life from any form of cricket in the West Indies, some Caribbean governments were entertaining the idea of refusing the rebels re-entry.

Regular phone calls to his wife revealed the extent of the hostility in his homeland. 'She didn't want me to come back because it was so rough. People were saying they were going to kill us on arrival.'

There's a photograph from the first tour of a smiling Mattis with Bernard Julien, Joe Pamensky, his son and an attractive young woman at a party at Pamensky's house. They have their arms linked. Mattis, the tallest of the bunch, is wearing a long-sleeve, white open-necked shirt and nimbly holding a cigarette and glass of spirits in one hand. Booze-fuelled or not, he looks happy. In Mattis's mind it can only be an illusion. 'To be honest, no moment from those tours sticks out as a happy one,' he says now.

The crushing realisation of what the outside world thought of the rebel cricketers was immediately apparent as the first tour ended. Returning to Jamaica via a short stay in the US 'to let things die down', Mattis found his government coaching job terminated and he was barred from even practising with Lucas club team-mates. The cricket fraternity, which had sustained him into early adulthood, now cast him adrift.

A pall of exclusion greeted him at every turn. His Rasta friends snubbed him. 'Jaghi, an Indian Rasta man, never spoke to Peashead again after South Africa, and they were real close,' Mattis's brother Michael says.

'They turned on me real bad.' Mattis laughs again. 'But I was just trying to provide for my family.'

The ostracism sent Mattis into a tailspin. He tried to get out of the second leg of the tour, but the contract was binding. That tour, a much longer ten weeks, became something of a drag, as his uncertain future tainted any joy he derived from the Windies XI winning both the 'Test' and one-day series. 'I started worrying about what I was going to do without cricket and what was going on back home. There was even a rumour that the house we were living in got burned down. My family were telling me not to come back.'

But he had nowhere else to go. He says there was an offer to play Currie Cup cricket in South Africa, but he feared returning to the apartheid country without the support network of a well-financed international tour. He moved his family out of Barbican, where he'd long since ceased to be a local hero, and lived off the rand he made in South Africa.

Work enquiries fell on deaf ears. Random people in the street would taunt him, yelling 'sell-out'. He began to smoke and drink heavily.

Lifelong friends let him down. A business deal with a Jamaican team-mate to import hacksaw blades from New York went awry, when, Mattis claims, the profits were hidden from him. 'I invested a lot of money in it, but because of my South African connections I couldn't be at the front of the operation, so he was supposed to take care of it – but I never saw a dime. We had grown up together.'

One night, driving through the Kingston business district of Half Way Tree with his then wife Joan, he was pulled over by two policemen. According to Mattis, they yanked him out of the car and one of them shoved a gun in his mouth. 'You're lucky your wife is here with you,' he yelled, 'because I would blow your head off right here and now, you fucking traitor! You deserve to die!' Then he took Mattis by the back of the head and slammed his face on the car bonnet.

'My wife was crying her eyes out, begging them not to kill me,' Mattis says. They locked him up for the night. It was the final straw. 'I knew I had to get out. It was getting serious. I called a friend in New York. I had to go.' Mattis didn't want to leave his young family in Kingston but he couldn't help them if he was dead. He would never return.

It was 1987. New York was in the grip of its own crime epidemic, as cheap crack cocaine flooded the city. Mattis, separated from his country, family and the sport he loved, was vulnerable. 'I was depressed,' he says. 'I started to use heavier drugs – not just marijuana. Cocaine. I made some bad choices I regret to this day.'

The long-distance relationship with his wife was already under strain. Drug addiction killed it. He was dealing on the streets of Brooklyn. 'I was dealing to survive,' Mattis says by way of justification.

He holds his head in his hands. 'But when you're taking drugs you make irrational decisions.'

A friend had suggested he move to historic Poughkeepsie, an hour and a half north of New York, to play cricket in the

Metropolitan League. But drugs and the torment of South Africa followed him.

His wife filed for divorce in June 1990. Five months later, he was charged with selling narcotics to an undercover policeman. The *Poughkeepsie Journal* reported that 'after the officer bought the narcotics, Mattis led police on a five-block foot chase until he was arrested after a struggle'. He was also charged with bail jumping and a misdemeanour on an active warrant.

In his lounge room surrounded by the touchstones of family life, it's hard to square this image of Mattis the cop-evading street fighter, with the peaceable middle-aged father sitting on the sofa. 'I made poor decisions – you do things you wouldn't normally do,' he says, gazing at a display cabinet of daughter Treasure's achievements. 'I'm not proud of that part of my life.'

His arrest was part of a pattern of reoffending that would dog Mattis throughout the 90s. Whenever Mattis tried to get his life back on track, South Africa would return to haunt him. Former Jamaica team-mate Jeff Dujon refused to play a New York exhibition match for a West Indies XI against a US Invitational XI that included Mattis because of his apartheid connection. Faced with the choice between a West Indies wicketkeeping legend and a four-Test batsman, the promoter sided with the former and Mattis was forced to sit the game out.

'That really hurt my feelings, for a fellow countryman to say that.' Mattis shakes his head. 'We had come up through the ranks together.'

There's a two-inch scar on the left side of Mattis's jawline. It's another reminder of the life he's forever trying to leave behind. It's yet another reminder of South Africa. In 1997, a year after he'd met Tasha, Mattis says he was sitting in a bar on Main Street talking sports and drinking with friends. The bar, no longer in use, is flanked by a crumbling concrete and tar driveway. It's here that Mattis says he was shot.

A couple of expat Jamaicans recognised the Test cricketer – there's a small but significant Caribbean population in Poughkeepsie – and in Mattis's words began to 'yap their mouths off', telling him he'd taken 'blood money' to play in South Africa. They argued momentarily about drugs then stepped outside on to the driveway. 'One of them pulled a gun on me,' Mattis says. 'He started shooting, saying I had to die because I was a traitor to the black man. I started to back up, but the first shot hit me in the leg, and I fell on to the concrete. He kept on shooting until there were no bullets left. I don't know how I didn't die.'

The assault wasn't over yet: 'His friend came with a knife and tried to stab me in the neck, and I tried to hold his hand, but he got me on the side of the face. That's how I got the scar.'

Mattis's left leg was a mess. The bullet had almost destroyed his femur, and doctors thought the entire limb would have to be amputated. He spent two months in hospital as the bone was reinforced by a steel plate and his leg allowed to heal. Mattis now sees the shooting and miraculous recovery as evidence that God had intervened to spare him. 'He was on my side,' Mattis says. 'That's why I repay him every day.'

Tasha, a native New Yorker, has also been by his side for the past 23 years. 'He has a good, kind heart and he is a good dad,' she says. She was by his side when his son, 27-year-old Sugar Ray, was beheaded defending his father's honour in a gangland murder in Kingston in 2009. She was waiting for Mattis when he was released from detention. She will be by his side when the deportation case is resolved. 'We have a good attorney, we are confident,' she adds.

Jamaicans have long memories. Grudges die hard in a land where the lingering effects of slavery are lived out daily. Mattis is fearful that if he returns to the island he will be shot. His fears may seem paranoid to outsiders, but there can be little doubt that his welcome would be less than friendly.

Mark Neita understands. He says Jamaica can be a very unforgiving society. 'We want to be the moral guardians of the

Caribbean, to set the standard. We hold on to things a lot longer than anywhere else.'

The Smith Metropolitan AME Zion Church is an imposing edifice. Built in the Gothic revival style early last century, its two-storey bell tower stands watch over the local neighbourhood and industry. It's also witness to Poughkeepsie's growing drug problem. Dealers sell heroin and other drugs outside the church's front gate.

The city and surrounding Dutchess County was once home to the IBM empire, employing over 30,000. Now that figure is closer to 3,000. Economic collapse has led to social problems. 'It's very challenging to resist drugs in Poughkeepsie,' says Pastor Edwrin Sutton. 'On every street corner it's there.'

So far, Mattis, with the help of the congregation, has been able to keep himself clean and to avoid temptation. 'But there is a lot of hopelessness in this city,' Sutton adds. 'A lot of poverty and senseless violence.'

'I can see he is very level-leaded and has the heart to do the right thing,' Sutton says of Mattis. 'Coming to the church gives him a sense of hope, inspiration and fight to go on to the next day.'

At Pat's Kitchen, a small Jamaican restaurant on Main Street, Mattis is something of a celebrity. The sparse lunchtime crowd fist-bump him even if they are not quite sure of the exact nature of his sporting achievements. 'You played for the West Indies,' a guy who is too young to have seen Mattis at the wicket says. 'You were a pace bowler!'

'I was a batsman!'

'You play with Viv Richards?'

'Yeah, mon.'

'Ha. He played with Clive Lloyd and Vivian.'

They both laugh. It's the kind of banter that makes Mattis feel more comfortable with who he is. 'This time of my life is the happiest I have been – I am at peace,' he says, as the cook signals that his oxtail stew is ready. 'I just want to go out gracefully.

Every man deserves a second chance. This is my life here, not in Jamaica.'

Back in the car, the man on the radio continues to expound on the evils of temptation. 'No temptation has overtaken you except such is common to man,' he quotes from Corinthians. 'God is faithful who will not allow you to be tempted beyond what you are able, but with the temptation will also make the way of escape, that you may be able to bear it.'

Mattis will be hoping that God keeps his end of their bargain.

As we were going to print, I learned that Mattis's deportation case was likely to be resolved favourably.

Colin Croft

'He reminds one of a heavyweight boxer'

'THE REASON I haven't answered any of your many emails or phone calls is because I want nothing to do with you or your project.' At least I could be certain the man abruptly hanging up the phone was Colin Everton Hunte Croft, the brute of a man all his team-mates told me would happily bowl bouncers at his grandmother to get her out; the gruff, straight-up-and-down guy (except when he was veering into umpires with an extended elbow) with a public reputation for terrifying fans and batsmen alike.

'Tell him if he doesn't speak to you, he'll be in big trouble,' pint-sized Faoud Bacchus joked. His former team-mate had offered to act as a go-between and help me to contact Croft somewhere in the urban sprawl north of Orlando. Instead he ended up reeling off anecdotes about the gruff hitman in the car park of the Embassy Hotel in downtown.

'He would run in the midday sun,' Bacchus says. 'He would say when you're playing cricket, you're not playing at six o'clock in the morning, you are playing in the midday sun, so that's when you should train. He would also run on the concrete and the road instead of grass. Why? He would say, "Faoud, when you are a fast bowler and you plant your foot down, it feels harder than concrete, so I have to train for the same." That's the mentality he had. Colin has one mindset and that's it. He was hard. He

301

doesn't care what people think.' Others described him as a neat-freak teetotaller, who would get pissed off if his room-mate came in after 10pm.

The most famous photograph of Croft places him second in order of height in a line of four of the most destructive fast bowlers known to cricket-kind. While 6ft 8in Joel Garner and the inscrutable Andy Roberts peer into the Port of Spain horizon and Michael Holding gazes angelically, Croft leers at the camera, his long face twisted with contempt and 'you looking at me?' venom. The ultimate hatchet man in a gang of miscreants.

And it was Croft who did the dirty work, often bowling unchanged for marathon spells without dropping pace or psychological intensity. He was, so legend has it, the only member of the pace battery to question Clive Lloyd's insistence on having a drink with the opposition after a day's play. 'Why would I want to drink with guys I want to kill?'

But unlike most pacemen who dished it out with almost homicidal glee, he could also take it. 'He bowled a lot of bouncers,' says former Australian captain Ian Chappell. 'But he came in as nightwatchman a few times and he never once complained if he got bounced.'

However, his code of honour was tested one ignominious afternoon at Lancaster Park, Christchurch, when his elbow momentarily became a truncheon of defiance against the perceived injustices of an umpire out of his depth. Normally, Croft lurched out wide to the extremities of the popping crease, opening up his view of the batsman's ribcage before angling the ball at his prey's solar plexus. This time, frustrated by dubious decisions – Croft had petulantly flicked off the bails en route to his bowling mark – he went the other way, clattering into the back of umpire Fred Goodall, a small, ferret-like man in a white coat, and carried on down the pitch as if nothing had happened.

Today, he would have endured a multi-year ban and eternal social media damnation, but in 1980, when aggressive, rebellious fast bowlers were key to putting eyeballs on television screens and building up cricket's new gladiatorial image, it only burnished his reputation. But it was a reputation that told only half the story. Croft was smart. He was a qualified air traffic controller and had worked as a maths teacher in his native Guyana. Even if team-mates knew him as 'Goofy', because of his resemblance to the Disney character, they respected his intellect and strength of character.

It was the growling hitman who SACU board member Ali Bacher wanted to kick-start momentum for a proposed rebel tour of South Africa. Croft's 125 wickets in 27 Tests and his status as a current West Indian fast bowler would add immediate prestige and attract waverers to the cause. At 29, Croft was at his peak, but a nagging back injury was threatening his career, and Bacher, a doctor, could link him up with South Africa's top specialists. Croft also had a wife and son, and a mortgage to pay off. A generous lump sum would set him up and enable him to attain his commercial airline pilot's licence. There was life beyond cricket, and he knew it.

Yet right up until the rebels left for South Africa, the Caribbean public could have been forgiven for thinking that Croft was still aspiring to represent Guyana in the 1982/83 Shell Shield and the West Indies in the subsequent five-match Test series against India. According to WICBC president Allan Rae, Croft was receiving treatment for his back in Jamaica from renowned orthopaedic specialist Sir John Golding while staying at a hotel in Kingston – all on the WICBC tab. Rae and selector Steve Camacho would take him to rehab sessions during the day and Croft dined at the president's St Andrew home, never once mentioning South Africa. 'He started spinning me the yarn about dying to play for the West Indies again and he was going to get well,' Rae told Tony Becca of Jamaica's *The Gleaner*.

But when Camacho went to collect Croft from his hotel the following morning, staff informed him that he'd checked out. The next thing they heard he was in Johannesburg. 'Of all the players who went to South Africa he was the one I was most annoyed about. A pen went through his name as far as I was concerned,' Rae said.

News of Croft's arrival stoked a sense of panic in the South African cricket community. All-rounder Peter Willey, himself a former English rebel, and now representing Eastern Province, warned South Africa's batsmen they were about to encounter aggressive pace bowling the likes of which they had never experienced before. 'You haven't seen anything as fast in this country for a long time,' he told the *Rand Daily Mail*. 'They have about six of them in the squad, and at least three could play in any Test side in the world.'

The proposed spearhead was of course Croft. He had more Test wickets than the rest of the squad combined. But despite the constant attention of Bacher, and the intervention of medical specialists, he was more often seen in the dressing room cradling files of X-rays than he was marking out his run-up. His failure to launch disappointed the local media. They had built the 'brooding meanie' into public enemy number one. 'He reminds one of a heavyweight boxer – no more so than when he goes through a vigorous skipping routine in a sweat suit emblazoned with his name,' wrote one scribe.

Even though Sylvester Clarke soon usurped him as aggressor-in-chief, and little-known Jamaica paceman Ray Wynter was drafted as his substitute, the press still harboured a masochistic desire to see Croft fit and tormenting Springbok batsmen. Journalists spent time with him in the pavilion attempting to tease out his motivations and locate the man behind the monster myth. In one profile for the *Rand Daily Mail*, a diligent reporter carefully waded beyond Croft's moat of monosyllabic answers.

The burly paceman revealed that he was enrolled at an American university to do a degree in aeronautical engineering with the aim of becoming an aerospace engineer. Unlike many of his rebel brothers, Croft was already preparing for life outside the professional cricket bubble.

He alluded to a poor upbringing as the son of a shipping clerk and nurse's aide and seemed unfazed by the prospect of a life ban from the sport that had made his name. 'I knew what to expect,' he said. 'We had to weigh up whether what we were being offered was worth the consequences we would have to face.' Nor was he spooked by the spectre of apartheid. 'We haven't much time to move around so all we've really seen of this country are hotels and cricket fields. Listen man, cricket is cricket. All tours are much the same.'

But he still harboured a desire to show South African audiences that he could cut it one last time. 'I feel real bad about my back injury. But I suppose life is like that. Man, I just want you to know that I just hate to be sitting down when there is cricket to be played.'

The second tour had all the hallmarks of a second coming. In the interim, the SACU financed an operation on that troublesome back, which was referring pain down his left leg and preventing him from bowling at top pace. The recovery was swift. 'Croft back with a bang' boomed a newspaper headline – even though he'd merely bagged two wickets against Johannesburg's Mondeor High, a schoolboy XI – such was the public's appetite for his resurrection. Croft, too, was keen to demonstrate his enthusiasm, arguing vociferously with the umpire who had the temerity to call him for bowling too wide of the crease. 'I have never been no-balled for that in my life before,' he shouted. His team-mates had to calm him down – the opposition were only schoolboys after all.

In the Northern Transvaal tour match, Croft's six scalps for next to nothing impressed Northern's captain Lee Barnard so much that he warned: 'He's going to give the guys a lot of trouble with his height and a good line.' Sponsors salivated. Little-known company Dazzle Video, inspired by his 'remarkable courage' in overcoming a career-threatening injury, offered Croft a handsome 300 rand for every wicket he took in the upcoming series. Everyone, it seemed, was keen to board the Croft train.

Not everyone, however, was keen for Croft to board theirs. On Monday, 29 November 1983, Cape Town's suburban railway system became the centre of an international incident that shone a light on the daily trials of apartheid and gave yet more ammunition to critics of the rebel tours. Travelling alone, Croft unwittingly sat in a whites-only carriage. The conductor, unaware of his celebrity, asked him to move to a more colour-appropriate car. A white passenger protested on Croft's behalf, but the conductor, enforcing the segregation laws of the land, stood firm and Croft and his defender moved to a non-white compartment for the rest of the journey. At least that was Newlands resident Raymond Roos's version of what happened. Croft maintains they didn't move cars, but it was of little consequence; the fact that he'd been made a victim of apartheid's racial code generated world headlines.

The South African government immediately apologised to Croft for any 'embarrassment' suffered, but critics pointed out that millions of black South Africans experienced the same discrimination every day, so why were they not also worthy of an apology? Hassan Howa, president of the Western Province Cricket Board, which opposed the rebels' presence in the republic, summed up the vibe: 'Perhaps the West Indians will now start to realise how blacks in this country feel.'

In the Caribbean, media outlets had a field day at Croft's expense, portraying his misfortune as a form of comeuppance. The Trinidadian *Guardian*'s front page led with 'Croft gets taste of apartheid' and the *Barbados Advocate*'s editorial declared 'Croft's moment of truth'. It went on to say: 'Like the cancer it is on the South African body politic, apartheid is still there even when some of us are prepared to look away and behave as if it is not. Call it poetic justice. See it as Croft getting what he deserved. The fact remains that all this shows that the talk about the rebel cricketers breaking down apartheid is just so much wishful thinking on the part of those who would not.'

Typically, Croft took the humiliating incident in his stride. 'The conductor was just doing his job,' Croft told reporters. 'Perhaps he could have been a little bit flexible, but he didn't have to be. In his eyes I was just a black man. He did what he was supposed to do. It could have been my fault too. I should have been reading the whites-only signs, but not being accustomed to that sort of stuff I didn't worry about it.'

Whether it was mere coincidence or emotional residue from the train incident, Croft's performances with the ball tended to fall away from that moment onwards. He was still quotable: 'When I start playing cricket, my character changes. I am not a very nice person to know,' and the length of his run-up – 15, 19 or 20 paces – was an enduring source of curiosity but, increasingly, the myth didn't quite match the reality. He featured in just the one Super Series match, claiming a creditable 3-48 from ten overs, but against the might of Transvaal and with 'Test' spots up for grabs, his 18 overs leaked 95 runs. Tellingly, he wasn't called on by Lawrence Rowe to bowl in the second innings. He was now being called 'wayward' and 'erratic'.

Off-spinner and room-mate Derick Parry says that Croft didn't really want to play anymore. 'Was he injured? [Laughs] I don't think he was injured – he'd come to collect.'

Berea Park, Pretoria, was the venue for Croft's swansong – ten wicketless overs for 51 – seriously expensive figures in an era of thin bats and long boundaries. His Dazzle Video sponsorship had yielded only three victims and 900 rand. The career of one of the most intimidating bowlers in the history of cricket had petered out in a haze of injury, poor form and indifference.

Not that Ali Bacher was too concerned. Without Croft's prized signature, the tours may never have succeeded in attracting so many top-level West Indian cricketers, and fit, lame or aloof, he was always good copy for journalists. Croft, too, benefited from a massive payout he could never have imagined had his career flatlined in county or Shell Shield cricket where money was scarce. Retiring to Florida, he finished his university degree and skilfully repositioned himself as a cricket commentator and journalist. As always, he was a man in control of his destiny.

Former Australian captain Ian Chappell shared the microphone with him. 'You thought of him as mad when you played against him, but he was far from that,' Chappell says. 'He had a lot of ideas and he was always pushing himself as a commentator. But the competitive instinct was never far away. I remember we were having a discussion and he said I once got you out lbw, and I said, that can't be right, Crofty, you never pitched one over halfway – it's never going to be bouncing under the height of the stumps. He looked quite hurt for a while.'

In 2010 Croft addressed the controversy surrounding the rebel tours in *Fire in Babylon*, a documentary and book on the West Indies' rise to cricket dominance in the 1980s. For once, he seemed torn. 'Money is everybody's god,' he railed. 'Let's be honest, you had to look after yourself.' He took umbrage at the idea that he fattened his bank account while black South Africans suffered. 'I'm a mercenary? When I went to World Series Cricket, was I not a mercenary then? I'm not sure I understand the difference. This is not a game. This is my livelihood. It's my job.'

But he also expressed regret. 'I suppose in retrospect it was not a good decision. Maybe from naivety, maybe from singularity, I may have made a mistake there ... A lot of people could say I embarrassed the Caribbean. I take whatever comes with it.'

And then, in the most revealing moment of all, as the camera zoomed in on a black-and-white photograph of Croft and his suited team-mates during the official West Indies 1979/80 tour of Australia, the hard man appeared to crack. 'It hurts not to be a part of that team,' he said, as if realising that South Africa had tainted his legacy. 'Being able to walk down the street and hold your head high – that was better than gold, than being a millionaire.'

Ezra Moseley

'I'm not bowling anymore on
this shit-heap, man'

EZRA MOSELEY was never as rude to me as Colin Croft. But he was definitely as fast – most say faster. Battle-hardened former England opener Robin Smith said Moseley generated more pace off the wicket than any bowler he faced. Barry Richards rated him equal with the sharpest of all the rebel Caribbean hitmen.

He was also elusive. Still is. Various coaching posts with the BCA and Cricket West Indies (formerly the WICB) – he mentored the 2017 women's World Cup side – and a natural reserve have rendered him a reluctant contributor to history's pages. Although he denies it, there's clearly a sense that raking up old rebel tour issues might not be in his best professional interests. They still have the power to divide.

Our congenial seven-minute WhatsApp conversation ended in stalemate; he promised to divulge career secrets only if I wrote his biography first, which without a publishing contract wasn't feasible. Nor does he, as a two-Test bowler, have the box-office pull of a Joel Garner or Malcolm Marshall. We agreed to meet in Barbados to talk about his contemporary and friend, the late Sylvester Clarke, but he was called away to Jamaica with the national women's side just before my LIAT Airlines flight landed at Grantley Adams International Airport. It was a pattern of frustration that would characterise our communication.

There are two deliveries, seven years apart, that define Moseley's legacy. Both are preserved in YouTube perpetuity for future students of the psychological terrors of combating fast bowling. The first ties South African opener Jimmy Cook up in an ungainly tangle of fear as his neck snaps back whiplash-like to avoid the 90mph orb rocketing towards his right cheek. When he regathers himself, Cook's crucifix necklace is still dangling over his shoulder blades, the momentum from his instinctive survival dance having pushed it there, and his dark green Springbok cap sits up comically like a steam train driver's hat.

Barry Richards – sensible pale blue helmet and blond curls – witnessed Moseley's monster ball from the safety of the bowler's end. 'Ezra wasn't big and he only had a short run-up, but he was very deceptive,' the master batsman says. 'And as we were going out to open the batting I had one of those half helmets on – just with the ear pieces, and I said to James, "Are you wearing a helmet?" He said proudly, "No, I will show them the badge, the cloth badge." So, out we go, and Ezra bowled him the quickest bouncer and it nearly killed him. He was an S-bend trying to avoid it. And within 15 seconds of shaking his head, he was waving away to the pavilion to bring the helmet out. I'll never forget the look on James's face when he looked down the other end. His eyeballs were just fixed.'

Moseley's near decapitation of Cook took place on a placid Newlands wicket in 1983 during the opening 'Test' of the first rebel tour. He was 25.

The second delivery turned a Test series in 1990. His quarry this time was England captain Graham Gooch, a man at the peak of his batting capabilities, steadily guiding his side towards a fourth innings 151-run target and a 2-0 lead over the invincible West Indies. Moseley, at 32, was making his Test debut but he was no greenhorn. He had hundreds of first-class wickets under his belt and the confidence to match. He'd replaced the mini-

Afro he sported in his youth with fashionable Lionel Richie-style Jheri curls, and his approach to the stumps was marginally slower, but smoother. When the spitting cobra of a ball rose unexpectedly from just short of a length, Gooch, who had already been struck once by Moseley, hoisted his bat in self-preservation. But he was too slow – as any mortal batsman would have been. The ball cannoned into the back of his left hand, fracturing the base of his little finger in two places. Unshaven and normally unbending, Gooch dropped his bat on the Queen's Park pitch.

Television commentator Tony Lewis, the former England captain, was incredulous: 'It wasn't doing this for Curtly Ambrose,' he said, referring to Moseley's ability to extract lift where others had failed. The Bajan debutant had out-bowled a man who would take 399 more Test wickets than him.

First drop Alec Stewart, also in his maiden series, was Gooch's partner at the crease. He says that Moseley surprised Gooch – and the English batsmen – with his zip and bite from the southern end on that final day of the third Test. 'He was short, but he bowled quick and he was probably the quickest bowler in that series. With his trajectory, it was like Malcolm Marshall. He was on you all the time and could still get the ball to bounce, despite being a little bit more skiddy than the others. Goochie was as tough as anyone I played with and you knew when he showed pain, there was an issue. And he was in proper pain.'

Without their moustachioed talisman – and frustrated by stand-in captain Desmond Haynes's stalling tactics – England's run chase inevitably petered out. Gooch was ruled out of the last two Tests and not for the first time the champion West Indies side retrieved a rubber that had appeared beyond their grasp.

What made Moseley's appearance even more significant was that he was the only rebel to be selected for the official West Indies side after their life ban was rescinded in 1989. His form had been irresistible during that 1990 Red Stripe Cup season – 22 wickets at 24.64 – but there were still rumblings in certain corners of the Caribbean that it was too early to welcome a 'race traitor' into the Test side.

The freeing of Nelson Mandela from prison early that year only heightened opposition. Jamaican politician A. J. Nicholson summed up the mood in a letter he wrote to the *Jamaica Gleaner*: 'To my mind there is something utterly wrong in witnessing the jubilation of the release in February of Nelson Mandela after 27 years in bondage and the inclusion of Moseley in March.'

By the fifth Test in Antigua, the home of proud anti-apartheid champion Viv Richards, there was talk of a crowd boycott as local politicians and radio DJs ramped up the rhetoric, no doubt hoping their countryman, all-rounder Eldine Baptiste, would be preferred over Moseley. Even the normally impassive Andy Roberts entered the debate, pointing out, somewhat ironically, that when he was pensioned off by the selectors he must have been an 'old 32', whereas debutant Moseley was obviously a 'young 32'. Ultimately, a strained hamstring that Moseley had acquired in the fourth Test forced him off the team, dulling the controversy, but there were still those who wondered whether the injury was fabricated in order to avoid a stand-off.

He also had strong-willed and highly opinionated team-mates to deal with. Apart from Richards, wicketkeeper Jeff Dujon was a fierce opponent of apartheid – he'd knocked back the SACU's offers of luxury cars and bags of cash – while Malcolm Marshall and Desmond Haynes famously bailed out of the tours at the last moment. How would they respond to a rehabilitated rebel in their midst?

'It's true, I wouldn't have gone to South Africa and I was against the rebel tours,' Dujon says. 'But the West Indies team was a very cohesive unit at that point in time and anything like that was put aside for the good of the side,' Dujon says. But he's not sure whether he would have chosen Moseley had he been on the selection committee. 'I don't know. I know what you're getting at, but I would only have been one of the selectors.'

Why did Ezra Moseley, a bowler capable of dislodging and disfiguring the world's best batsmen, end up on the wrong side of history, an anathema to black opinion-makers and even some of his team-mates? Superficially, the early signs were positive: a county contract and Glamorgan cap before he'd even represented his native Barbados. But the fact that he had to decamp to England to taste first-class action spoke to the broader issue of the pace bowling logjam at the apex of Caribbean cricket. As muscle-bound countryman Hartley Alleyne also discovered, the market for shorter, skidding quicks under six feet tall was already cornered by Malcolm Marshall. Not that Moseley was deterred. Seven wickets on his county debut, a hat-trick against Kent in the Benson and Hedges Cup, followed by a 6-23 splattering of the touring Australians, including the prized wicket of Allan Border – leg stump flattened – signalled a young paceman of international class.

The 23-year-old 'who used to serve drinks at the Grantley Adams Airport in Barbados' confessed to *The Guardian*'s match reporter that his purple patch was 'the best nine days of my cricketing life'.

The cricket gods ensured it didn't last. On the back of that Glamorgan success he was finally selected for Barbados alongside Joel Garner and Sylvester Clarke, but after collaring 16 Shell Shield wickets in the 1981/82 season, he succumbed to every fast bowler's nightmare injury – a lower back stress fracture.

Replaced at Glamorgan by tall Vincentian quick bowler Winston Davis, and forced to undergo a long period of rehabilitation, Moseley's fledgling career was in limbo. There was no guarantee he would recover his pace or his import spot at Sophia Gardens.

Such was, in part, the backdrop to his choice to sign for the rebel tour of South Africa and surrender all claims to an official maroon West Indies cap. He was 24. It was a life-changing decision that even the most rusted-on rebel struggled with.

On the journey to the republic, Barbados team-mate Franklyn Stephenson says Moseley and Alvin Greenidge were fretting about touching down in South Africa and would have happily turned the aeroplane around if they could have. But, on arrival, Moseley could still conjure a smile for the *Rand Daily Mail*'s front page as a white Johannesburg tailor measured him for the tour blazer.

Beefy Sylvester Clarke hogged the headlines in South Africa, introducing a brutal brand of fast bowling that shocked the Springboks' sheltered batsmen. But a fit Moseley earned high praise from commentators and, most importantly, the opposition. Barry Richards's assertion that he was potentially quicker than Croft, Clarke, Alleyne and Stephenson was borne out by the Cook ball, which the opening batsman wrote 'almost killed me', and stats of 34 'Test' and ODI wickets at 25.

His reputation as a no-frills assassin encouraged Eastern Province to sign him for the 1984/85 Currie Cup season after the tours ended. As a professional cricketer, it also helped him to plug the financial gap that yawned after being banned from Caribbean sides. He didn't disappoint the St George's Park faithful, blasting out 34 wickets at a miserly average of 16.38, often on a docile home pitch.

His opening bowling partner was rangy blond seamer Mike van Vuuren. They were room-mates and are still good buddies. 'He's a great guy who I got on very well with,' van Vuuren says, 'but sometimes he was temperamental and just did not want to bowl.'

Van Vuuren says that Moseley had a tendency to become uninterested when he wasn't charging in against the best batsmen. He needed the spur of authentic competition to be at his most potent. Van Vuuren remembers a match against Transvaal, the so-called 'Mean Machine', at Port Elizabeth in early 1985. Transvaal were probably the strongest provincial side in the world at the time – Cook, Pollock, Kourie, McKenzie, Jennings, Rice and Sylvester Clarke rounded out a team full of hard-nosed pros, but the wicket was flat and unresponsive, and van Vuuren says that Moseley wasn't impressed. 'He walked past me after two or three overs and said, "I'm not bowling anymore on this shit-heap, man,"' van Vuuren says.

But when the great Graeme Pollock strode to the crease, Moseley perked up at the prospect of doing battle with the man who averaged 61 in Test cricket. He demanded the ball. 'He bowled four overs of high pace, knocked off Pollock for 15, but as soon as he was gone, if I remember rightly, he buggered off back to fine leg.'

It was understandable, van Vuuren says, that Moseley preferred to test himself against the best, especially when the prospect of Test cricket had been snatched from him. And he knew that bagging blue riband wickets generated the biggest headlines back in England and the Caribbean. But his flighty behaviour was a headache for captain Gavin Cowley.

At a day-night match in Pietermaritzburg, during a fiery spell, Moseley asked for an extra slip. His request was denied. The paceman returned to the start of his run-up, sat down and refused to bowl. 'He was not always the easiest,' van Vuuren says. 'He was great with his circle of friends but there were some he didn't take too kindly to.'

After a card game, opening batsman and team-mate Philip Amm was one of them. 'It was a rain delay and Philip ridiculed Moses for throwing away a joker during a game of rummy. As a result he received 13 consecutive bouncers in the nets from Ezra.'

But the descriptors 'hot-blooded' and 'difficult' never harmed a fast-bowler's CV, and another stint with Glamorgan followed in 1986. The years leading up to the reversal of the Test-playing ban in 1989 were spent roughing up amateur batsmen for Littleborough in the central Lancashire League and representing Spartan in the BCA alongside former Test and Barbados team-mates. When the ban was ultimately lifted, Moseley was required to sign a form promising not to return to South Africa. He and fellow rebel Franklyn Stephenson were then included in the Barbados squad for the 1989/90 Red Stripe Cup season.

After cracking Gooch's pinkie and entering Caribbean fast-bowling folklore, Moseley was included on the three-Test tour of Pakistan under Desmond Haynes's captaincy in late 1990 – regular skipper Viv Richards was undergoing an operation for persistent haemorrhoids.

With Malcolm Marshall fit, Moseley was relegated to fifth in the pecking order behind young Trinidadian Ian Bishop and the emerging duo of Curtly Ambrose and Courtney Walsh. Still, all the pre-tour debate was about whether Marshall, the same age as Moseley, and with 329 Test wickets to his credit, was over the hill. Marshall's reputation prevailed and Moseley's contribution was limited to two one-dayers.

Back at Kensington Oval, Moseley nurtured his bone-splitting reputation, breaking Guyana number three Andrew Jackman's forearm with a trademark lifter. And 16 Red Stripe Cup wickets at 22.75 kept him in the picture for West Indies selection for the five-Test tour by Allan Border's Australians in 1991. Writing a tour preview in the *Sydney Morning Herald*, Phil Wilkins observed: 'There is a lot of Merv Hughes in Ezra's wild man make-up. He is a tough bully boy who spares no batsmen. Marshall, Ambrose and Bishop are the headline stealers, but Moseley could be remembered as the head hunter this year.'

It wasn't to be. Bishop withdrew from the series with a stress fracture of the lower vertebrae, but the hulking Jamaican Patrick Patterson squeezed out Moseley in the race to fill his spot. At 33, Moseley's obsolescence was confirmed later that year when Winston Benjamin and rookie Ian Allen were preferred for the tour of England.

Moseley's fragmented West Indies career was over, a victim of international politics and a fast bowling production line that seemed to stretch far into the Caribbean sunset.

* * *

True to his enigmatic public persona, his utterances in cyberspace have been minimal since. Interviewed by *Wisden India* magazine a few years ago, he refused to expound on the rebel tours and wished he'd retired earlier so he could have devoted more time to coaching. In a 2011 ESPN video he bemoaned the current fast bowlers' casual attitude to training and nominated Malcolm Marshall as the best paceman of his generation: 'He was a terrific bowler ... his ability to assess a player and the conditions and know exactly how he wanted to get them out.'

It was a generous assessment – Marshall, a great of the game, but only three months younger, had occupied a central role in West Indies cricket that could, with better choices, have been Moseley's. As it turned out, six Test wickets was his career harvest. That and the trembling testimonies of some of the greatest batsmen to have played the game.

Franklyn Stephenson
'Yes, he drank my Coke!'

'POW FUL' is an old Barbados term meaning someone who speaks their mind without fear of ramifications. It's an adjective Franklyn Stephenson wears with pride. At his eponymous cricket academy in the parish of St Thomas on the western side of the island, the man often referred to as the 'best all-rounder the West Indies never had' is training both barrels on his country's leading academics.

Professor Alan Cobley, who has said the rebel tours did nothing to advance cricket for black people in South Africa, is a 'jackass. You can talk about the tour; you're talking in the dark. This is crazy. Criminal.' Sir Hilary Beckles, the superstar of Caribbean academia and long-time apartheid critic 'wants putting in jail. He's got to comment on every situation, and he knows absolutely nothing.'

But Stephenson's 35-year-old sense of indignation must wait. His under-11 boys are limbering up for a match against Bayley's Primary School in the Herman Griffith competition, so-named for the second Bajan to bowl in Test cricket. Stephenson, clad in the bright orange and green colours of his academy, is manoeuvring a Rust-Oleum striping machine to mark out the required length of pitch for the age group. The muggy morning air is discordant with the sound of kids clamouring for his attention, tugging on his black Queensland Valleys Cricket Club

318

cap – one legacy of a peripatetic career – and jostling for batting order promotions.

The academy is a testament to Stephenson's indomitable spirit. Once a rocky outcrop off Highway 2A, he has transformed it into a top-line facility, even hosting his old county side Nottinghamshire. Inside the pavilion, a portrait of a smiling Stephenson in his 100-wickets-and-1,000-runs-in-a-season pomp hangs above the doorway, just as an image of the Queen might adorn a club or royalist institution.

In fact, Stephenson is bereft of airs and graces; a toothy, megawatt grin is never far away. Team-mates called him Cookie Monster because of his resemblance, when bearded, to the furry *Sesame Street* character, but whereas the loveable muppet had an insatiable lust for sweet biscuits, Stephenson has an insatiable lust for life – and cricket. Like his teenage hero and former team-mate Collis King, he's a forceful presence, a fearless practitioner of the *carpe diem* principle with a perpetual contempt for the besuited fools of administration, academia and politics. 'That is their right, to do crap and still be part of society,' he rages, returning to the subject of Beckles and Cobley. 'I've been there to South Africa. Get these jackasses to come in front of me!'

His young batsmen are also causing him grief. 'That should be a single every time, Andre! Look at the fielders and know who can't save a single – if they're too deep, run!'

To lighten the mood, I hand him an archived clipping from the *Rand Daily Mail* newspaper of a beautiful blonde Johannesburg model named Mandy leaning in close to him during a day trip to Sun City, the luxury resort and casino that featured international entertainers and became a rallying cry for anti-apartheid activists in the 1980s. 'My wife has gone home – you just missed her,' he laughs in mock fear. 'That was a promotional set-up,' he adds.

On the same wall as his signature portrait there's a framed newspaper clipping with the headline 'Stephenson – the best since Sobers'. The story relates to his 13-75 against Yorkshire at Headingley in 1989, 'the outstanding achievement' of the county season so far, the writer enthuses, as good as Richard Hadlee, the man he'd replaced at Nottinghamshire.

He wasn't the first West Indian all-rounder to be saddled with Sobers comparisons, but whereas contemporary Bernard Julien played as if it was a burden, Stephenson, naturally fearless and self-confident, felt no pressure. It also helped that he was then 30 years old, and he never had to reproduce on a Test cricket pitch, because those 'jackasses' in officialdom, he says, had ripped the best years of his career from his CV.

That bullet-proof self-confidence was honed and tested across the 2A at St John the Baptist School in Holders Hill, the beachside community famous for producing Desmond Haynes, and the surrounding villages of Durants, Hoytes and Halls where he grew up. In the classic Caribbean tradition, after-school games on the 'pasture' or roads involving 20 or 30 boys would last until dusk or their mums' patience ran out.

The best batters, like Seymour Nurse, could dig in for days on end, which only increased the pressure on everyone else to make the most of their 'hand'. There was also a sorting out process for newcomers. 'I remember when I went out to bat one time and I batted three balls. And a guy says, "He looks good; give him 'the thing'." "The thing" was a beamer – and they were accurate.'

When you'd survived 'the thing' you could survive anything. 'You had no fear of fast bowlers after that,' Stephenson laughs. It was inbred fearlessness that set him apart.

Peter Clough was a journeyman medium-fast bowler in the Sheffield Shield for Tasmania and later Western Australia. He roomed with the Barbadian during the 1981/82 season when Stephenson was based in Launceston, playing for Mowbray Cricket Club. They opened the bowling together for the state, which hadn't yet been granted full status in the competition proper. 'He was a fun-loving guy. He wasn't scared of anyone. He had so much self-confidence,' Clough remembers.

An audacious innings hooking Colin Croft's skull-seeking bumpers at the TCA ground particularly stands out. 'He only had a cap on, and Croft was bowling bouncer after bouncer and he just kept on hooking. It was a barrage. Croft had said to him, "You gonna hook dem, man? You gonna hook dem all." And he did. Things I couldn't have done.'

What was playing out was a classic confrontation between the younger man trying to stamp his mark on the game – and what he hoped might be his future Test team-mates – and the established gun keen to assert his own dominance.

In the touring West Indies first innings, Croft emerged as nightwatchman to protect Larry Gomes from the fading light. Stephenson seized the opportunity, cannoning a short delivery into the badge of the surly Guyanese's helmet. He went on to snare 5-46, including the scalp of Viv Richards. 'It was an interesting thing to see,' Clough says. 'The young pup if you like, having a go at the old dog. And the young pup won the day.'

Curiously, that season marked Stephenson's first-class debut. With Joel Garner, Malcolm Marshall, Wayne Daniel, Sylvester Clarke, Ezra Moseley, Hartley Alleyne and Collis King clogging up the fast-bowling ranks in Barbados, Stephenson, 22, had to ply his trade elsewhere. At Rawtenstall in England's Lancashire League that northern summer he'd out-bowled Michael Holding, Andy Roberts and Kapil Dev to capture 105 wickets at 9.3. He'd also debuted his idiosyncratic and devastating slow ball as a way to conserve energy during long spells.

It came of age in the Australian summer. Battle-scarred local batsmen had spent years steeling themselves against the fear of the rising ball from a succession of leering West Indies pacemen. They were war-weary and primed for anything aimed at their heads. Stephenson exploited their fears almost at will. Utilising his full 6ft 4in frame, his slower ball came disguised as a fast beamer. The effect was almost comical, as the ball suddenly dipped and dropped at the batsman's quivering, recoiling feet, gently nudging into his pads or the stumps. Nowhere was it more devastating than in his first game for Tasmania, against Victoria on a low-playing MCG pitch.

'With silver and gold pendants thumping he represented an awesome sight to the Victorian batsmen, who had no idea at what height the ball would reach them,' wrote *The Age*'s Mike Coward of Stephenson's destructive 6-19 figures. Five of his victims, including Test players Graham Yallop, Jeff Moss, Ray Bright and Max Walker were out lbw or bowled, as the slower ball messed with the most experienced of minds.

Peter Clough was his opening bowling partner. 'It was a game where the slow ball took everyone by surprise. They were thinking here's a new West Indian fast bowler, and this will land on my head, but it lands at their feet. You can tell yourself "hey, this is going to be a slow ball", but when the guy has been bowling really quick and it looks like it's coming at you head-high, your body doesn't react like it's a slower ball.'

Tasmania's victory was their first on the Australian mainland, and Stephenson's debut 10-46 match analysis, in a season where he bagged 30 wickets at 16.63, was a declaration of serious intent to the wider cricket world.

But there were no Sobers comparisons yet. In the Caribbean, a sense of mistrust, consistent with the West Indies' dominant position in world cricket, tended to cloud the assessment of performances from outside the region. It was one thing to bag ten wickets in the semi-professional leagues of Lancashire or the fledgling backwater of Tasmania, but it was another to repeat that feat in the Shell Shield, the world's toughest domestic competition.

But Stephenson's 1982 form was irresistible, even if his habit of roughing up team-mates in the nets with short deliveries could be a source of irritation. His break came when Sylvester Clarke and Wayne Daniel were unavailable, and all-rounder George Linton dislocated his shoulder in a one-dayer.

Unsurprisingly, Stephenson's first Shell Shield wicket came from a slower ball, trapping Leeward Islands number three Ralston Otto in front for 18.

But it was with the bat that Stephenson smote all his doubters. With Andy Roberts at his unsmiling best, there were few volunteers to replace the departing Alvin Greenidge as Barbados slumped to 8/2 a quarter of an hour before stumps in Basseterre, St Kitts. The normally elegant opener was out fending off a ball that was homing in on his right ear. The Bajan dressing room was spooked. But not first-cap Stephenson. He'd experienced 'the thing' after all.

Utilising all his Holders Hill street smarts as nightwatchman, Stephenson stood his ground against the great Antiguan, who peppered him with bouncers. But the intense concentration it took to ward off Roberts left him vulnerable to lesser practitioners of the fast arts, local favourite James Harris spearing a bumper into Stephenson's shoulder. He wasn't deterred.

The next day, Stephenson hammered 20 fours and four sixes to record 165, an innings CANA described as 'scintillating' with 'fine technique' on the on side. Whereas the previous evening they were baying for his blood, the 4,000 spectators at Warner Park now gave him a standing ovation.

In the English summer, Stephenson returned to Rawtenstall, accompanied by his wife Julia and newborn daughter Amanda, and played for Gloucestershire when he wasn't required in Lancashire. He topped the bowling averages for his county, but how would his feats be received back home? On the surface, his first trial match back with Barbados was going well. He'd taken two wickets, and on the practice day he spent his time diligently in the nets as usual, when he was confronted by legendary 1960s quick bowler Charlie Griffith, who was helping out with the selection process. According to Stephenson, the fast bowler got stuck into him straight away, telling him that since he'd scored the 165 on debut he'd become 'Pow ful'; too big for his boots.

Stephenson was stung. Griffith was no shrinking violet himself; he'd had his own battles with cricket's establishment and he'd also coached Stephenson at St John the Baptist School. 'He said I was full of chat. But I'd been in England doing my own things. I'm still wondering why and what I did to deserve it. Seeing this authority figure telling me all was not well, was really, really weird.'

Was Stephenson being overly sensitive or was there something else behind Griffith's dressing down? Had his cards been marked?

At the same time, the Caribbean was abuzz with talk of a rebel tour to South Africa. It was well known that several Bajans had committed, but organiser Gregory Armstrong was desperate to bolster the squad's bowling stocks, especially with the withdrawal of St Vincent pacer Winston Davis.

Stephenson was targeted. At first he was offered US$80,000 but said no because he felt the timing was wrong – he was trying to establish himself in the Barbados side and he didn't want to be banned from Test cricket. He also says he had 'personal' reasons, which he won't disclose, for rejecting the deal.

When Armstrong upped the offer to US$100,000, Stephenson stonewalled him again. But the Griffith incident put doubt in his mind. 'Was he trying to tell me something? Absolutely, the thought of being banned troubled me'. Stephenson says. 'But I thought, what was I going to be banned from? I wasn't a member of the West Indies team. There was no West Indies A or B. It gets to the stage where you're not going forward.'

What clinched his signature was a strange, almost spiritual incident at the Holders Hill playing field where he was hanging with old friends, discussing his options. 'They all had their opinions about what happened with me and Griffith and it started to rain. I was so deep in thought, standing in the middle of the road, but I wasn't getting wet. It was a sign. In Barbados when the rain starts to fall you have to get out of it quick. I felt it was my destiny to go on this tour.'

Stephenson was only 23, the youngest man in the squad. Had he terminated a potential West Indies career on the basis of a tongue-lashing from a has-been bowler and a bizarre meteorological event? Of course, it wasn't that simple. Stephenson had his wife and baby daughter to support, and he was, despite his tender years, inured to the nomadic demands of a professional cricketer's existence.

Still, some thought he'd acted prematurely. Peter Clough was one of them. 'I was surprised, but only in part,' he says. 'Franklyn was always a man in a hurry. He was keen to get ahead. And I think sometimes when you take the quickest path, it's not always the best path. He was impulsive. That's the way he played the game. I think if he looked at it in hindsight he might have made a different decision. The next season we had Michael Holding come to Tasmania and I became good friends with him too, and he was against the tours, so it made it difficult for me having two friends on opposing sides.'

Respected West Indies commentator Reds Perreira was shocked by Stephenson's defection. 'The one name on the list of players going that caught my thoughts was Franklyn Stephenson. I really thought he was making a rash decision, because there was no doubt he was going to play for the West Indies. He was totally outstanding.'

It was also certain that with the exit of so many seasoned Bajan and West Indies players to South Africa, Stephenson would have been closer than ever to making his Test debut.

Countryman Malcolm Marshall definitely saw the tours in that way – a chance to advance his own West Indies interests. He figured that with Croft and Clarke chasing rand, it opened up an opportunity to cement his own position in the famous pace battery. Some feel it's why he entertained Dr Ali Bacher's mega-dollar advances right until the death, until he was sure which of his bowling competitors were going.

Whatever the ramifications, Stephenson's call had been hard on everyone involved. 'I had lots of difficulties with Franklyn Stephenson,' Armstrong says. 'He had his views, that had to be respected. The irony was he liked South Africa more than anyone else.'

And the mainly white South African crowds liked him, too. Perhaps because he'd been forced to pursue a career outside the

Caribbean, Stephenson was more adept at mixing in diverse social situations, and his natural gregariousness marked him out as approachable – and a prized autograph. He slotted into the role of unofficial goodwill ambassador.

Second tour batsman Monte Lynch reckons both Stephenson and Sylvester Clarke, whose astonishing bowling captivated the republic, had a massive impact that went way beyond their cricket heroics. 'I think they should have been knighted for what they did,' he says. 'They helped the P. W. Bothas of this world see that, yes, we are human beings.'

In the first 'Test' at Cape Town, a parable-like 'Stephenson and the Coke bottles' incident unfolded on the Newlands boundary. As he returned to his position near the fence after fielding a ball, a white boy approached him with a bottle of Coke, asking the big Barbadian to take a sip. 'I said, thank you, but I had my own drink bottle,' Stephenson says. But the young boy was persistent. Once again Stephenson politely refused. On the third occasion, Stephenson gave in. 'I thought this isn't working, so I said give me the Coke and I had a drink.'

Chuffed, the young boy ran off shouting, 'Yes, he drank my Coke!' At the next ball there were more than 15 young white boys brandishing Coke bottles at their new hero. In the tourists' eyes, it was the kind of innocent racial interaction that reinforced their claims that they were achieving something more than just winning cricket matches.

Lynch remembers Stephenson at the centre of another poignant inter-racial moment during the second tour. A white boy offered the fine leg fieldsman a lick of his ice cream. According to Lynch, Stephenson pretended to lick it. 'But he didn't give it back to the white kid,' Lynch says. 'He gave it to a black kid, who licked the ice cream. Then the black kid gave it back to the white kid.' Lynch was moved. 'You're watching that happen and thinking that would not normally happen on the street. I wish I had a camera. It was a serious moment.'

But Stephenson was aware that what occurred inside the rarefied confines of a sporting stadium bore little resemblance to the outside world. He saw with his own eyes the destructive effect apartheid had on the black psyche. 'They kept their heads down when they walked – they weren't like boisterous people in the West Indies,' he says. 'There were people without a smile who looked apologetic for being where they were. It was very moving. Black people there couldn't believe we spoke English, the white man's language.'

He says the majority of his exchanges with the indigenous population occurred at hotels, where most of the staff were black and often spoke under their breath for fear of being seen fraternising with guests.

On the pitch, Stephenson was typically explosive. In *Calypso Cavaliers*, a contemporary review of the 1983 tour, Brian Cowley wrote: 'His style of play epitomised for South African spectators their vision of the typical West Indian player – a tearaway fast bowler and uninhibited attacking batsman.' But Stephenson knew that if he wanted to be selected for the 'Test' side he would have to moderate his attacking instincts. With Croft's back injury ruling him out, he saw a niche as the third seamer bowling holding spells while speedsters Sylvester Clarke and Ezra Moseley recharged their batteries. It was a successful ploy, consigning experienced Test all-rounder Bernard Julien to the drinks cart.

Was it an honour representing the West Indies for the first time, even in an unofficial capacity, alongside legends Rowe, Kallicharran et al? 'It didn't bother me too much,' Stephenson says. 'In the Lancashire League I got 105 wickets, Holding got 86, Roberts and Kapil Dev 71, so I never felt overawed by any situation. Any game I played was the one I focused on.'

Nor did he feel any pangs of conscience about making colossal sums of money while his black South African brothers and sisters suffered at the hands of a discriminatory regime. 'Yes, we were going to get paid, but we were also going to be ostracised for doing our work. My job at hand was to represent my colour, my country and the institution of cricket.'

Some back in Barbados felt he'd betrayed his colour. At a department store in Bridgetown, a policeman called him an 'honorary white'. And his attempts to play with local club Maple – Barbados rebels weren't banned from club cricket in between the tours – were stymied by a ludicrous amount of paperwork, which Stephenson believes was a ruse to keep him out of the club. However, he did turn out for Spartan thanks to Ezra Moseley's intervention. In any case, his major professional focus was still on England, where in Zaheer Abbas's absence he had a stint at Gloucestershire, and with Oldham in the Lancashire League.

In the second South Africa instalment, Stephenson made a determined effort to ramp up his output – he felt the side's performances in the first campaign lacked a killer punch – but the hectic ten-week schedule took its toll on everyone, and with many of the older players hurtling towards a career dead end, tempers frayed.

As part of his renewed focus, Stephenson advocated for team meetings to plan strategies. He got his wish, but the result wasn't pretty. 'So many guys were late for the meeting ... There was a scuffle that spilled into the corridor. People were having a go at each other ... David Murray was always on somebody's case. He gave Albert Padmore a lot of stick. He's the smallest guy in the group but the most antagonistic. He got on to Ezra Moseley's case and Moseley grabbed him by his beard.'

What was Lawrence Rowe doing? 'Just whistling, cool as a cucumber,' Stephenson laughs.

Even when nine of the squad visited Sun City, the *Rand Daily Mail* reported that the tourists were 'unimpressed by their surroundings' and kept their Walkmans on in the presence of their Bophuthatswana government host throughout lunch. Stephenson's companion for the day, 'Mandy', the model he stressed was part of a promotion, was reported as an encumbrance, as she pawed all over him despite the obvious presence of his wedding ring and her own admission that she hoped his wife wouldn't be 'cross when she sees this picture'.

* * *

At Stephenson's academy there's a moment of high farce. A young charge on strike has dropped his bat mid-delivery and sprinted to the pavilion in search of a drink. 'You can't casually stop the game like that and come and get water.' Stephenson shakes his head as the thirsty boy sups from a plastic bottle. 'You have to let the water come to you. You have to ask the umpire! Or in the water break.'

Among the memorabilia on the walls of the academy pavilion is a Nottinghamshire Cricket Club-certified piece entitled 'The Double'. It celebrates the unique fact that both Stephenson and Kevin Cooper captured more than 100 wickets each in the 1988 county season. What it neglects to relay to the impressed observer is that Stephenson also blasted more than 1,000 runs, recording a rare all-rounder's double that only one other man, New Zealand great Richard Hadlee, has achieved in the past 50 years. In a typical touch of theatre, Stephenson waited until the last game on the fixture list, against Yorkshire, to knock off the required 210 runs, battering two centuries and snaring 11 wickets in the match, in what *The Guardian*'s match report described as 'the finest individual all-round performance in a cricket match for 82 years'.

It's his defining achievement, a two-fingered salute to the Caribbean authorities that dared ban him from Test cricket for life, an achievement *Wisden* recognised by naming him one of their five 1989 cricketers of the year.

But how would his disbelieving critics back in Barbados rate it? It was an important question because in early 1989, on the back of an ICC resolution, the WICBC offered to lift the Test and first-class ban on the rebels provided they agreed not to play in South Africa again and applied to the board for reinstatement.

It's a bittersweet memory for Stephenson. 'I sort of wish that I could have been strong enough to tell them to take a flying leap,' he says, 'because I had been wrongfully banned for so long. I was thinking: who was going to apologise for banning me for six and a half years? But I worded the statement to say that if this has offended anybody, I'm sorry, but it was my decision. I remember at the time: here's the world waiting to see what this man is going to do in Test cricket.'

There was certainly no welcome mat laid out for him in his homeland. Cammie Smith, a veteran of the 1961 tied Test, and former West Indies assistant manager, says Barbados selector Keith Walcott was never a fan. 'I think Stephenson was a very useful player, but he ran aground with Keith Walcott,' he says. 'It was alleged Keith met him in Bridgetown with an official from England who told Walcott that Stephenson did the double last year.'

According to Smith, Walcott's reply was damning: 'Don't you think the standard of cricket has deteriorated in England?'

Somewhat begrudgingly, it seems, Stephenson was included in the Barbados squad but already there were murmurs of disapproval. 'There was this big outcry,' he says. 'These 30-year-olds should be at the YMPC – the geriatric hospital, because they're too old. They should be letting the youngsters play.'

The protracted manner of his selection demonstrated how reluctant the Barbados establishment was to have him return to the fold. Initially named in a squad of 13, he was told by a team-mate that he wasn't playing in the XI, but Malcolm Marshall, who was carrying a wrist injury, took him aside and assured him he would take the paceman's place. At a team dinner a few days later, Stephenson says, his inclusion was informally announced, but the selectors, sticklers for protocol, then informed the team that no selection meeting had actually taken place.

What made it even more frustrating was that the proposed 13th man, Sherwin Campbell, was a future Test batting opener, a wholly unsuitable replacement for Marshall. I was thinking 'What's going on?' Stephenson says. 'It was all part of this big underlying thing where they had this plan of me not actually playing for them.'

On the morning before the start of Barbados's opening match against Leeward Islands, the selection farce continued. After a hit-out in the nets, the rest of the squad returned to the dressing room to kit up for the first innings, leaving Stephenson to face throwdowns from members of the crowd. He'd seen Keith Walcott arrive earlier but had had no contact until 28 minutes to 11. 'He walked over to me and said in his own inimitable way, "Franklyn, Malcolm isn't fit so we've decided you will take his place."'

Stephenson also found Desmond Haynes's captaincy hard to fathom. 'He was the worst captain I've ever come across,' he says. 'He didn't have a clue about setting fields and how to manage things, and he was very egotistical.'

After top-scoring in the first innings with 77 not out from number seven, Stephenson was watching his side's second innings unfold from the comfort of the pavilion. 'I was just sitting there with my pants on, underwear, jockstrap, no socks,' he says, when Haynes called to him from the Kensington Oval dressing room. 'He says to me, "Are you padded?" Padded? I am batting seven – we were only three wickets down.'

Another wicket fell, and wicketkeeper Ricky Hoyte, who had batted at six in the first innings, began his walk to the centre square … until Haynes intervened. 'He said, "No, Stephenson is in,"' he recalls. 'I said, "Desmond?" He said, "I just ask if you were padded."' Stephenson was dumbfounded. 'I said, "What did that mean?" The batsman is out there waiting, and he tells me I'm in. When I ran on to the field, it must have been five minutes later; my pads were running behind me. There was no communication. He was terrible. I think between him and Gordon Greenidge, those were the worst two captains Barbados ever had.'

Despite the backroom subterfuge, Stephenson top-scored again, this time with 46, and won the man of the match award, but he was plagued by hamstring soreness throughout the Shell

Shield season and his respectable return of 12 wickets at 28 and 180 runs at 36 did nothing to silence his critics. 'I shouldn't have been playing, but having the opportunity to play, you would have to take me off the field with a bulldozer.'

Reds Perreira also observed that Stephenson was rarely given the chance to bowl at the tail and convert a two-for or a three-for into the headline-grabbing five-wicket hauls that all bowlers crave.

He never played for Barbados again. Stephenson says the following season Haynes made it clear he didn't want anyone over 30 in the squad. The irony was that Haynes himself was 34. 'They just didn't want me to play,' Stephenson says. 'I was too pow ful.'

In South Africa and England, his 'pow' was sought after. Orange Free State coach Eddie Barlow wanted him to help turn the province and its band of next-generation Proteas into a Currie Cup-winning powerhouse. Back in the republic for the first time since the rebel tours, and with apartheid in its death throes, Stephenson witnessed a country grappling with change. He enjoyed playing alongside Hansie Cronje, who he says wanted him to qualify for South Africa. He also rubbed shoulders with Allan Donald and Omar Henry, the first 'coloured' man to represent the Proteas. But in the heart of the old Boer Republic, there were still pockets of intolerance. 'They ate so much meat and drank so much alcohol they got pissed very quickly,' Stephenson says of the Afrikaner good ol' boys.

In a Bloemfontein hotel, he almost felt their wrath. 'I went to the bathroom,' he says, and four white men followed him. 'It was quite scary. I was cornered by them, and I was thinking, it's gonna happen, somebody's going down. Luckily, somebody else pushed the door open. I think the incident was racially motivated.'

Two titles and a slew of one-day trophies were earned during Stephenson's tenure, as he wound down his career in the northern hemisphere with Sussex.

* * *

Bayley's Primary School's opening batsmen are taking guard on the truncated wicket as Stephenson dispenses advice to his stiff-legged wicketkeeper: 'Keeping is about moving your feet and keeping your knees bent,' he says. 'So, the first thing about keeping is you gotta get fit, you gotta get ready to move.'

It's fair to say Stephenson has made a success of life post-cricket. Google his name and there are references to his other great passion, golf, and his celebrity as the first person to birdie the world-famous Extreme 19th in Limpopo, South Africa. There's also a link to an after-dinner speaker agency.

None of the depressing headlines associated with rebels Austin, Chang, Mattis and Murray, nor the moral opprobrium visited upon Rowe. But there are still vestiges of anti-rebel sentiment in Barbados – people in high places who would rather Stephenson stopped voicing his opinion so loudly. Stopped being so damn 'pow ful'.

Eric Bynoe, the Bayley's coach, says local authorities encourage touring professional sides to give Stephenson's academy a wide berth. Fellow rebels Ezra Moseley, Alvin Greenidge and Emmerson Trotman have been appointed to high-profile coaching jobs; their outspoken team-mate nothing. It's why he established the academy; a way of giving back to the game he loves *sans* the petty politics and ancient grudges. 'Sometimes I don't feel myself as Barbadian,' Stephenson says in frustration. 'Because you can't be that stupid in thought.'

Looking back at the tours now, Stephenson is supremely confident they advanced the course of freedom in South Africa. 'We had shown white people blacks could be more than miners and cleaners. They were liberty tours.'

He cites the repeal of beach segregation laws a couple of years after the tours finished as evidence of their indirect impact, although it's hard to imagine then-President P. W. Botha, an architect of apartheid, changing his world view on the basis of a Sylvester Clarke yorker or sweet Lawrence Rowe cover drive.

From Stephenson's perspective, the tours were a form of soft power that produced greater advances than any of the moralising from critics afar could ever do. Which brings him back to academics and critics Cobley and Beckles. 'Why after all this time do they come and put nonsense in people's heads? Why not bring a South African who lived through the time to talk? They just invite people to come and talk crap.'

He believes the rebels had the courage to tread where politicians and cricket officials feared. 'In 1976 there was Soweto,' Stephenson says, referring to the black student uprising against the use of Afrikaans as the language of instruction in South African schools. 'There was a big flare-up about it in the Caribbean, about what we could do. But there was nothing you could do. In 1983 I got a chance to actually do something. There were all these songs being sung: 'Free Nelson Mandela', 'Free South Africa', liberate this and that, and then we get a chance to go there and do what we do best, and we weren't coming in through the back door – the people in power were actually inviting you. It was a no-brainer.'

Many rebel tourists draw a link to WSC, asserting that even taking into account the question of apartheid, their motives – lining their pockets as professional cricketers – were the same as their Kerry Packer-paid brethren.

Stephenson pushes the argument one step further. 'Packer was worse than us. It was just about come and play for my team for money. There was no feeling. But we went to South Africa and they were asking us to come break down barriers. It was something they needed us to do.'

Out on the field, the best all-rounder the West Indies never had is annoyed by what he's seeing from his 11-year-olds. 'You have to walk in with the ball. You're like statues. Nobody is moving!'

He hopes the academy will produce a generation of cricketers who might one day be able to resist the slide in the region's fortunes – and walk in with the bowler. But he knows the ongoing battles with the Caribbean cricket hierarchy won't go away. 'They don't pay the price for losing because they're sitting in administration. They say the players are no good.' He pauses, to amplify his disgust. 'Imagine going from top to bottom and nobody's going to prison. Crazy, man.'

Acknowledgements

PROJECTS LIKE these are never the toil of one person. I'd like to thank Ivan Butler and Dean Rockett for their diligent work on the manuscript, Philip Gore for flagging editorial no-balls and for narrative inspiration, Brian Williams for copy smarts and the immortal phrase 'you've got a triple-century in your notebook', Reds Perreira for his Caribbean address book and encouragement, and my wife Elizabeth for just about everything else.

Seamus Caplice, Rob McCormick, Mitchell Hall, Michael van Vuuren, Leonard Chambers, Patrick Terrelonge, Delano Franklyn, Eric Bynoe, Peggy RockClarke, Molly Biggenot-Austin, Mark Audain, Jeremy Chunn, Tony Becca, Crispin Andrews, Robert Caine and Rohan Bodman all pitched in with timely assistance from contacts to commentary.

I'm also very grateful to past players Ian Chappell, Dennis Lillee, Bobby Simpson, Gary Cosier, Barry Richards, Graeme Pollock, Jeff Dujon, Joel Garner, Deryck Murray, Jimmy Adams, Maurice Foster, Alan Butcher, Alec Stewart and many more, who generously shared thoughtful insights on their peers.

And lastly, a big shout-out to the rebels, their families and friends. Without them there would be no book.

*To watch home videos of the rebels recreating their favourite shots and deliveries, head to The Unforgiven Facebook page.

Scorecards
Tour 1 – 1982/83

1st 'Test', West Indies XI versus South Africa at Cape Town, Jan 21-25, 1983

Result: South Africa 449 & 108/5 (30 ov)
West Indies XI 246 & 309 (f/o)
South Africa won by 5 wickets

South Africa 1st Innings

SJ Cook	c †Murray b Stephenson	73
BA Richards	c Rowe b Moseley	49
PN Kirsten (c)	lbw b Parry	2
RG Pollock	b Moseley	100
CEB Rice	lbw b Parry	16
KA McKenzie	lbw b Parry	4
AJ Kourie	c †Murray b Moseley	69
RV Jennings †	b Parry	15
GS le Roux	c & b Stephenson	30
VAP van der Bijl	c Stephenson b Parry	10
ST Jefferies	not out	40
Extras	41 (b 18, lb 13, nb 8, w 2)	
TOTAL	449 all out (132.4 Overs, RR: 3.38)	

Fall of wickets: 1-85, 2-98, 3-201, 4-264, 5-270, 6-276, 7-351, 8-371, 9-382, 10-449

	O	M	R	W	Economy rate
ST Clarke	34	9	88	0	2.58
EA Moseley	25	3	87	3	3.48
FD Stephenson	23.4	0	93	2	3.92
DR Parry	43	10	117	5	2.72
RA Austin	7	1	23	0	3.28

West Indies XI 1st Innings

RA Austin	c †Jennings b van der Bijl	93
AE Greenidge	b Jefferies	4
EH Mattis	lbw b le Roux	0
AI Kallicharran	b van der Bijl	21
LG Rowe (c)	c Kourie b van der Bijl	9
CL King	c †Jennings b van der Bijl	19
DA Murray †	b Kourie	3
DR Parry	b Kourie	18
FD Stephenson	run out	56
EA Moseley	st †Jennings b Kourie	8
ST Clarke	not out	5
Extras	10 (b 1, lb 7, nb 2)	
TOTAL	246 all out (75 Overs, RR: 3.28)	

Fall of wickets: 1-8, 2-9, 3-46, 4-66, 5-86, 6-89, 7-129, 8-212, 9-232, 10-246

	O	M	R	W	Economy rate
GS le Roux	17	4	56	1	3.29
ST Jefferies	9	4	28	1	3.11
VAP van der Bijl	20	6	44	4	2.20
AJ Kourie	28	6	101	3	3.60
PN Kirsten	1	0	7	0	7.00

1st 'Test' continued

West Indies XI 2nd Innings (following on)

RA Austin	b Kourie	23
AE Greenidge	lbw b le Roux	23
EH Mattis	c †Jennings b le Roux	19
AI Kallicharran	st †Jennings b Kourie	89
LG Rowe (c)	lbw b Jefferies	26
EA Moseley	c Kirsten b van der Bijl	25
CL King	b Jefferies	13
DA Murray †	c †Jennings b le Roux	27
DR Parry	lbw b Jefferies	29
FD Stephenson	b Jefferies	16
ST Clarke	not out	0
Extras	19 (b 3, lb 9, nb 4, w 3)	
TOTAL	309 all out (f/o) (122.4 Overs, RR: 2.51)	

Fall of wickets: 1-43, 2-70, 3-73, 4-127, 5-177, 6-198, 7-253, 8-280, 9-308, 10-309

	O	M	R	W	Economy rate
GS le Roux	21	5	71	3	3.38
ST Jefferies	35.4	17	58	4	1.62
VAP van der Bijl	22	4	46	1	2.09
AJ Kourie	31	4	94	2	3.03
PN Kirsten	13	3	21	0	1.61

South Africa 2nd Innings (target: 107 runs)

SJ Cook	c Rowe b Moseley	6
BA Richards	c Parry b Clarke	7
PN Kirsten (c)	b Parry	13
RG Pollock	not out	43
CEB Rice	lbw b Clarke	6
KA McKenzie	lbw b Parry	0
AJ Kourie	not out	12
Extras	21 (b 8, lb 5, nb 3, w 5)	
TOTAL	108/5 (30 Overs, RR: 3.6)	

Did not bat: RV Jennings †, GS le Roux, VAP van der Bijl, ST Jefferies

Fall of wickets: 1-14, 2-18, 3-65, 4-82, 5-85

	O	M	R	W	Economy rate
ST Clarke	15	4	22	2	1.46
EA Moseley	8	1	25	1	3.12
DR Parry	7	1	40	2	5.71

Umpires: Barry Smith and Oswald Schoof

2nd 'Test', West Indies XI versus South Africa at Johannesburg, Jan 28-Feb 1, 1983

Result: West Indies XI 267 & 176
South Africa 233 & 181 (71.2 ov)
West Indies XI won by 29 runs

West Indies XI 1st Innings

RA Austin	c Pollock b van der Bijl	4
AE Greenidge	not out	42
EH Mattis	lbw b le Roux	3
AI Kallicharran	b Kourie	37
LG Rowe (c)	b van der Bijl	0
CL King	lbw b Kourie	101
DA Murray †	c Pollock b van der Bijl	8
DR Parry	b Kourie	20
FD Stephenson	c Pollock b Kourie	0
ST Clarke	c Rice b Kourie	25
RR Wynter	b Kourie	9
Extras	18 (lb 9, nb 7, w 2)	
TOTAL	267 all out (78 Overs, RR: 3.42)	

Fall of wickets: 1-13, 2-16, 3-39, 4-104, 5-164, 6-185, 7-185, 8-222), 9-233, 10-267

	O	M	R	W	Economy rate
GS le Roux	17	2	58	1	3.41
ST Jefferies	16	3	62	0	3.87
VAP van der Bijl	16	3	74	3	4.62
AJ Kourie	29	9	55	6	1.89

South Africa 1st Innings

SJ Cook	c Wynter b Stephenson	0
BA Richards	c Kallicharran b Clarke	0
RV Jennings †	c Parry b Clarke	0
PN Kirsten (c)	b Clarke	56
RG Pollock	b Stephenson	73
CEB Rice	c Austin b Parry	38
KA McKenzie	c Rowe b Wynter	27
AJ Kourie	lbw b Clarke	17
GS le Roux	lbw b Wynter	0
ST Jefferies	b Clarke	11
VAP van der Bijl	not out	1
Extras	10 (lb 7, nb 2, w 1)	
TOTAL	233 all out (78.3 Overs, RR: 2.96)	

Fall of wickets: 1-1, 2-1, 3-8, 4-122, 5-151, 6-199, 7-203, 8-204, 9-230, 10-233

	O	M	R	W	Economy rate
ST Clarke	23.3	4	66	5	2.80
RR Wynter	11	3	26	2	2.36
FD Stephenson	18	1	68	2	3.77
CL King	7	2	29	0	4.14
DR Parry	17	5	25	1	1.47
RA Austin	2	0	9	0	4.50

2nd 'Test' continued

West Indies XI 2nd Innings

RA Austin	c McKenzie b van der Bijl	14
EH Mattis	b Jefferies	21
AI Kallicharran	b van der Bijl	13
LG Rowe (c)	b Jefferies	0
DA Murray †	c Cook b Jefferies	4
AE Greenidge	c †Jennings b le Roux	48
DR Parry	b Kourie	15
FD Stephenson	c Pollock b le Roux	4
ST Clarke	c Kourie b le Roux	0
CL King	lbw b Kourie	39
RR Wynter	not out	0
Extras	18 (b 4, lb 4, nb 5, w 5)	
TOTAL	176 all out (62.1 Overs, RR: 2.83)	

Fall of wickets: 1-33, 2-56, 3-56, 4-57, 5-65, 6-70, 7-70, 8-105, 9-176, 10-176

	O	M	R	W	Economy rate
GS le Roux	15.1	3	46	3	3.03
ST Jefferies	22	8	66	3	3.00
VAP van der Bijl	16	7	24	2	1.50
AJ Kourie	9	2	22	2	2.44

South Africa 2nd Innings (target: 211 runs)

SJ Cook	c King b Clarke	27
BA Richards	b Parry	59
PN Kirsten (c)	b Clarke	7
RG Pollock	c King b Clarke	1
CEB Rice	c Austin b Clarke	12
KA McKenzie	not out	26
AJ Kourie	c †Murray b Clarke	5
RV Jennings †	c †Murray b Clarke	0
GS le Roux	lbw b King	2
ST Jefferies	run out	31
VAP van der Bijl	b Clarke	2
Extras	9 (b 1, lb 4, nb 3, w 1)	
TOTAL	181 all out (71.2 Overs, RR: 2.53)	

Fall of wickets: 1-87, 2-97, 3-97, 4-100, 5-111, 6-117, 7-119, 8-124, 9-179, 10-181

	O	M	R	W	Economy rate
ST Clarke	22.2	10	34	7	1.52
RR Wynter	9	0	33	0	3.66
FD Stephenson	18	3	47	0	2.61
CL King	1	0	3	1	3.00
DR Parry	20	3	51	1	2.55
RA Austin	1	0	4	0	4.00

Umpires: Dudley Schoof and Cyril Mitchley

SCORECARDS

Tour 2 – 1983/84

1st 'Test', West Indies XI versus South Africa at Durban, Dec 23-27, 1983

Result: West Indies XI 529/7d
South Africa 333 & 59/0 (24 ov) (f/o)
Match drawn

West Indies XI 1st Innings

SFAF Bacchus	retired hurt	19
EN Trotman	c Pollock b le Roux	21
MA Lynch	c Hobson b Kourie	26
AI Kallicharran	c Hobson b le Roux	103
CL King	c Jefferies b Rice	0
LG Rowe (c)	lbw b Jefferies	157
DA Murray †	c Kourie b le Roux	32
FD Stephenson	b Hobson	53
DR Parry	not out	63
EA Moseley	not out	33
Extras	22 (b 5, lb 9, nb 6, w 2)	
TOTAL	529/7d (135 Overs, RR: 3.91)	

Did not bat: ST Clarke
Fall of wickets: 1-34, 2-86, 3-87, 4-241, 5-311, 6-392, 7-468

	O	M	R	W	Economy rate
GS le Roux	27	2	88	3	3.25
ST Jefferies	31	3	132	1	4.25
AJ Kourie	36	5	123	1	3.41
CEB Rice	21	4	65	1	3.09
DL Hobson	19	1	95	1	5.00
PN Kirsten	1	0	4	0	4.00

South Africa 1st Innings

SJ Cook	c †Murray b Clarke	69
HR Fotheringham	lbw b Moseley	0
PN Kirsten (c)	c †Murray b Moseley	84
RG Pollock	b Parry	62
KS McEwan	c sub (HL Alleyne) b Moseley	11
CEB Rice	c & b Parry	7
AJ Kourie	b Clarke	32
RV Jennings †	b Clarke	18
GS le Roux	c Stephenson b Clarke	11
ST Jefferies	b Clarke	0
DL Hobson	not out	12
Extras	27 (b 4, lb 9, nb 13, w 1)	
TOTAL	333 all out (106.1 Overs, RR: 3.13)	

Fall of wickets: 1-2, 2-132, 3-219, 4-239, 5-249, 6-257, 7-302, 8-313, 9-313, 10-333

	O	M	R	W	Economy rate
ST Clarke	32.1	11	105	5	3.26
EA Moseley	26	5	76	3	2.92
FD Stephenson	21	5	61	0	2.90
DR Parry	25	7	62	2	2.48
CL King	2	1	2	0	1.00

1st 'Test' continued

South Africa 2nd Innings (following on)

SJ Cook	not out	30
HR Fotheringham	not out	22
Extras	7 (b 2, nb 5)	
TOTAL	59/0 (f/o) (24 Overs, RR: 2.45)	

Did not bat: PN Kirsten (c), RG Pollock, KS McEwan, CEB Rice, AJ Kourie, RV Jennings †, GS le Roux, ST Jefferies, DL Hobson

	O	M	R	W	Economy rate
ST Clarke	3	0	9	0	3.00
EA Moseley	4	2	8	0	2.00
FD Stephenson	6	1	16	0	2.66
CL King	6	2	13	0	2.16
AI Kallicharran	5	2	6	0	1.20

Umpires: Dudley Schoof and Denzil Bezuidenhout

2nd 'Test', West Indies XI versus South Africa at Cape Town, Dec 30 1983 – Jan 3, 1984

Result: West Indies XI 252 & 268
South Africa 404 & 117/0 (21.2 ov)
South Africa won by 10 wickets

West Indies XI 1st Innings

EN Trotman	c †Jennings b Kourie	28
EH Mattis	lbw b Jefferies	6
MA Lynch	c †Jennings b Kourie	2
AI Kallicharran	c Fotheringham b Kourie	8
CL King	c Kourie b Jefferies	83
LG Rowe (c)	c & b Kourie	0
DA Murray †	lbw b Rice	39
FD Stephenson	c Pollock b Kourie	7
BD Julien	not out	33
DR Parry	c & b le Roux	30
ST Clarke	lbw b Jefferies	0
Extras	16 (b 4, lb 7, nb 4, w 1)	
TOTAL	252 all out (87.4 Overs, RR: 2.87)	

Fall of wickets: 1-31, 2-38, 3-46, 4-49, 5-49, 6-156, 7-183, 8-183, 9-247, 10-252

	O	M	R	W	Economy rate
GS le Roux	17	6	34	1	2.00
ST Jefferies	20.4	6	63	3	3.04
AJ Kourie	22	6	66	5	3.00
DL Hobson	20	5	49	0	2.45
CEB Rice	8	1	24	1	3.00

South Africa 1st Innings

SJ Cook	c †Murray b Clarke	45
HR Fotheringham	c Julien b Stephenson	20
PN Kirsten (c)	c Parry b Julien	88
RG Pollock	c †Murray b Parry	102
KS McEwan	c †Murray b Clarke	32
CEB Rice	not out	71
AJ Kourie	lbw b Clarke	1
RV Jennings †	lbw b Parry	8
GS le Roux	c Mattis b Clarke	11
ST Jefferies	c Julien b Parry	1
DL Hobson	c & b Clarke	1
Extras	24 (lb 17, nb 1, w 6)	
TOTAL	404 all out (132.5 Overs, RR: 3.04)	

Fall of wickets: 1-61, 2-84, 3-267, 4-273, 5-315, 6-317, 7-364, 8-393, 9-398, 10-404

	O	M	R	W	Economy rate
ST Clarke	37.5	13	92	5	2.43
BD Julien	24	5	71	1	2.95
FD Stephenson	27	5	95	1	3.51
DR Parry	36	8	79	3	2.19
CL King	5	1	21	0	4.20
AI Kallicharran	3	0	22	0	7.33

2nd 'Test' continued

West Indies XI 2nd Innings

EN Trotman	c †Jennings b Jefferies	1
EH Mattis	c Rice b Kourie	26
MA Lynch	run out	23
AI Kallicharran	lbw b Kourie	17
CL King	c Pollock b Jefferies	26
DR Parry	c Pollock b Rice	58
LG Rowe (c)	c Cook b Hobson	31
DA Murray †	c Fotheringham b Kourie	40
FD Stephenson	lbw b le Roux	7
BD Julien	c Kirsten b le Roux	18
ST Clarke	not out	3
Extras	18 (b 4, lb 7, nb 1, w 6)	
TOTAL	268 all out (96.3 Overs, RR: 2.77)	

Fall of wickets: 1-5, 2-53, 3-63, 4-86, 5-100, 6-178, 7-206, 8-232, 9-260, 10-268

	O	M	R	W	Economy rate
GS le Roux	17.3	5	50	2	2.85
ST Jefferies	16	6	62	2	3.87
AJ Kourie	27	11	61	3	2.25
DL Hobson	15	2	36	1	2.40
CEB Rice	15	8	21	1	1.40
PN Kirsten	6	1	20	0	3.33

South Africa 2nd Innings (target: 117 runs)

SJ Cook	not out	40
HR Fotheringham	not out	71
Extras	6 (lb 5, w 1)	
TOTAL	117/0 (21.2 Overs, RR: 5.48)	

Did not bat: PN Kirsten (c), RG Pollock, KS McEwan, CEB Rice, AJ Kourie, RV Jennings †, GS le Roux, ST Jefferies, DL Hobson

	O	M	R	W	Economy rate
ST Clarke	6	0	23	0	3.83
BD Julien	2	0	11	0	5.50
FD Stephenson	2	0	11	0	5.50
DR Parry	8	0	36	0	4.50
CL King	3	0	22	0	7.33
AI Kallicharran	0.2	0	8	0	24.00

Umpires: Sydney Moore and Cyril Mitchley

3rd 'Test', West Indies XI versus South Africa at Johannesburg, Jan 13-17, 1984

Result: South Africa 160 & 236
West Indies XI 193 & 205/9 (53.2 ov)
West Indies XI won by 1 wicket

South Africa 1st Innings

SJ Cook	lbw b Clarke	7
HR Fotheringham	b Moseley	8
PN Kirsten	c †Murray b Alleyne	67
RG Pollock	c Moseley b Alleyne	41
KS McEwan	c †Murray b Alleyne	0
CEB Rice (c)	c Trotman b Stephenson	4
AP Kuiper	lbw b Alleyne	16
AJ Kourie	not out	7
RV Jennings †	c sub (BD Julien) b Moseley	1
WK Watson	lbw b Moseley	0
RW Hanley	c †Murray b Moseley	0
Extras	9 (lb 4, nb 5)	
TOTAL	160 all out (45.4 Overs, RR: 3.5)	

Fall of wickets: 1-16, 2-24, 3-91, 4-92, 5-102, 6-151, 7-154, 8-160, 9-160, 10-160

	O	M	R	W	Economy rate
ST Clarke	13	6	17	1	1.30
EA Moseley	10.4	2	45	4	4.21
HL Alleyne	12	1	54	4	4.50
FD Stephenson	9	2	34	1	3.77
CL King	1	0	1	0	1.00

West Indies XI 1st Innings

EN Trotman	c Fotheringham b Hanley	3
AE Greenidge	c †Jennings b Kuiper	20
EH Mattis	lbw b Watson	0
MA Lynch	lbw b Rice	9
CL King	c †Jennings b Watson	54
DA Murray †	c Pollock b Kuiper	43
AI Kallicharran (c)	lbw b Hanley	18
FD Stephenson	not out	30
EA Moseley	c Pollock b Kuiper	0
ST Clarke	lbw b Kuiper	9
HL Alleyne	c sub (ST Jefferies) b Kuiper	0
Extras	7 (lb 3, nb 3, w 1)	
TOTAL	193 all out (52.5 Overs, RR: 3.65)	

Fall of wickets: 1-6, 2-11, 3-23, 4-69, 5-106, 6-142, 7-154, 8-154, 9-189, 10-193

	O	M	R	W	Economy rate
WK Watson	16	5	42	2	2.62
RW Hanley	13	4	26	2	2.00
CEB Rice	6	1	46	1	7.66
AP Kuiper	11.5	0	50	5	4.22
AJ Kourie	6	1	22	0	3.66

3rd 'Test' continued

South Africa 2nd Innings

SJ Cook	c Greenidge b Alleyne	17
HR Fotheringham	lbw b Moseley	4
PN Kirsten	c King b Moseley	61
RG Pollock	b Stephenson	46
CEB Rice (c)	c †Murray b Clarke	47
AP Kuiper	c Mattis b Alleyne	10
RV Jennings †	lbw b Alleyne	0
KS McEwan	c Stephenson b Alleyne	0
AJ Kourie	b Alleyne	31
WK Watson	not out	6
RW Hanley	c Stephenson b Clarke	0
Extras	14 (b 3, lb 5, nb 2, w 4)	
TOTAL	236 all out (56.3 Overs, RR: 4.17)	

Fall of wickets: 1-6, 2-44, 3-127, 4-149, 5-169, 6-169, 7-169, 8-216, 9-236, 10-236

	O	M	R	W	Economy rate
ST Clarke	24.3	5	74	2	3.02
EA Moseley	14	1	55	2	3.92
HL Alleyne	14	1	62	5	4.42
FD Stephenson	4	0	31	1	7.75

West Indies XI 2nd Innings (target: 204 runs)

EN Trotman	c Pollock b Watson	4
AE Greenidge	c Kourie b Kuiper	43
EH Mattis	b Watson	32
MA Lynch	c †Jennings b Rice	7
AI Kallicharran (c)	c Pollock b Watson	7
DA Murray †	c Pollock b Rice	3
FD Stephenson	c †Jennings b Kuiper	20
CL King	c sub (ST Jefferies) b Rice	42
EA Moseley	c Hanley b Watson	14
ST Clarke	not out	23
HL Alleyne	not out	0
Extras	10 (lb 3, nb 5, w 2)	
TOTAL	205/9 (53.2 Overs, RR: 3.84)	

Fall of wickets: 1-4, 2-72, 3-86, 4-94, 5-97, 6-99, 7-143, 8-172, 9-200

	O	M	R	W	Economy rate
WK Watson	16.2	3	63	4	3.85
RW Hanley	9	1	27	0	3.00
CEB Rice	12	0	50	3	4.16
AP Kuiper	11	0	32	2	2.90
AJ Kourie	5	1	23	0	4.60

Umpires: Dudley Schoof and Sydney Moore

4th 'Test', West Indies XI versus South Africa at Port Elizabeth, Jan 27-31, 1984

Result: South Africa 277 & 127
West Indies XI 199 & 206/4 (49 ov)
West Indies XI won by 6 wickets

South Africa 1st Innings

SJ Cook	c †Murray b Stephenson	26
M Yachad	c †Murray b Moseley	6
PN Kirsten	c †Murray b Clarke	0
RG Pollock	c Mattis b Clarke	0
KS McEwan	c Kallicharran b Moseley	120
CEB Rice (c)	c †Murray b Clarke	23
AP Kuiper	c †Murray b Stephenson	5
AJ Kourie	not out	63
DJ Richardson †	lbw b Alleyne	13
WK Watson	c †Murray b Clarke	8
RW Hanley	b Clarke	0
Extras	13 (b 2, lb 8, w 3)	
TOTAL	277 all out (82 Overs, RR: 3.37)	

Fall of wickets: 1-11, 2-16, 3-16, 4-54, 5-100, 6-117, 7-205, 8-264, 9-277, 10-277

	O	M	R	W	Economy rate
ST Clarke	23	7	36	5	1.56
EA Moseley	20	2	93	2	4.65
FD Stephenson	18	2	61	2	3.38
HL Alleyne	16	2	55	1	3.43
CL King	5	1	19	0	3.80

West Indies XI 1st Innings

SFAF Bacchus	c Kirsten b Rice	66
EN Trotman	c Pollock b Hanley	43
EH Mattis	c Kourie b Kuiper	15
AI Kallicharran	c Cook b Watson	16
CL King	c Kuiper b Watson	0
LG Rowe (c)	lbw b Kuiper	16
DA Murray †	run out (Kirsten/†Richardson)	8
FD Stephenson	not out	19
EA Moseley	c Kourie b Kuiper	4
ST Clarke	c Kuiper b Watson	0
HL Alleyne	lbw b Kourie	4
Extras	8 (b 1, lb 5, nb 1, w 1)	
TOTAL	199 all out (81 Overs, RR: 2.45)	

Fall of wickets: 1-83, 2-113, 3-136, 4-136, 5-160, 6-170, 7-176, 8-180, 9-185, 10-199

	O	M	R	W	Economy rate
WK Watson	24	10	46	3	1.91
RW Hanley	15	4	30	1	2.00
AJ Kourie	11	1	23	1	2.09
AP Kuiper	18	3	57	3	3.16
CEB Rice	13	2	35	1	2.69

4th 'Test' continued

South Africa 2nd Innings

SJ Cook	c †Murray b Clarke	2
M Yachad	lbw b Alleyne	31
PN Kirsten	b Clarke	4
RG Pollock	c †Murray b Clarke	42
KS McEwan	c †Murray b Alleyne	0
CEB Rice (c)	c Clarke b Stephenson	12
AP Kuiper	c Alleyne b Clarke	14
AJ Kourie	c †Murray b Stephenson	4
DJ Richardson †	b Stephenson	3
WK Watson	not out	4
RW Hanley	b Clarke	0
Extras	11 (b 3, lb 4, nb 2, w 2)	
TOTAL	127 all out (46.4 Overs, RR: 2.72)	

Fall of wickets: 1-4, 2-9, 3-66, 4-87, 5-103, 6-109, 7-117, 8-122, 9-124, 10-127

	O	M	R	W	*Economy rate*
ST Clarke	13.4	3	32	5	2.34
EA Moseley	8	1	22	0	2.75
FD Stephenson	15	2	47	3	3.13
HL Alleyne	10	3	15	2	1.50

West Indies XI 2nd Innings (target: 206 runs)

SFAF Bacchus	c sub (GS Cowley) b Watson	76
EN Trotman	c Kuiper b Kirsten	77
EH Mattis	lbw b Hanley	1
AI Kallicharran	not out	32
FD Stephenson	c sub (RV Jennings) b Kourie	1
CL King	not out	10
Extras	9 (lb 4, nb 3, w 2)	
TOTAL	206/4 (49 Overs, RR: 4.2)	

Did not bat: DA Murray †, LG Rowe (c), EA Moseley, ST Clarke, HL Alleyne
Fall of wickets: 1-130, 2-133, 3-182, 4-186

	O	M	R	W	*Economy rate*
WK Watson	9	0	46	1	5.11
RW Hanley	8	0	38	1	4.75
AJ Kourie	19	5	65	1	3.42
AP Kuiper	4	0	25	0	6.25
CEB Rice	3	0	9	0	3.00
PN Kirsten	6	1	14	1	2.33

Umpires: Herbert Martin and Cyril Mitchley

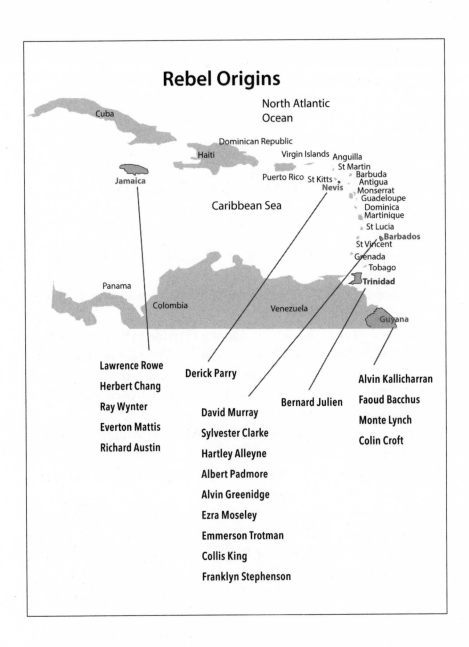

Rebel Origins

North Atlantic Ocean

Cuba

Dominican Republic

Haiti

Virgin Islands Anguilla
St Martin
Barbuda
Puerto Rico St Kitts Antigua
Nevis Monserrat
Guadeloupe
Dominica
Martinique

Jamaica

Caribbean Sea

St Lucia
Barbados
St Vincent
Grenada
Tobago
Trinidad

Panama

Colombia Venezuela Guyana

Lawrence Rowe

Herbert Chang

Ray Wynter

Everton Mattis

Richard Austin

Derick Parry

David Murray

Sylvester Clarke

Hartley Alleyne

Albert Padmore

Alvin Greenidge

Ezra Moseley

Emmerson Trotman

Collis King

Franklyn Stephenson

Bernard Julien

Alvin Kallicharran

Faoud Bacchus

Monte Lynch

Colin Croft

Selected Bibliography

Calypso Cavaliers: The Story of the 1983 Tour, by Brian Crowley (Ibbotson, 1983)

The Rebel Tours: Cricket's Crisis of Conscience, by Peter May (Sportsbooks, 2009)

Ali: The Life of Ali Bacher, by Rodney Hartman (Viking, 2004)

Indian-Caribbean Test Cricketers and the Quest for Identity, by Frank Birbalsingh (Hansib Publications, 2014)

Indo-West Indian Cricket, by Frank Birbalsingh (Hansib Publications, 2016)

A History of West Indies Cricket, by Michael Manley (Guild Publishing, 1988)

Whispering Death, by Michael Holding, with Tony Cozier (Andre Deutsch Ltd, 1993)

Marshall Arts, by Malcolm Marshall with Patrick Symes (Queen Anne Press, 1987)

Clive Lloyd: The Authorised Biography, by Trevor McDonald (Granada Publishing, 1985)

Cricket the Game of Life, by Scyld Berry (Hodder & Stoughton, 2016)

Jamaica at the Wicket, by Arnold Bertram (Research and Project Development Company Limited, 2009)

Beyond a Boundary, by CLR James (Yellow Jersey, 2005)

A Spirit of Dominance: Cricket and Nationalism in the West Indies, edited by Hilary Beckles (University of the West Indies Press, 1999)

SELECT BIBLIOGRAPHY

The Development of West Indies Cricket, by Hilary Beckles (Pluto Press, 1999)

From Lilliput to Lord's, by Greg Young (Silverwood Books, 2017)

Desmond Haynes Lion of Barbados, by Rob Steen (Weidenfeld & Nicolson, 1993)

Living my Dreams, by Joseph 'Reds' Perreira (AuthorHouse, 2011)

Fire in Babylon, by Simon Lister (Yellow Jersey, 2016)

The West Indies: 50 Years of Test Cricket, by Tony Cozier (The Book Service Ltd, 1978)

Films

Fire in Babylon, directed by Stevan Riley (2010)

Windies Whirlwind: West Indies in South Africa 1983/84

Also available at all good book stores

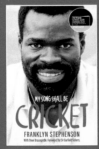

9781785316920

9781785315053

9781785314889

9781785314865

9781785314377

9781785311628

9781785314070

9781785315053

9781785311314